CONTEMPORARY
URBAN JAPAN

Studies in Urban and Social Change

Published by Blackwell in association with the *International Journal of Urban and Regional Research*. Series editors: Chris Pickvance, Margit Mayer and John Walton

Published

Forthcoming

CONTEMPORARY
URBAN
JAPAN

A SOCIOLOGY OF CONSUMPTION

John Clammer

BLACKWELL
Publishers

First published 1997

Blackwell Publishers Ltd
108 Cowley Road
Oxford OX4 1JF
UK

Blackwell Publishers Inc.
350 Main Street
Malden, Massachusetts 02148
USA

British Library Catloguing in Publication Data

A CIP catalogue record for this book is available from the British Library.

Library of Congress Cataloging in Publication Data

Clammer, J. R.
    Contemporary urban Japan : a sociology of consumption / John Clammer.
        p.   cm. — (Studies in urban and social change)
    Includes bibliographical references and index.
    ISBN 0-631-20301-X. — ISBN 0-631-20302-8
    1. Sociology, Urban—Japan.   2. City and Town life—Japan.
3. Consumption (Economics)—Social aspects—Japan.   4. Consumer
behavior—Japan.   I. Title.   II. Series.
HT147.J3C63   1997
307.76′0952—dc21   97–12661
                                                              CIP

Typeset in 10½ on 12 pt Baskerville
by Ace Filmsetting Ltd, Frome, Somerset
Printed in Great Britain by Hartnolls Ltd, Bodmin, Cornwall

This book is printed on acid-free paper.

'Modern Japan is surely now the heartland of contemporary consumption, and John Clammer's book represents a long-overdue analysis of its significant features. Rich in illustrative detail and theoretically sophisticated, this is a thoroughly engrossing work which at its core contains a compelling and original thesis. It deserves to be read not only by those with an interest in Japanese society and culture but by anyone wanting to see a glimpse into the form a possible future Western consumer society may take.'

Martyn Lee, Coventry University

Contents

Preface

In the past three decades there have been dramatic changes in the fortunes of cities and regions, in beliefs about the role of markets and states in society, and in the theories used by social scientists to account for these changes. Many of the cities experiencing crisis in the 1970s have undergone revitalization, while others have continued to decline. In Europe and North America new policies have introduced privatization on a broad scale at the expense of collective consumption, and the viability of the welfare state has been challenged. Eastern Europe has witnessed the collapse of state socialism and the uneven implementation of a globally driven market economy. Meanwhile the less developed nations have suffered punishing austerity programmes that divide a few newly industrializing countries from a great many cases of arrested and negative growth.

Social science theories have struggled to encompass these changes. The earlier social organizational and ecological paradigms were criticized by Marxian and Weberian theories, and these in turn have been disputed as all-embracing narratives. The certainties of the past, such as class theory, are gone and the future of urban and regional studies appears relatively open.

The aim of the series Studies in Urban and Social Change is to take forward this agenda of issues and theoretical debates. The series is committed to a number of aims but will not prejudge the development of the field. It encourages theoretical works and research monographs on cities and regions. It explores the spatial dimension of society, including the role of agency and of institutional contexts in shaping urban form. It addresses economic and political change from the household to the state.

Cities and regions are understood within an international system, the features of which are revealed in comparative and historical analyses.

The series also serves the interests of university classroom and professional readers. It publishes topical accounts of important policy issues (e.g. global adjustment), reviews of debates (e.g. post-Fordism), and collections that explore various facets of major changes (e.g. cities after socialism or the new urban underclass). It urges a synthesis of research and theory, teaching and practice. Engaging research monographs (e.g. on women and poverty in Mexico or urban culture in Japan) provide vivid teaching materials just as policy-orientated studies (e.g. of social housing or urban planning) test and redirect theory. The city is analysed from the top down (e.g. through the gendered culture of investment banks) and the bottom up (e.g. in challenging social movements). Taken together, the volumes in the series reflect the latest developments in urban and regional studies.

Subjects which fall within the scope of the series include: explanations for the rise and fall of cities and regions; economic restructuring and its spatial, class and gender impact; race and identity; convergence and divergence of the East and West in social and institutional paterns; new divisions of labour and forms of social exclusion; urban and environmental movements; international migration and capital flows; politics of the urban poor in developing countries; cross-national comparisons or housing, planning and development; and debates on post-Fordism, the consumption sector and the 'new' urban poverty.

Studies in Urban and Social Change addresses an international and interdisciplinary audience of researchers, practitioners, students and urban enthusiasts. Above all, it endeavours to reach the public with compelling accounts of contemporary society.

Editorial Committee
John Walton, Chair
Margit Mayer
Chris Pickvance

Acknowledgements

As in any study of this kind, numerous individuals have contributed to the formulation of ideas and their expression. Help in the first category has come from Rob Shields, who prompted me to write a first version of Chapter 4, which appeared in a collection edited by himself (*Lifestyle Shopping: The Subject of Consumption*, Routledge, 1992). I was aided by Lise Skov and Brian Moeran through their invitation to participate in the workshop on Women, Media and Consumption in Japan held at the Department of Japanese Studies at the University of Hong Kong and for their detailed editorial comments on my paper for that conference, a very much shorter version of which appeared in the proceedings (Curzon 1995) and which has been greatly expanded to comprise Chapter 6 of the present volume. Chapter 5 also began as a conference paper, at the Japan Anthropology Workshop session at the European Association of Japanese Studies conference at Copenhagen in 1994, and has benefited from the feedback of participants.

In the second category I would especially like to mention Hirose Takashi, who took on the burden of typing much of the manuscript and who has been a constant stimulus and friendly critic throughout the period of writing and revising, and also Ozawa Chikako, for her help with numerous details, assistance with word processing and unfailing support. Special thanks too must go to the Department of Sociology and the Contemporary Japan Centre at the University of Essex, where from April to September 1996 I was a visiting fellow in an environment that gave me both the leisure and the stimulation to complete the writing of the manuscript. Particular thanks at Essex to Tony Woodiwiss for his personal and institutional support and to Tanaka Hiroko for her friendship and advice.

1

Approaching Japan through the Study of Consumption

The study of consumption has recently emerged as a central concern in the sociology of culture. Rescued from its domination by marketing specialists, consumption has come to be recognized as an essential part of a constellation which links interest in the body, the nature of selfhood and the emergence of late (or post)modern society to older concerns with material culture, the organization of the everyday life world, the presentation of the self and the micro-economics of households, whether comprised of families or of individuals. These issues are in turn located within the broader context of macro-social change, including urbanization, globalization and shifts in the economies of both developed and developing societies. The fact that such major contemporary social theorists as Jean Baudrillard have placed the analysis of consumption at the heart of their total theoretical projects (e.g. Baudrillard 1970) should alert us to the potential centrality of consumption behaviour in the organization of everyday life in the contemporary world. But despite the growing recognition of the significance of consumption for anthropological and sociological analysis, few attempts have been made to explore in any detail the ethnography of consumer behaviour in non-Western societies, to link such a sociology of consumption to wider social, economic and political changes in such societies or to consider critically the relevance of theories of consumption in such contexts.

Of all the cases that might present themselves as candidates for such comparative analysis, Japan is certainly one of the most prominent. The first non-Western society to achieve industrialization under its own steam and without ever experiencing colonization, Japan is now the world's second biggest economy and one of its most populous states. Famous for its achievement of a highly efficient export-oriented capitalist industrial system and the creation of a mass consumer society at home characterized by its scale and intensity, and equally for the quality of its products and services, Japan cries out for analysis as the most conspicuous example of mass consumption in Asia. While a number of other Far Eastern societies share some of these characteristics – Hong Kong, for example, Singapore certainly and to an ever-increasing extent the urban sectors of Taiwan, Malaysia and Thailand – Japan stands out for two reasons. The first of these is the sheer scale of mass consumption: a large population (123 million), heavily concentrated in large cities, apparently committed to consumption as a way of life, which is reinforced by media saturation and an intensity of advertising and information without equal in Asia (or possibly in the West, for that matter).

The second relates to the debates that have sprung up in Japan about the meaning and direction of the massive social and cultural changes brought about by the very rapid and very complete expansion and penetration of mass consumption since the 1960s, debates ranging from discussions of the significance of Tanaka Yasuo's best-selling 1980 novel *Nantonaku, kuristaru (Somehow, crystal)*, with its minimal plot and extensive lists of brand-name products, to analyses of Japan as the quintessential postmodern society of the modern world (e.g. Miyoshi and Harootunian 1989). These debates are of some significance since they pose in a very fresh form and in a radically different social context issues that are currently at the heart of social theory. Addressing these systematically both creates the possibility of discovering fresh ways of approaching and exploring Japanese society beyond the frequently sterile and repetitive categories of so much contemporary Japanology, while establishing the dialectical possibility of reflecting back to Western social theory an entirely new perspective on its assumptions and preoccupations and claims to universality (Clammer 1995a).

Two sets of issues emerge here then: the analysis of consumer behaviour in Japan from a sociological point of view in the context of its urban, economic and political environment; and the theorizing of this behaviour, an exercise that has the potential both to change the nature of Japanese studies and the study of Japan, and also to modify substantially the nature and content of general social theory, theory often weakened by its ethnocentric biases or by its lack of rooting in the social reality of living societies, especially those of a different cultural form. Both of these levels will be addressed here, through the analysis of selected aspects of contemporary Japanese consumption activities and through dialogue with social theory, both Western and Japanese. Implicit here is the project of locating consumption as a subject of sociological and anthropological analysis, especially as it relates to concerns with embodiment, selfhood, globalization and the nature of late modernity.

JAPAN AND CONSUMPTION

A society of the complexity of Japan naturally attracts and can tolerate a number of different and competing approaches, and no single one can hope to exhaust the riches of such a large-scale and actually diverse culture. But nevertheless it must be said that much has happened in social theory in the 1980s and 1990s, a lot of which has not reached Japanology. Such developments, however, need to be assimilated as much into the understanding of Asian societies as they have been into the analysis of European and North American ones. Significant among these approaches is the rising interest in consumption and the nature and culture of consumer societies – ones, that is, in which mass consumption is now entrenched as the dominating principle of everyday life. This concern itself is part of a wider movement involving interest in the understanding of so-called postmodern society, the problem of sociological methodology after structuralism, engagement with critiques of mass society, recognition of the rising significance of media studies, and the establishment of the study of popular culture as an area of legitimate scholarly investigation – and with it the analysis of the cultural forms and economic networks of everyday life.

The premise here is that the study of consumption reveals cultural patterns and economic organization in a clearer light than competing approaches that are central to the understanding and explanation of Japanese social life. And in the case of Japan it is especially important that such analysis be undertaken to offset the frankly marginal nature of a great deal of anthropological investigation in particular, which still tends to focus on tiny and often unrepresentative corners of Japanese life while ignoring the actual culture and life-paths of the majority. While aspects of Japanese consumer culture will be explored in detail in the chapters to come, here it may be useful to give some idea of the potential scope of the approach to Japan through the study of consumption.

Everyday life, behind its rituals and routines, is in practice very much taken up with economics – the micro-economics of consumption decisions, shopping patterns, thinking about food not only in terms of nutrition but also in terms of affordability, its effect on one's figure and as an expression of lifestyle. Many of the patterns of everyday life are to be understood as dominated by consumption. Saving (or not), participation by housewives and students in part-time work, spatial movement and the use of time throughout the day (and weekly, monthly or even annual cycles – paying the rent, the visit of the co-op van, the school bazaar, sales at the departmental stores, eating out at weekends) are all aspects of this. So too of course are leisure activities and in many cases networks of friendships; in many societies (whatever the cultural ideology) relationships are actually organized around economic interactions – in Japan often shopping and the sharing of consumer information among housewives, window shopping among teenagers, competitive eating and drinking among male businessmen and salaried workers, and gift-giving and receiving among all social categories.

If everyday Japanese life is dominated by consumption, so too are some of its less visible aspects. A central sociological problem in Japanese society is that of the nature of social stratification. Japan is clearly a very hierarchical society, with universities, companies, occupations and practically everything else ranked in a usually clearly defined order. The language itself makes egalitarianism impossible, with its speech levels, codes of politeness, male and female versions and situational kinship terminology. But yet class consciousness appears to be very low, and the language of class rarely enters everyday discourse despite the evident existence of objective social inequalities. How is one to solve this conundrum? One possibility, and the one that will be argued here, is that stratification in Japan is based on status competition which, in the case of everyday life, is heavily implicated in acts of consumption. This competition, while largely symbolic, has objective social outcomes which, given the ethos of Japanese society, must be played down in order to minimize the disruptive effects of too much overt competition. To consume and to be known to consume, while simultaneously maintaining an ideology of equality, is a fascinating dimension of Japanese life ignored in most studies of social stratification and mobility, but one which will be explored in much further detail here.

Closely connected to the question of social stratification is that of gender. Many observers of contemporary Japan consider Japanese women to occupy a distinctly second-class status, a position based upon lower earnings and lack of access to high-level posts in business, the bureaucracy or politics. Interestingly, some prominent Japanese feminists disagree with this characterization, citing as counter-evidence the almost absolute control by Japanese wives of their household budgets (earned by the husband but spent by the wife), decisions and lifestyles, which revolve around children (their command of socialization and the education of their offspring), culture (free time for self-cultivation and often the practice of the traditional arts) and consumption (especially shopping). Seen from this point of view it is Japanese men who, while possessing greater symbolic power, do not actually hold the real micro-power that controls everyday life and who, furthermore, are trapped into a lifestyle of long commuting journeys, long working days and very little leisure.

Their wives on the other hand, while having little symbolic power, actually oversee most major decisions, spend without producing and have substantial leisure time. The gendered nature of consumption in Japan, while it does not address the problem of women's exclusion from high-level corporate or political positions, does make this thesis fairly convincing at the level of everyday life.

This range of issues could be extended in several directions. One would be to relate consumption as an everyday activity to the availability of information, images and stimuli endlessly purveyed through advertising, the media in general and magazines in particular. There is a vast market for magazines in Japan, and almost all magazines contain large amounts of advertising; most include consumer information in the form of articles and many are devoted virtually exclusively to promoting consumption of things – foods, services, fashions, holidays or whole lifestyles. Friendships, as we have noted, often involve the sharing of such information, in some cases to the degree that 'friends' can sometimes be defined as the network of those with whom one regularly exchanges such consumption information. The much discussed issue of *kokusaika*, or the 'internationalization' of Japanese society, is interesting in this respect. While the rhetoric occurs at the national and occasionally at the local political level, the practice, insofar as it exists, takes place mostly through consumption activities – eating in restaurants that specialize in 'ethnic' foods, consuming foreign products, and learning (or pretending to learn) foreign languages, especially English. The consumption of language classes is now so great that the language-school business has grown into an enormous industry, so much so that there is literally at least one school adjacent to virtually every major railway station, and probably a third of the advertisements that adorn every suburban train carriage will be for such schools (one such chain actually advertises itself as the *eki-mai* school – 'one in front of every major station').

Another set of questions revolves around the place of material culture. Japan is well known as a society in which high aesthetic standards tend to prevail (there are of course exceptions) in the design and presentation of quite everyday objects. The discovery of consumption as a subject of anthropological and sociological investigation has interestingly, and quite correctly, gone hand-in-hand with the rediscovery of material culture, a subject that until very recently had dropped out of the anthropological repertoire almost entirely (Miller 1994a). Social life is in fact largely made possible by material objects, and their manufacture, exchange and consumption provides the framework and means of most forms of social interaction and cultural interchange. Clearly most forms of consumption involve the circulation of objects, not only as means of creating and maintaining social networks, but also as one of the chief ways through which identity is established and maintained and through which it is represented to others. Status competition, for example, is pursued largely through the accumulation of cultural capital and through the acquisition, display and exchange of things. Although at first sight material culture and the creation of a sense of selfhood might seem to fall into entirely different categories, they are intimately linked. The issue of the body – its constitution and presentation – which has also become a major topic of discussion in contemporary cultural studies, is the mediating link here, relating the world of things to the sense of self.

Finally, consumption behaviour takes place in a context initially created, and subsequently constantly modified, by larger forces. The first of these is obviously the economy itself, its institutional structures, its cultural patterning through models of employment and work and its evolving nature. Only a growing economy with a large domestic market and a very good infrastructure of communications, distribution and information can sustain mass consumption, and such a situation has come into being in Japan only since the early 1960s, aided by close collusion between business and bureaucracy, a protected market, export-led industrialization, a high savings rate and, from Japan's point of view, generally positive international system. Closely allied with this was and is the political situation. Japan's postwar economic growth has been encouraged by a combination of international factors (e.g. US military protection and open markets abroad) and domestic politics, starting with the income-doubling plan formulated in the early 1960s by the then prime minister, Kishi Nobusuke, and carried out by his successor Ikeda Hayato, and continuing through three subsequent decades of political stability (or inertia) marked by the pro-business policies of the Liberal Democratic Party. During this period enormous corporate expansion took place. Japanese businesses and capital moved abroad and began their colonization of local markets, at first in East and Southeast Asia, and soon just about everywhere else, and the availability of consumer goods expanded enormously, together with, as incomes rose, the ability to possess them for an ever-widening segment of the Japanese population. Political direction (or at least bureaucratic direction), an expanding economy and rapid urbanization gave birth in a little over two decades to an intensely consumer-oriented society. The factor of urbanization should certainly not be overlooked, as in the same period Japan moved from a still heavily agricultural society to a heavily urbanized one (Fukutake 1982). This was one in which not only were the majority of the population living in cities, but, as a result, the nature of occupations and employment had radically shifted and, equally importantly, national culture became dominated by urban culture – culture created in and reflecting the big commercial/industrial cities (and especially the Tokyo/Yokohama conurbation and the Osaka/Kobe conurbation and its outlier at Nagoya) and disseminated to the countryside and small towns by the urban-dominated media. The history of consumption in modern Japan runs directly parallel to the history of urbanization, and indeed consumption is in many ways simply contemporary urban mass or popular culture. Urban culture and consumption have become inseparable in the Japan of today.

Consumption is a complex phenomenon. It meets needs certainly, but it is also a response to desires and a means of seeking a variety of satisfactions. It is *asobi* – play – as much as it is utilitarian. It articulates with a range of central social issues, including, as was suggested above, stratification and gender, it potentially broadens the nature of sociological explanation as the consideration of desire – the basis of a high percentage of consumption – and it involves wrestling with one of the least developed areas of sociological analysis: that of the emotions, a theme that will constitute a major sub-text in what follows.

THINKING THROUGH JAPANESE CONSUMPTION

Almost any popular book on Japan will be bound to mention the propensity of the Japanese to transform what they have received (from abroad presumably) into something characteristically their own, marked by a distinctive cultural style. While there is some truth in this, it overlooks the fact that Japan is also very much a society of innovation, and much of what is consumed in the rest of Asia and throughout the world is now Japanese in origin – fashions, foods, electronic equipment, cars, television serials, to name just a few. In the creation and dissemination of the consumer society, Japan is the leader in Asia. This is important because the spread of consumption means not only the multiplication of material things, but also the colonization of lifestyles. In a somewhat different cultural context, Bryan Turner has argued that the threat to the integrity of Islam in the Middle East particularly is not the contamination of Western ideas or communist ideologies, but precisely the spread of consumerism, which undermines and quietly subverts values and practices without in some cases anyone noticing what is going on, since the same countries are of course pursuing 'development'. Islam, in other words, is not problematized by conflicting rational arguments, but by the fact that 'everyday life has become part of a global system of exchange of commodities which are not easily influenced by political leaders, intellectuals or religious leaders' (Turner 1994: 10). Turner is no doubt right in discussing Islam (or Christianity for that matter). What he overlooks, however, are two points. The first is that there are societies in which religion and consumption have reached a fairly cosy accommodation. There may not be many of these, but Japan is certainly one of them. The second is that consumption itself contains creative possibilities. It may undermine, but it also creates new possibilities and, often, new freedoms.

The key reason for this is that consumption is not just economic behaviour. It must be placed in the context of, and in some cases is itself, social, ritual, religious, historical and even deep psychological process. It comprises, in other words, a cultural system. This means that it creates forms of social behaviour and social interaction peculiar to itself. It also means that attempts to understand or to 'explain' it must also be culturally rooted. This is a subtle point. Most general sociological attempts to discuss consumption fall back on a combination of critical theory, structuralism and psychoanalysis; some indeed (e.g. Bocock 1993) turn out to be little else. This has two deleterious results: one is the lack of real description of concrete consumer behaviour and its cultural peculiarities, and the other is the use of inappropriate explanatory frameworks. It is instructive, for instance, that, while Western accounts of consumption are heavily Freudian in orientation, psychoanalysis is unpopular in Japan and has never taken root. The rival indigenous theories of psychotherapy are premised upon quite different assumptions (Lebra 1982: 201–31). To apply a quite culturally inappropriate model of psychological organization to Japanese consumption behaviour is likely to lead to a curiously distorted picture of that activity. If it is true, as we might assume that it is, that consumption is closely linked to a sense of identity, to begin with the wrong model of selfhood is to initiate the analysis on the wrong premise. The alternative possibilities need instead to be clearly set out.

This must be done in the context of both postwar culture and postwar political economy. Japan has seen a long period of postwar peace. For half a century the country has been embroiled in no wars or major international disputes. Despite the claims of the now old left that the postwar Japan–USA security treaty had drawn Japan into conflicts in Asia not of its own making, the fact is that Japan benefited economically from both the Korean and Vietnam wars. Sheltering under the US umbrella while the rest of Asia has seen a half century of unrest, without the need to divert more than a tiny percentage of GNP to defence, and with capital benefiting from the suppression of leftist labour organizations during the latter half of the US occupation, Japan was encouraged to prosper, initially by the Americans, who saw this as the route to establishing Japan as an anti-communist bulwark in East Asia, and subsequently by indigenous governments with a keen sense of national pride. The result was indeed rapid economic growth, spreading prosperity, widespread urbanization and the appearance of a distinctive style of state-led capitalism.

It is important to stress that mass consumption is a late phenomenon in Japan, something that did not begin to appear until the 1960s when the income-doubling policy began to take hold – roughly a decade after mass consumption really began to take hold in Britain, for example. This is important, because the transition from purely industrial capitalism, with its production-oriented ethos, to consumer capitalism marks a major social change. The appearance of consumer capitalism marks the origin of a culture based increasingly on desire rather than need, one in which signs rather than just economic/materialist forces are dominant. And this desire is not simply the 'desire to become a certain type of person through consuming objects such as clothes, or styles of furniture' (Bocock 1993: 3), but represents an entire reorientation to life, to what is possible and to the realization of the idea of the making of the self as an at least partly autonomous project rather than as simply the plaything of history or of social forces beyond the control of the individual. The body, for example, becomes eroticized in new ways: clothes are no longer simply a covering or a socially approved uniform, but a way of presenting that body in ways previously barely conceivable. If the advent of Western-style clothing created one such revolution in Japanese sensibilities, the choices associated with consumerism surely created another.

While the appearance of consumer capitalism is a new phenomenon in Japan, as it is in the rest of Asia, there are of course antecedents. The basis for hedonistic consumption was laid in the late Meiji (1868-1912) and especially in the succeeding Taisho period (1912-26). One of the revolutionary changes of this period was the appearance for the first time of departmental stores, which evolved for the most part from the great dry goods stores of the late Edo period. Since then, to an extent never found in the West, departmental stores have been central institutions in the physical layout of urban centres: they have become major places of resort for shopping, eating and cultural activities (many contain art galleries, almost all have at least one book store and many promote classes in a variety of arts) and are of key significance in disseminating fashions, new foods and gadgets, promoting gift-giving at the mid- and end-of-year gift seasons and encouraging aspects of Japanese traditional culture (they are, for instance, often the best place to buy a kimono, folk pottery or lacquer ware). The appearance of such stores, innovative in some directions and profoundly conservative in others, marked the beginning of a revolution in shopping behaviour. The same period that saw the expansion of the departmental stores also saw the expansion of efficient public transportation in Japanese cities, and to this day such stores are to be found concentrated around the major railway stations (they are often members of the same company that owns the railway: see Chapter 3), with their branches spread out along suburban lines. The period after the great earthquake of 1923 also witnessed the growth of cafe life and a big increase in leisure facilities such as theatres, music halls, cinemas and sports stadia (Seidensticker 1983, 1990). These developments were not unconnected with the emerging role of women as central to consumption. The Taisho period was a lively one in terms of the appearance of Japanese feminism, and there was a spill-over effect, if not exactly on economic independence, then at least on the shopping power of women. The phenomenon of women emerging as central to consumption that was noted by Veblen in the United States at the turn of the century arrived in Japan a decade or so later (Veblen 1953).

This transition marks not only the emergence of consumption as central to social life, but also the first appearance of a principle very apparent in the structure of Japanese consumption – the differentiation of consumers into categories marked by wealth, gender and age, a factor underlying the practical organization of much of Japanese life into consumption as well as occupational classes. After the war these earlier patterns soon reasserted themselves, combined in complex ways with the deliberately introduced Americanized culture of the occupation years. Interestingly, Japan may now be once again at a point of transition: the postwar hegemony of the Liberal Democratic Party (LDP) began to crack in the early 1990s, just as the price of affluence (pollution, overcrowding, high prices, Japan's role in Southeast Asian deforestation, etc.) began to be questioned, when the problem of those excluded from the economic 'miracle', especially foreign workers, was being raised with increasing stridency and when so-called 'disorganized capitalism' began to make its appearance.

THE STRUCTURE OF JAPANESE CONSUMPTION

While the following chapters will detail some of the conspicuous features of contemporary Japanese consumption behaviour, it may be useful to start with a more general sketch of consumption patterns that provides a context for the understanding of those segments of life. The differentiation of consumers just alluded to is interesting for several reasons. One is that it does not necessarily reflect 'objective' social differences, but rather represents categories invented by advertising people and the media for the purpose of targeting marketing ploys at fairly discrete groups, or at groups who can be made to think of themselves in that way. Such differentiation into age and sex categories (or 'tribes' – *zoku* – as they are sometimes called) is driven especially by the magazine and comic book (*manga*) industry, which targets very distinct groups – pre-teen children, teenage girls, teenage boys, university students, young 'OLs' (i.e. 'office ladies' – clerks and secretaries), young salaried male workers, older house-wives, and so on. The advertising and information content is geared to the supposed tastes (or industry-created tastes) of the appropriate group. Some of the results might look surprising to Western eyes, such as the magazines targeted at young men and full of fashion advice, suggestions for accessories, hairstyles, and even perfumes. These are not designed for (although they are read by) young gay men, but for men in their late teens and early twenties, who, as many Japanese are, are fashion con-scious and have money to spend – money often generated not from indulgent parents, but from part-time jobs taken on precisely to feed the consumption habit. Movement between such groups (except for such special-interest groups as, say, surfers or motor-bike enthusiasts) is largely the result of age: one moves more or less automatically, and in this respect Japan represents nothing so much as a vast age-grade society. While fixed-status groups do exist, from the point of view of consumption classes there is considerable fluidity, especially for those already in the 'middle class' of Japanese society.

Consumption and social stratification are then both interrelated and evolving, just as there are both continuities and changes in Japanese senses of identity. This is partly because consumption itself is driven by a mixture of the desires, needs and fantasies of the consumer, the innovat-ing tendencies and marketing skills of industry, and the relationship of the latter to larger social forces. As alienation appears to increase, in Japan as elsewhere, consumption, in the absence of other traditional forms of management, may become a mechanism for attempting to overcome estrangement and to manage the 'risk society' of increasing uncertainty and economic complexity.

These reflections suggest that a central anthropological issue in the analysis of Japan is the balancing of apparent paradoxes. Consumption in some ways promotes individualism – freedom of choice, ability to select artefacts and to define lifestyles. Japan, however, also tends to be a formulaic society, and this is itself reflected in the nature of consumption – the availability of (and often there is no choice) prepack-aged, coded and standardized items. In the West, where novelty and being different is given more stress, Japanese consumers must seem uni-form and passive. And indeed the wearing of a 'uniform' – the salaryman's blue suit, or its job-hunting season equivalent the 'recruit-suit', the golf-ing outfit, the intellectual's beret, and so on – is very characteristic of a society where dressing alike – or at least corresponding to one's social role – is expected. Attendance at a Japanese wedding, where all of the men present (the women here are given slightly more latitude) will be wearing identical black suits and white ties, easily confirms this.

The massification of consumption in fact fits very well with at least two major themes in Japanese culture. The first is a tendency to conformity laid down during the Tokugawa era (1603–1868), with its strict sumptuary laws, and certainly reinforced during the period of prewar militarism, the war years themselves and the period of postwar austerity. This desire for uniformity, a kind of socialism of fashion, often criticized as 'groupism', should in fact be respected as a deeply held cultural value. Japan is actually a very conservative country in which, as in traditional Japanese aesthetics, innovation takes place within generally very strict boundaries. The second is the pre-eminent place given to emotions. So when Bocock says that 'consumption is more than ever before an experience which is to be located in the head, a matter of the brain and mind, rather than seen as the process of simply satisfying biological bodily needs' (Bocock 1993: 51), he creates a fundamental distortion at two levels. The first is to negate the role of desire and feeling in consumption, and the second, while consumption is not only about 'needs', suppresses the place of the body – the fact that much, indeed probably most, consumption is primarily to do with a body project.

Desiring to consume (as much as actually doing it) is itself a major feature of consumption behaviour, and is in turn related not only to the social construction of the body (both conceptually and literally through such mechanisms as fashion and diet), but also to the social construction of the desires themselves. This of course occurs in a number of ways – through the media and advertising, obviously, but also through the process of socialization. One learns to consume even as one learns other essential social skills. Consumption does very much involve the mastery of a set of values, practices and cultural symbols – values which are acceptable, diffusable and reproducible. Again advertising is a major source of such values, but they come from elsewhere too: shopping expeditions with mother as a small child, interaction with peers, information available in books and magazines. Much socialization in Japan, if carefully examined, turns out to be education for pleasure, and of course education, being one of the major forms of cultural capital, is itself consumed voraciously (that is one reason for the high savings rate – to pay for it all).

A characteristic of Japanese consumers is that they are highly informed (the information which encourages consumption also provides the means to discriminate between competing alternatives) and aesthetically sophisticated. They are actively involved in creating their sense of identity in terms of gender, age, lifestyle and as Japanese, even when this has to be done vicariously. With the transition of consumption from that based on need to that based on desire, people desire to 'consume' (at least through their gaze) even when they cannot afford actually to buy. The notion of desire then requires a little unpacking. For while in its simplest sense it can refer just to wanting, in its fuller sense it implies rather more than that, since desire involves symbolic and imaginative as well as material levels, and certainly embraces emotional and erotic components.

Baudrillard's view that desires are surface phenomena, not things of depth, needs to be firmly rejected. In Japan they are certainly stimulated by advertising, the constant creation of new products by industry (beers, chocolates, fashions and many other items change with the seasons), the influence of the global economy and tourism, and are encouraged by decreasing identification with work roles and 'life outside school' among younger students. But desires are also linked to, and indeed motivate, social and cultural practices, are rooted in socialization, and may form specific cultural complexes such as the *amae*, or dependency syndrome identified and made popular by the psychotherapist Doi Takeo (Doi 1973 [1988]). Consumption furthermore involves a set of performances, successful execution of which provides both status and inner satisfactions. Consumption as such crosses the boundaries between the cultural and the psychological, as it must insofar as it is based on desires, which are fluid, form and reform and tap into the unconscious. Even if much consumption in Japan is still the domain of women, men are increasingly expected to be discriminating consumers, and changing images of masculinity are closely tied to self-presentation and cultural performances that relate rather more closely to consumption (being able to order food fluently in a 'foreign' restaurant, for example) than with anything to do with the endlessly invoked 'samurai' ethics or aesthetics of the real or mythical past. In a society that provides apparently endless sites for consuming, no social category is exempt from its influence and no identities can be untouched by its transforming power.

A very clear example of this can be found in Merry White's discussion of the role of consumption in the lives of Japanese teenagers (White 1994). Her book, which is primarily an ethnography of Japanese teenage life with some comparison with teen life in the USA, is valuable not only as a descriptive account, but also for the theoretical points that it makes. As she suggests at the very beginning, in Japan there is a diversity invisible to most short term visitors. Her account shows very clearly the way in which one social category has been incorporated into the market, partly through the clever exploitation of cultural characteristics of teens, such as their being what White calls 'friend slaves', by advertisers and by departmental stores such as those clustered in the Shibuya district of Tokyo which, with their trendy names ('Parco', 'Seed', 'Loft', 'Wave'), cater especially to the young. Media and advertising have created a youth market by emphasizing the separateness of a 'youth culture', not least by taking pains to understand the contradictions of teenage life: the need to seek an individual sense of self and the need to conform; the attraction of materialism and the simultaneous attraction to idealism; the economic significance of teenagers and their social marginality.

An important feature of White's analysis is her emphasis on class differences: the difference between the affluent child cramming for university entrance and the high-school or night-school dropout destined for the factory floor, both of whom are probably *infomaniaktu* – 'informaniacs' – highly informed about consumer trends and who read widely the magazines targeted at their age group. Character, according to White, is linked not to the spending (or saving) of money (as in the USA), but to school achievement. In Japan there is less puritanism and no negative moral connotations attached to acquiring material goods. Japanese children quickly learn their 'material' and educational 'selves' – what White terms 'complementarity': 'the valued and functional fit between opposites in Japan' (White 1994: 21), which is not the same as being a hypocrite – as being different things to different people. White's study is essentially one of socialization – of the growth of ideas about relationships, parents, school, sexuality and consumption. Although her model is essentially a comparative one – Japanese teens in relation to US ones – what she is actually suggesting is a model of character structure which, if laid down in childhood, extends into adulthood and contains the same principle of complementarity: low on puritanism while capable of hard work and perfectionism, of pursuing rarefied high cultural activities while being equally busy accumulating material goods, reading foreign literature and *manga*, but without any sense of incongruity between these activities. These characteristics of course shed a good deal of light on later patterns of consumer behaviour of adult Japanese – patterns that will appear constantly in subsequent discussion.

Most Japanese teens then are 'part-time' consumers: the amount of schoolwork expected of them sees to that. This objective constraint (combined with relatively little money) works together with cultural perceptions that do not, in Japan, constitute teens as a 'problem', such as the deeply held idea of continuity rather than conflict between generations. Shopping together is an important way of creating and reinforcing friendships among peers, in particular because the peer culture (rather than 'groupism') which dominates much of Japanese social life creates a uniform market, participation in which further reinforces a sense of belonging. At the same time teen demands create quality and to some extent diversity (there are different teen sub-cultures) in the youth market, and promote a rapid turnover in styles, even though at any one point in time a single style for a given age group will dominate a particular area (in Tokyo or Osaka first and then spreading to smaller towns and the countryside).

There are of course gaps between the haves and the have-nots, important when the ability to 'keep up' with peers is a significant part of social acceptance. White indeed suggests that parents work, especially mothers who take part-time jobs, to support their children's 'needs' for things, which include not just shopping, but such modern essentials as piano lessons (very popular in Japan), trips and almost certainly a home computer. Here again there is an interesting complementarity: age is certainly a major factor in Japanese consumption and can be used as a very accurate predictor of the events of the life-course – entering and graduating from university, age of marriage, and so on – and teens as one such category are very much targeted by marketers. At the same time, and this is very clearly reflected in magazines for teenagers, for instance, there is a very genuine concern for their well-being, creativity and potentiality. Much of the advice and information proffered should not be seen as manipulation, but as motivated by the desire to help. The segmented population from the point of view of marketers – the 'micro-masses', as they are now often called in Japan – prove to be an interesting point of intersection between the constructions of the market and the actual life-cycle as perceived by the majority of the Japanese themselves.

THE POWER OF THE GIFT

In the last two decades economic anthropology has evolved from a preoccupation with exchange (a trend initially established by Marcel Mauss in his classic essay on gift exchange, and continued through a tradition including the work of Malinowski on the *kula* exchanges of Melanesia, the writings of Marshall Sahlins and Mary Douglas among others). In the late 1960s a reaction to this domination of interest in exchange was challenged by French Marxist anthropologists who moved debate from structures and processes of exchange to structures of production. In doing so, links between economic activity and social stratification were uncovered, including the possible existence of classes in societies that claimed to have none or were traditionally represented in this way (for a discussion of this whole movement, see Clammer 1978). A decade later saw the emergence of the current interest in consumption among anthropologists and cultural sociologists. Sometimes these three phases, exchange–production–consumption, are seen as an evolutionary sequence. In fact, closer examination of actual economic interactions, specially at the micro-level, shows that they are all implicated in one another.

Gift-giving, the original paradigm of the exchange model, demonstrates this very clearly.

It is well known that Japan, pre-eminently among the industrialized societies of the world, is very much a culture in which gift exchange continues to play a very major role, and has done so despite (or because of?) the rapid modernization experienced since the 1960s (Befu 1968). Gift-giving, while apparently part of the 'exchange' end of the spectrum, actually represents a major form of consumption in contemporary Japan, so important in fact that it is necessary to devote some space to discussing it as a specific phenomenon, one which casts considerable light on consumption behaviour and its underlying culture.

Gift-giving, in all cultures where it is practised, attempts to establish stable and lasting relationships between groups or individuals who are initially isolated from each other or even actually or potentially hostile. Some form of reciprocity is assumed, although moral considerations as such may be entirely absent, or, if they are present, are focused on the recipient rather than the giver. As Bauman puts it, interestingly in the context of a discussion of ethics in postmodern societies, 'whatever moral obligation appears in this context, arises at the far end of the gift-giving act, as its consequence, not the beginning' (Bauman 1994: 57). Gift-giving then, although it is sometimes posed in moral terms, or in terms of a language that appears to carry moral connotations ('obligation', for example), can actually be, and frequently is, amoral. The obligations assumed are not necessarily moral ones at all, but can be purely functional or social in nature. Material things, including the things given as gifts, have multiple roles. Material and social relations are aspects of each other. There are no 'pure' social relationships seen from this perspective, but rather what the social archaeologist Gosden calls a 'social ontology' – which is 'a structure of being springing from social and material relations in which material existence and thought are intermixed' (Gosden 1994: 62), in which objects encapsulate memory, create identity and penetrate the future, and enter into the human colonization of both space and time.

In much anthropological theory, gift exchange is seen as somehow 'containing' the giver in a way that commodity exchange does not. But in fact contemporary Japanese gift-giving involves the exchange of commodities, which are valued precisely as such. Commodity exchanges do not necessarily simply represent transactions between individuals who remain independent of each other. Even in the context of shopping, relationships are often created between purchaser and vendor; how much more so in the context of gift-giving. This means that, in practice, mutuality is usually created around consumption activities, including, in contemporary Japan, the exchange of commodities. Things, despite being frequently thought of as permanent, are actually unstable – they decay and change and, in modern Japan, simply go out of fashion. Objects do not in themselves have essential properties, but derive their significance from the meanings that are attached to them. Gift-giving in Japan then involves not only the constant renegotiation of relationships through the gifts, but equally the constant social construction of the objects themselves and an awareness of shifting meanings. Cultural capital is accumulated not so much by the act of exchanging itself, or in correct timing, but rather through the demonstration of mastery of the current (it is always evolving) semiotics of the objects themselves. While the consumption of culture through visible activities such as visiting museums is also important, to a great extent command of cultural competence in Japan is encapsulated in the gift relationship, which can as such become very easily a relationship of reciprocity rather than power. Objects, like images, are ideologically loaded, and signs, material or otherwise, are multivocal. In such a situation power derives not so much from the relationship between the subject (the person) and the sign, but in understanding and being able to manipulate the relationships between signs. Since objects are expressive symbols they enter immediately into symbolic interaction (Gottdiener 1995). Much of Japanese life can be understood rather better if it is seen not in terms of conventional anthropological and Japanological analysis (*uchi/soto* – inside/outside; *tatamae/honne* – public face and private or true face; *giri* and *on* – reciprocity and obligation, and so forth), much of the responsibility for which must be laid at the door of Ruth Benedict and her half century of influence on the categories of Japanological analysis (Benedict 1946), but rather in terms of symbolic struggle within the context of a society ideologically committed to the public presentation of itself as organized on the principle of *wa* – harmony. Gift-giving shares in this fundamental ambivalence, combining the ideology, and often the practice, of reciprocity with low-intensity symbolic warfare.

This can be seen in the actual ethnography of gift-giving in urban Japan. Gifts, while they may be given on an individual basis (e.g. on birthdays or Valentine's Day), or even to oneself – so-called 'monadic giving' (Sherry, McGrath and Levy 1995) – often reflect a system of obligation rather than freely willed choice. The chocolates given to men by women on Valentine's Day are often called *giri choco* – 'obligation chocolates' – and are presented to bosses or superiors in the organization rather than to friends. However, the greater part of visible gift-giving occurs not between individuals, but between households, much of it the year-end (*oseibo*) and mid-year (*ochugen*) seasons. Gifts are then bestowed largely out of gratitude from inferiors to superiors or to acknowledge favours granted. The precise nature and value of gifts is carefully calculated in terms of the size of the obligation and the relative social standing of the two parties. Etiquette manuals are easily available and are frequently consulted for advice on the correct forms. Careful lists are kept of what is given to whom and what is received.

Traditionally, gift-giving was expressed in the idiom of *on* (indebtedness) and of *giri*, or obligation, historically in the context of the *ie*, or corporate household, and while the rhetoric stressed the maintenance of group solidarity and neighbourliness, formal gift-giving did and still does frequently mask or reinforce objective inequality of status. While genuine gratitude and loyalty can indeed be expressed through gift-giving, dependency – *amae* – and also the incurring of substantial socially induced expense, can also be fostered. For presentations are stimulated not only by the two approved gift-giving seasons, but also by weddings, funerals, the opening of a new business or clinic, promotions, illnesses and the setting off for or returning from abroad. *Depatos* – departmental stores – have built very successfully on Japanese cultural values, or rather have gone a long way in commercializing those values, and are now among the biggest promoters of gift-giving. Any departmental store and most supermarkets provide gift delivery services, often have special gift departments or desks, provide elaborate wrapping services for items purchased in the store, widely advertise their suggestions for appropriate gifts, and are tireless in creating or importing an ever-expanding range of occasions for gift exchange or giving, which now includes such distinctly non-Japanese events as Christmas (one of the biggest), Hallowe'en, Valentine's Day (and its reciprocal White Day), Mothers' Day, Fathers' Day and Secretaries' Day. At the same time the network of those to whom gifts should be given widens, now to include bosses, colleagues, parents, the family doctor, lawyers, teachers, local politicians, and go-betweens (*nakodo*) who have been involved in brokering marriages. And the range of potential gifts grows ever bigger and is slowly changing. While fairly conventional gifts still dominate the market – foods, cooking oil, seasonings, seaweed, beer, mushrooms, liquor and certain kinds of fruit, especially melons – innovations include gift certificates and coupons (cash is given at weddings and funerals, but on few other occasions) and regional specialities, many of which can be ordered (and delivered) through new marketing outlets such as the post office.

Gifts then are as much to do with status as with reciprocity, and they are a huge business that involves not only stores and public agencies such as the post office (any branch has advertisements and pamphlets on the wares available for order there), but also a range of secondary industries such as the *takubin*, or parcel and baggage delivery services, which are to be found all over Japan. The symbolic and economic levels of the gift do not then turn into one another – they are in reality merged from the outset. But while using the language of reciprocity, Japanese gift-giving also constitutes the Other, since gifts, while establishing or signifying social bonds, also establish social distance. Interestingly, Japanese society, while very conspicuously a gift-giving one, is not primarily a commensual one, promoting an image of sharing and reciprocity, but not on an oral basis – unlike, for instance, Chinese society, where eating together is often the basis of social bonding. Gift-giving then appears as a commercialized form of modern intimacy, or rather as the form of intimacy without its substance, of creating bonds without a moral substance.

CONSUMPTION AND THE ORGANIZATION OF EVERYDAY LIFE

Acts of consumption then enter into the constitution of contemporary Japanese society at many levels, some at least of which have fundamental implications for the ways in which Japan is understood and interpreted. The peacefulness of Japanese society – the absence of overt opposition to its main institutions and customs – for instance, is often traced to the ideology of harmony – *wa* – a set of values, in other words, that somehow pervades Japanese life. Such appeal to cultural values does indeed take place in everyday discourse as well as in some genres of Japanese social thought, but sociologically rather more understanding might arise from the recognition of the mechanisms which transform 'low' or oppositional culture into trends and fashion. The difficulty of resistance in Japanese society lies primarily in the tendency of oppositional forces (whether political or cultural) to be co-opted, not least by the media, which is in Japan quite literally the 'mediating' link between genuinely popular culture and the absorption or transformation of such culture into the mainstream. While this can be seen operating at many levels, its place in relation to consumption is significant at two levels. The first is the co-opting of genuinely popular culture – innovations in taste or fashion, for example, taking place outside of the commercialized realm. Such innovations, once discovered, quickly become publicized and, if successfully co-opted, trendy. The second is the way in which such transformations in the consumer realm act as a paradigm for wider social processes. That is to say, both the way in which certain socio-cultural changes take place in Japan, and the way in which others are prevented from occurring, derives not primarily from political control, but from 'cultural' control. This notion of 'culture', once deconstructed, turns out very frequently to mean consumption behaviour. New fashions, new TV personalities, new politicians, new ideas about 'internationalization' are all constructed and presented in much the same way and are marketed essentially as commodities, to be used and discarded once a new trend appears. Cultural nationalism in Japan occurs largely today (although certainly not in the past) through consumer culture. This is a profound and subtle transformation, one which pervades the society and without recognition of which modern Japanese history simply cannot be adequately grasped.

In Japan what one sees is a national culture of a strongly centripetal character attempting to maintain itself in the face of globalization. The detailed means through which this attempt is made by those who create opinion and manage images of national identity, who in practice are frequently businessmen and intellectuals, including in the Japanese context local-level schoolteachers (Yoshino 1992), are interesting. For example, very little reference is made to religion or religious values. Instead an indigenous model of culture is formulated which has several key characteristics. The first of these is the recognition, apparently very belatedly arrived at by Western sociologists, that culture is indeed constructed and the practice of culture takes place through the experience of culture as artificial and constructed, although of course as essential. People are not then deluded about this, but recognize the construction of culture as the central project of human beings, but in ways that interestingly differentiate Japanese understandings from those of the West. This differentiation occurs in two main ways, the first being the perception of culture as an essentially collective enterprise in which individualism in the Western sense plays little part, the understanding of culture being based on a social psychology which sees self and society fundamentally as reflections of each other, and the second being the place of nature in relation to culture. For whereas until very recently, with the spread of the ecological movement in the West, nature was seen as over against society and as something in some sense to be resisted and controlled – excluded from society, in other words – in Japanese social thought nature is part of the constitution of society and enters into the nature of social relationships (Clammer 1995a: 59–81). This has several direct implications for the wider understanding of Japanese society, and specifically for the understanding of the place and nature of consumption within that society.

The first of these is that the Japanese sense of personal being is very much an *embodied* one. Again Western sociology has apparently only just caught up with this fact, as the plethora of recent books on the place of the body in society attests. The creation of bodies as essential aspects of selfhood is a central part of the project of constructing a humane culture. Emphasis on self-cultivation – historically through ideas derived from Chinese Confucianism and indigenized through ideas of aesthetic practice, meditation and the martial arts – and in the contemporary world through consumption – diet, sport and the presentation of the body through fashion in particular – has long been part of Japanese culture and actually performs a moral function. The body, seen in Japan as being the gift of one's parents, is to be cultivated not for narcissistic motives, but as the vehicle for enlightenment or self-realization. Abandoning the body (as in many forms of Western asceticism) is thus unthinkable, as is its mortification. Cultivation rather reflects a whole mind–body philosophy which assumes their basic harmony (Yuasa 1987).

What is interesting here are the differing sociological implications of this. The 'reflexivity', again recently discovered by Western sociologists, has always been present in Japanese society in the form (somewhat different from that of the West) of self-cultivation and a culturally specific conception of the life-cycle, in which distinct attributes are attached to the expected characteristics and expected behaviour of each way-station in the cycle, and in which continuity rather than conflict between generations (as was suggested in the preceding discussion of teenagers) is assumed. Aging, now an important theme for many sociologists, is cast in a different light in Japan. It is a natural process to be affirmed rather than denied; valuable attributes are attached to age, and aging is expressed not in terms of attempting to appear young, but rather in the form of the modification of consumption and self-presentation to accord with chronological age. The style and colour of dress and the consumption of foods and entertainments is expected to evolve over the life-cycle. Old age then is in an important sense socially constructed through consumption which signals and reflects the social categories into which chronological aging is culturally organized. The 'life-projects' identified by sociologists such as Anthony Giddens as characteristic of late modernity in the West (Giddens 1991) do not have identical equivalents in Japan, where life-projects are much more likely to be organized around the expected characteristics of phases of the life-cycle (itself culturally patterned). Thus they have rather more uniformity than Western ones, based on ideas of autonomous selves and fuelled by self-help manuals, to which anxious Europeans and North Americans, beset by the anxieties of late modernity, are increasingly turning.

What might in the West be seen as modernist constraints have, insofar as that vocabulary applies to Japan, been retained in unexpected ways. The replicability and reproducibility of cultural elements identified by such writers as Walter Benjamin as characteristic of modernity have long been part of Japanese culture. Consumption, trends, 'tribalism', the pursuit of fashion – the loss of modernist constraints, in other words – coexist with social order in Japan in ways that do not occur elsewhere. Social anxiety does exist in Japan and can express itself in materialism – as in some of the so-called New Religions, for example – but even this must be understood in terms of a culture in which the quotidian – the mundane and the everyday – is elevated to an art form and seen as constituting the core of life rather than as detracting from it (Hasegawa 1982).

Per capita income in Japan now exceeds that of the USA. Per capita consumption, which until recently lagged behind, partly as a result of the high savings rate, is now on par with the USA. From the late 1970s a high annual growth in the rate of consumption was recorded, and, when different pricing structures are taken into account, this growth is even more remarkable. Today a colour TV, a refrigerator and a washing machine are standard equipment in almost every home. Over 80 per cent of households own at least one camera, and ownership of stereos, cars, microwaves, air-conditioners and pianos is high and growing. Huge numbers of Japanese are now travelling for leisure both at home and abroad, and the internationalization of consumption proceeds apace with substantial ownership of foreign cars (especially European ones), the proliferation of Western-style fast-food outlets and a big growth in the habit of eating out, often in 'ethnic' food restaurants. Furniture, cutlery and tableware has become highly Westernized, increasing significance is attached to leisure and there is growing demand for sporting, recreational, hobby and educational activities of a non-functional nature. Added together these trends point to a wide-ranging quiet revolution in the organization of everyday Japanese life (Hernadi 1990).

This quiet revolution, while it has effected the entire society, has not applied equally to every stratum of the society. Foreign workers, who have been brought to Japan because of the revolution, have not necessarily participated in its benefits. Nor have all Japanese. William Kelly rightly argues against the idea of total middle-class homogenization. Contrary to popular foreign images, most working Japanese are employed not in large corporations and with the benefits of life-time employment and total job security, but in small and medium companies where employment is not guaranteed and where mid- and end-of-year bonuses – a very important and substantial part of annual income for salaried workers – are variable and can shrink or disappear altogether. A large number of people, especially women, students and retired people, are in part-time or temporary employment. And there is still a substantial old middle class of shopkeepers, small business people and farmers, including large numbers of urban farmers – people who, often for tax purposes, have retained land in cities (or cities have expanded to encapsulate their land) and continue rice growing or market gardening. And even within an identifiable middle class there are substantial variations in lifestyles signalled by both consumption patterns and social differentiation, achieved, for example, through membership in one of the New Religions. As Kelly points out (Kelly 1993), the emergence of white-collar workers as a mass phenomenon is in any case a relatively recent thing and one that cannot be seen as an isolated social event; rather it must be related to the impact of institutional changes in postwar society, such as schooling, family and housing, access to which is a major determinant of social mobility in Japan.

A critique of the view of Japan as homogeneously middle class also needs to take into account the ways in which discourses of public culture have developed a series of new social categories – the 'micro-masses' referred to earlier. The dominant discourse among media commentators and intellectuals in the 1970s was that of *churyu ishiki*, or 'middle-class consciousness', reflecting the new affluence and consumer boom of those years. By the 1980s this had been replaced by talk of the 'new people', or *shinjinrui*, of that internationalizing decade, soon to be upstaged by the *shin shinjinrui* – 'new new people'. Before long talk had shifted to the identification of new 'micro-masses' and theories of *sedai*, or generation cohorts, with discussion of the *raifu kosu*, or 'life-course', and most recently with debates about Japan as a *koreika shakai*, or 'aging society'. Interwoven with these larger categories have been smaller ones, the 'tribes' which the Japanese media delights in discovering – the *futenzoku*, or hippies, of the early 1970s, the 'bamboo-shoot people' of Tokyo's trendy Harajuku district, the *takenokozoku* and the 'speed tribes', or consumer-oriented youth, of the current generation (Greenfeld 1994). The 'micro-mass' theory, originally propounded by the social commentator Fujioka Wakao, was that the 'old' (actually late 1960s and 1970s) middle-class consciousness was replaced by the 1980s with *shoshu*, or such smaller significant-group consciousness, and was closely associated with the idea of the simultaneous emergence of the *shohi bunka*, or consumer culture, complete with the appearance of what Fujioka called 'grasshopper consumers', flitting from trend to trend and consuming from hedonistic motives, having abandoned the frugality and economy-building mentality of the older generation (Fujioka 1984). Such ideas were rapidly embraced by some prominent intellectuals, many of whom in Japan build their careers in commenting on and promoting the trendy. Asada Akira, for example, developed a rather Baudrillardian-like theory in which advertising copywriters are the new heroes, in that advertising, for all its simulations and promotion of hyper-reality, promotes differentiation within consumer capitalism, within which consumption itself promotes liberation and new forms of subjectivity (Asada 1984).

So, as Marylin Ivy suggests, 'An analysis of mass culture in postwar Japan is thus crucial not only for understanding the domestic interrelationship of capitalism, aesthetics and technology but also for grasping the global implications of Japan's "economic miracle"' (Ivy 1993). In her survey of the evolution of a mass culture in Japan post-Meiji, Ivy suggests that, in the 'postpost war' period (i.e. from about 1955 on), the big changes that have really transformed Japanese life have been the interrelated forces of consumerism, urbanization and the expansion of the media – TV, publishing and the cinema, all forces that have flowered most comprehensively in the 1990s.

Starting in the late 'postpost war' (i.e. the 1970s), household budgets have shown interesting changes. The proportion set aside for necessities (food, utilities and functional clothing) has declined. So has the proportion spent on furniture and household goods. At the same time the amount spent on leisure and luxuries has increased, although there is still a high level of savings, reflecting the high costs of housing purchase and education. Gender differences also became very visible in the same period and continue down to the present. Between 1984 and 1989 the consumption expenditure of single women of all ages increased by 13 per cent and those of single women under the age of 30 by 15.8 per cent. Expenditure by men, however, rose far less rapidly, reflecting a tendency for young women, especially before marriage, to spend more on leisure, recreation and travel as well as on shopping. Japan is interestingly a society of high consumption despite high consumer prices, and a society of mass consumption and mass savings (Horioka 1993)

Such considerations are related to a number of other features of consumption culture in Japan. One of these is the association of high price with quality, hence the desire for brand-name goods and the following of expensive fads. Media and departmental stores do a lot to 'train' young people in shopping, and once a trend has taken hold people will flock to join it (e.g. the current craze among young children for pagers, among older youth for party telephone lines on which a number of teenagers can share and talk to each other, and among adults for portable telephones). Such trends are closely followed by the advertising industry (e.g. by the Hakuhodo Institute of Life and Living affiliated with one of Japan's biggest advertising agencies) so that more or less instant feedback is available. The industry knows what people are consuming, and alert consumers know what the media are promoting, almost simultaneously. In the UK people will boast about the cheapness of something they have purchased, in Japan about its expense. Objects are also discarded much more rapidly in Japan than probably anywhere else. Perfectly functional but simply out-of-date equipment, fashions or furnishings will be replaced rapidly by those who can afford to do so; possession of the very latest enhances cultural capital like almost nothing else. Variety or originality is not the point: newness is.

The place of consumption in everyday life – its role in daily routines, its transforming effects on social relationships, its attitudes to the body and its place in the construction of meaning systems – now needs deepening in two directions. The first of these is its place within the world of urban Japan, where mass consumption is principally concentrated and in which consumption powerfully orders the management of space and time. The second is the placing of consumption within a bigger picture of the political economy of contemporary Japan, both in order to examine its place within wider political and economic structures and to attempt to trace the role of consumption in hastening the evolution of Japanese society from one based on primary industrial production and the provision of associated financial services, to a 'postmodern' one. This latter is based increasingly on the production and consumption not of things, but of signs, on the manipulation of images and the colonization of space and time through new forms of econo-cultural practice; these create an economy of desire in which necessity itself is transformed and restructured and with it the whole way in which the entire society is constituted.

2

Consumption and Urban Cultures in the Japanese City

Consumption is a universal phenomenon in contemporary Japan from which no one is immune, not even monks in their temples. But patterns of consumption do vary substantially, and while, for example, farmers consume the products of industrial Japan as well as the literal fruits of their own labours, mass consumption – consumption indulged in intensely and as a way of life – is an urban experience. There are obvious reasons for this: density of population and its attendant concentration of opportunities and networks, the location of media organizations in the larger cities, and the fact that urbanites are most likely to define and create their lifestyles through consumption.

This very basic fact has two sociological consequences. Firstly, mass consumption must itself be analysed as an urban phenomenon, and popular culture, fashion and spatial and temporal behaviour are radically shaped by their urban context. Urbanism as it were sets the frame for contemporary consumption activities. Secondly, it follows from this that the nature of urban sociology and of much urban anthropology is transformed if the structures and rhythms of urban life are seen as created in large part through the pursuit of consumption. Consumption in contemporary Japan then has to be seen in its urban setting, and cities have to be understood not only in architectural terms or as sites of production, but also very much as arenas of consumption. While Japan has possessed cities and urban cultures for a long time, the large cities of the present coincide with industrialization and latterly with the appearance of mass markets and of affluence, which has brought about a transformation of the face of Japanese cities, with their contemporary concentrations of departmental stores and spreading suburbs and their lack of parks and public facilities outside of those created by commerce. This is an urban world in which many of the best art galleries are to be found within departmental stores or owned by large companies that attempt to combine the pursuit of capitalism and of culture.

THE URBAN CONTEXT OF CONSUMPTION

Japan is not a newly urbanized society. Urban centres — the location of the court and of religion — were already developed by the fifteenth century in the form of the successive capitals of Nara, Kyoto and Kamakura, cities which still exist and are revered as the foci of traditional culture, both secular and religious. During the period of the Tokugawa shogunate (1603–1868) a network of castle towns developed, both as centres of military control and as the locations of commerce, and with it a culture of the townsmen, a culture which reached its flowering in the great castle city of Edo (later renamed Tokyo) and its rival Osaka. Since the Tokugawa era the latter has been seen as a city of business and of an individualistic and colourful urban culture, a point noted by Umesao in his study of the comparative urban psychology of the inhabitants of the three focal cities of Tokyo, Osaka and Kyoto (Umesao 1987). This early urban experience is important, for the Japanese are no strangers to urban life, and Edo in its heyday was one of the world's biggest cities, with a highly developed urban infrastructure including sanitation and fire-fighting facilities that would have been the envy of European cities of the time. Urbanism has long been a component of Japanese life, and the experience of creating and sustaining urban cultures based on commercial lifestyles has deep roots (Nakamura 1993).

Today Japan is one of the most urbanized of countries, with almost 20 per cent of its total population concentrated in the greater Tokyo area alone. Indeed, this heavy concentration of population and functions in Tokyo has given rise to calls for the relocation of the capital and the dispersal of bureaucratic and corporate headquarters to provincial cities or to a new custom-built capital. The high prices, crowding and long commuting journeys that now characterize Tokyo life (and to a great extent those of Osaka too) might then, in theory, become a thing of the past. The problem, however, is that the large cities are also the centres of the media industries, of education, of cultural creation and dissemination and of consumption, and any kind of city planning in Japan has to take account of this multiplicity of activities, often existing in a symbiotic relationship with each other. This intense concentration of functions, and the sheer size of its economic base, has led to the characterization of Tokyo and Osaka as 'world cities' comparable not only in size, but more importantly in economic and cultural power, with any of the leading cities of the Western world (Miyamoto 1993).

Over time the characteristics spatially and socially of Japanese cities have changed. The socially controlled and spatially focused nature of the old castle towns (analogous to that of the life of the cathedral cities of medieval Europe) has been replaced with an uncentred sprawl. An often noted characteristic of Japanese cities is that they appear to have no centres and possess few landmarks, have few straight streets and no grand boulevards; addresses are almost impossible to locate without a map, one usually oriented from the nearest railway station. That this apparent disorder does in fact reflect a different spatial and social logic from that of European cities is undeniable (Ashihara 1989), although the argument that will be advanced here is that this does not simply represent spatial preferences somehow rooted in traditional culture. Some of the changes that have occurred in Japanese cities are very significant for patterns of social life. As in many North American cities, there has been a 'hollowing out' of the inner cities; however, unlike in America, these inner cores have not become ghettoes, but concentrations of large stores, corporate offices and cinemas. This still has the effect of creating areas in which no one actually lives and which are virtually deserted from late evening until late mid-morning on the succeeding day. Frequently what resident population is left behind in such zones are individuals, often elderly, who have refused to sell their property to developers, a problem that is worse in Osaka than it is in Tokyo, since the old inner-city areas of Osaka were once thriving commercial districts filled with small businesses, but are now characterized by a population of elderly dependent residents whose children have long since moved to suburbs.

The emergence of Japanese 'world cities', complete with their own international airports, which has been brought about by the transnationalization of Japanese trade and business (Fujita and Hill 1993), has also brought about very high land prices and an increasing gap between home-owners and renters. Both Osaka and Tokyo are now vast sprawling cities without apparent limits, characterized by lack of zoning, but with the inner cities defined by their concentrations of large stores and office buildings, the next-to-inner-city areas containing the still remaining pockets of older housing and family businesses, and the suburbs containing a mix of residential quarters. These comprise individual detached homes, 'mansions' or condominiums and *danchi*, or public housing blocks, commercial and industrial enterprises, and especially vast numbers of small firms – factories, shops and workshops – which are not only a numerically very significant sector of the Japanese economy, but are also the *nayedoko*, or 'seedbeds', from which innovations come – innovations which, once taken up by consumers, are often then manufactured on a mass scale by the bigger companies.

Outside of Tokyo and Osaka there are a variety of cities of rather different types. These include the old capitals of Nara, Kyoto and Kamakura, which are centres of small-scale commerce, education and traditional culture and which are major destinations for both local and foreign tourists because of their temples, historical sites and local delicacies. Then there are some of the old castle towns, such as Kanazawa, still noted for their traditional architecture and still dominated by what might be called the 'old upper-middle class' – merchant families established for generations (Wimberley 1973). Possibly also to be included in this group are towns that have been specially 'traditionalized' and quite deliberately turned into cultural centres and centres of local tourism, such as Kurashiki in Okayama Prefecture, where half of the city has been rebuilt and Meiji and pre-Meiji buildings restored, many of them converted into museums of the period, art galleries, traditional-style inns or souvenir shops.

A completely different category comprises cities that are almost entirely industrial in origin and contemporary in composition. Possibly the best example of this is Toyota City, adjacent to the old castle city of Nagoya (now itself a major commercial centre), which is a company town devoted wholly to the production of motor vehicles. Other examples would include Kawasaki, the industrial city situated between Tokyo and Yokohama, and the 'steel town' of Kita-Kyushu in western Japan. Many provincial cities combine several of these functions and still attempt to maintain some balance between their historical characteristics and their modern bureaucratic, commercial and industrial ones. Examples here would include the major prefectural capitals, sites as such of local government, regional business headquarters and the location of at least one national and several prefectural and private universities and colleges (e.g. Sapporo in Hokkaido, Sendai in Tohoku or Kagoshima in Kyushu). Also among them are medium-sized provincial cities once important as political or trade centres and now attempting to recover some of that former status through energizing their commercial sector or exploiting geographical advantages (e.g. Niigata, which, with its location on the Japan Sea coast, is well sited for trade with Russia and China, or Mito, an important political centre as capital of one of the great pre-Meiji fiefs and now a small city with some interesting historical sites, an important regional arts centre and theatre (the Mito Arts Tower) and accessible to Tokyo within two hours by train).

The most recent variety of Japanese cities are the new ones devoted to research and development activities – 'science cities' in intention. While there are plans for a number of these, at least two actually exist, both again within easy commuting distance of Tokyo, which in this context too acts as a mag-net. One of these is Tsukuba, a university and research city a short distance north of Tokyo and physically quite unlike other Japanese cities, with its straight roads, public plazas and orderly layout. Another of quite different character is the Kanagawa Science City, which is actually a large complex of buildings set in a typical small industry area at the intersection of the cities of Tokyo, Kawasaki and Yokohama and, unlike Tsukuba, immediately adjacent to manufacturing facilities and large population centres.

Two general sociological observations emerge from this brief typology of Japanese urban settings. The first is that, at one level, the variety of urban settings and the cultural styles associated with them (including in many cases very distinctive senses of local identity expressed through dialect differences, such as the language of old Kyoto residents or *Osaka Ben*, the indigenous form of speech of Kansai natives, regional cuisines and fashion and make-up – as with the 'Osaka face' sometimes referred to in Japanese women's magazines) contradict the familiar stereotype of Japanese cultural homogeneity. The second is that, at another level, what unites most urban Japanese is participation in a common culture of consumption. The same magazines can be read from one end of the (very long) country to the other, the same advertisements are viewed nationally, and fashions and trends of many kinds that begin in Tokyo diffuse rapidly to the rest of the country. It is the dialectical relationship between these two cultural forces – the unifying tendencies of a common consumer culture with its often internationalizing elements on the one hand, and the varieties of indigenous urban cultures with their regional characteristics on the other – that provides the fuel for much of the dynamics of everyday urban life: the desire, for example, to defend identity as a Japanese while simultaneously consuming the world.

Maintaining community life is increasingly difficult to sustain in the big cities, despite the valiant attempts of urban anthropologists such as Bestor (1989) and Robertson (1991) to argue for the vitality of local level politics and the *matsuri*, or festivals, which still regularly occur in city neighbourhoods. What both overlook is the emergence of new patterns of networking based on consumption, work and links to activities and cultural interests outside of the neighbourhoods. The neighbourhood (in Bestor's case) or the *shi*, or urban administrative unit (Robertson), are now of only very limited utility as the foci of analysis. Many people who live in them work outside of them, most inhabitants originated elsewhere, friendship networks entirely transcend them and patterns of spatial movement for shopping and entertainment entirely ignore them. In both cases conventional anthropological methodology has led to the misidentification of the unit of analysis as place rather than as network.

As cities change, links based on sociological factors other than locality increase in importance. Japanese cities are no longer a congeries of village-like neighbourhoods, but a messy mixture of huge stores and corporate offices coexisting with many small shops, petty commodity producers and residential units. Huge levels of in-migration, peaking in the mid-1960s in Tokyo, have been replaced by a hollowing out as high land prices and development policies force residents out of the inner cities into the suburbs, where the problem of declining public space (parks, for example) is also less acute. At the same time new multifunctional living/working/playing spaces, such as the Makuhari Messe, with its projected night-time population of 26,000 have begun to spring up on the outskirts of the major cities in an attempt to ensure something still rare in urban Japan outside of the old inner-city commercial districts with their family businesses: the proximity of work and home. Gaps between owners and renters are beginning to pose a potentially serious social problem, still papered over by daily participation in the common culture of consumption and the lack of overt class struggle in Japan. In those areas of cities dominated by renters, the traditional integrating role of the *chonaikai*, or neighbourhood associations, is steeply declining as identification with the local community fades. In neighbourhoods where companies have built *shataku*, or dormitory accommodation, for their workers (often single people or young families) this situation is exacerbated, since for Japanese employees it is the company rather than the neighbourhood that is the focus of identity, social networks and lifestyle.

These alternative patterns of urban life have been described in a number of settings, beginning with Dore's now classic ethnography of a Tokyo ward in the 1950s (Dore 1967). Today Dore's work stands as the most detailed description of Japanese urban life yet accomplished, and as a fascinating baseline against which to measure more contemporary developments. Dore's study was undertaken only a few years after the end of the war and before the 'economic miracle' was under way, and as such long before the era of mass consumption. Even so, shifts in leisure patterns were already apparent. The radio (not yet the TV) had become a major source of entertainment and information for a large number of city dwellers, and the movement towards the mass society was equally discernible. As Dore notes in the conclusion of his study:

> But today the age of economic individualism is all but over. The later
> stages of capitalist development have brought a new kind of collectivism of
> a vaster and more impersonal kind than that of the medieval village – the
> collectivism of the giant industrial corporation, of State welfare services

and nationalized industries, of shared fashions in clothes, enjoyments and values diffused by mass radio and television. (Dore 1967: 391)

Indeed, today Japan represents the interesting intersection of the older forms of collectivism and these new ones. Unfortunately, despite the general comprehensiveness of his survey, Dore did not investigate the nature of individual or household consumption apart from asking briefly about family incomes and expenditure and about gift-giving, which, in the late 1940s and early 1950s, was very important economically, especially to poorer families who were the recipients of gifts (something rarely true today), as well as reflecting the importance of kinship ties (Dore 1967: 57).

Interestingly, later ethnographies of Japanese cities have also ignored the same questions. In her study of Kodaira, for instance, Robertson traces the history of the town from its founding as an agricultural settlement on reclaimed and uncolonized land on the Musashino plain to its present status as an outer suburb of Tokyo. The theoretical core of her study is an analysis of the rivalry between the old Kodaira families ('the natives') and the mass of newer residents who have swollen the population of the town since the 1960s ('the newcomers') and the concept of neighbourhood is organized around an analysis of the local *matsuri*, in which both natives and newcomers participate (Robertson 1991). However, the extent to which any contemporary *matsuri* is motivated by commercial as much as by religious or local-level political factors is not discussed; nor is the extent to which Kodaira, while meaningful as an administrative unit, is much less so as a sociological one, given that significant ties of friendship, kinship, work and entertainment lie mostly outside the boundaries of the town, something which Robertson's own ethnography suggests, but which she does not pick up on.

A similar methodological limitation besets Bestor's ethnography of an inner Tokyo neighbourhood (Bestor 1989), a district that he dubs 'Miyamoto-cho'. Again the district forms a discrete administrative unit; it also has an annual *matsuri* and it has plenty of local politics. This latter point is part of the problem, since local-level politics, because of its self-referential nature, creates the sense of there being a community, even though in practice in Japan even fewer people pay any attention to local politics than do to national politics. In fact Bestors's ethnography is more of interest for the light that it sheds on the continuing existence in Tokyo of an old middle class. Except in a geographical sense, Miyamoto-cho is really only a community to these people. Tacitly Bestor himself admits this. For example, in describing the *kairanban* – the message-boards with announcements, news, warnings of public works about to begin in the neighbourhood, and so forth – Betsor notes that

In theory the system can pass information to or collect responses from all 750 households in a couple of days. But in practice kairanban often do not circulate to apartment dwellers. The responsibility for informing them of neighborhood events is left to the landlord or manager. As a result the chokai's (neighborhood association) messages often bypass these people, which both confirms and further reinforces their status as less than fully-fledged neighborhood residents. (Bestor 1989: 147)

This is not of course to deny that neighbourhoods do not exist in Japanese cities. They do, but to a majority of residents, except in pockets still dominated by members of the old middle class, they do not mean the kinds of things that many anthropologists of Japan ascribe to them, and the lifestyles of most residents, especially men and others whose work or cultural activities lie outside of the neighbourhood, do not involve them closely in political or social events within the locality. Indeed one of the factors which does tie people, especially women, to their residential local-ity is something hardly mentioned by either Robertson or Bestor – edu-cation. Having a child in school in a given neighbourhood links mothers in particular to the school or kindergarten, involves them in an effectively involuntary way in parent–teacher association meetings, sports days, fes-tivals in which the school takes part, and jumble sales and concerts. Relationship to a neighbourhood is highly gendered in Japan, and with-out a recognition of this the networks that actually comprise the social structures of such localities (which are often far from being communities) cannot be grasped adequately. Bestor's criteria for selecting his fieldwork site (Bestor 1989: 5) are such as to exclude the vast majority of Tokyo districts, but even within these closely defined limits the economic an-thropology of the area, the gendered nature of relationships to it, its class structure and its educational structure are every bit as significant as its neighbourhood association, its shrine and its festival – the attributes that for some reason still tend to attract anthropologists, even though, for the majority of residents, local life is no longer framed by them.

Japanese cities then are made up of a dense patchwork of districts, each itself diverse in terms of economic structure and social organization. Some of these districts are further described in later chapters: the world of the departmental stores and underground shopping complexes in Chap-ter 4 and the world of the suburbanite (especially housewives) in Chapter 5. Even these do not exhaust the range of types of neighbourhood, however: there would still be the 'new towns' of virtually identical hous-ing blocks on the peripheries of the big cities, the speciality areas such as Tokyo's bookshop area, Jinbo-cho, the 'Electric City' district of Akihabara, also in Tokyo, or the Gion quarter of Kyoto, associated with geisha and small bars and restaurants. Two things, however, are notable about all these districts: all are sociologically a complex mix of residential and commercial activity and all are devoted to a specific aspect of consumption. Often an individual street within a given neighbourhood will specialize in this way. In Tokyo's Ginza area the main street – Chuo-dori – is lined with the flagship stores of the big departmental store chains – Mitsukoshi, Tokyu, Takashimaya, Wako, Matsuya, Maruzen – among others. Major side streets, such as the well-known Miyuki-dori, specialize in up-market boutiques of designer goods. Still smaller side streets and the numerous alleyways are lined with the bars, small restaurants and night-clubs for which the area is renowned. At one end of the Ginza, surrounding the Yurakucho railway and subway stations, is a complex of departmental stores including large stores of the Sobu and Printemps chains and a considerable number of cinemas. Other districts also associated with shopping are similarly sub-divided into specialized zones. Tokyo's Shibuya, for instance, has a zone of departmental stores, one of small restaurants of a traditional style bordering the railway tracks adjacent to the enormously busy railway station, and another of night-clubs, cinemas, *pachinko* (pinball) parlours and bars – the famous Kabuki-cho district – while the same city's Shibuya has zones of departmental stores catering mainly to younger shoppers, an area of traditional bars catering mainly to middle-aged men, a cultural area (the *Bunka Mura*, or 'Culture Village', a large children's centre and the campus of the United Nations and Aoyama Gakuin universities), a large complex of cinemas and a district given over entirely to 'love hotels' – short-stay hotels, often of whimsical architecture, designed not for travellers but exclusively for romantic assignations. Such 'epitome districts' (Cybriwsky 1991), with their similar mix of enterprises, can be found in any large and many smaller Japanese cities, each one devoted to a range of consumption activities. These areas of course attract people who do not actually live there, but other neighbourhoods in which people do live are also areas in which people consume, and districts heavily populated with renters (usually near a railway station, since such people almost certainly commute) will be marked by the large number of convenience stores, often open 24 hours a day, small supermarkets, also open for long hours, and the usual mix of bookstores, coffee houses, dry-cleaning shops, cake shops, greengrocers and household goods stores characteristic of any suburban or inner-city residential area. Japanese cities then are certainly collections of neighbourhoods, but what does all this actually mean in more systematic sociological terms?

URBAN SOCIOLOGY AND JAPANESE SOCIETY

It has already been suggested that a better model than the community one for understanding Japanese urban neighbourhoods is that of the network – patterns of relationship (friendship, work or common interests) often based on consumption activities (shopping, eating, producing, selling) and which in many cases transcend the boundaries of any particular locality. While geography and spatial patterns (e.g. place of residence) greatly influence the empirical form that these networks take, networks are not identical with locality and, unlike a place, may be multiple in nature, are dynamic in character and appear and disappear over time. This can be seen in various ways. While residence in a locality commits one to a certain identification with that place, that identification is, firstly, gendered. Women, because of their social networks and the activities of their children, are more likely to be tied to a place than are men, whose work and leisure activities remove them from such spatial restrictions (Imamura 1987). Secondly, residence is related to kinship networks. Families not from the city in which they live are more likely to identify with their *furasato*, their home town of origin, than with their urban place of residence, and at New Year, possibly during the 'Golden Week' spring holidays, and certainly at *obon*, the mid-summer festival honouring the ancestors, will return 'home'. Families who are from the city in question but who have relatives in other neighbourhoods will often, especially again in the case of women, spend more social time outside of their locality than in it. Thirdly, it is related to religion. Residents of a neighbourhood are technically parishioners of its local shrine, if it has one. In practice few people actually contribute to or visit such shrines, but they may support a shrine or a Buddhist temple at a place of former residence or simply one elsewhere that they prefer for some reason. This pattern is especially marked in the case of Japanese Christians who, on moving place of residence, will simply cease to attend a church if their original church of membership is too far away to be easily attended. So while remaining nominally members of the original church which they no longer attend, they will ignore a 'strange' church in their immediate neighbourhood. Europeans or Americans, who are widely supposed to have a weaker sense of community than many Asians, would simply transfer their membership to, or at least attend, a place of worship in their new locality, thus establishing a new network near their place of residence. For a Japanese a sense of 'community' is constructed through kinship, work and common commitment to institutions (such as the school attended by one's children); for a European with weaker kinship bonds and higher job mobility, community is more likely to be defined in terms of a sense of place.

At a more theoretical level some of these questions are raised in a much debated paper by Ray Pahl on the issue of the adequacy of sociological theory in urban research (Pahl 1989). Interestingly, this paper itself starts with the very Eurocentric assumption that the issue of class is seen as being the problem. Although Pahl does not like the use of the catch-all concept of class in urban sociology, his argument is nevertheless phrased in terms of that concept. While from a Japanese point of view the debate is a somewhat unrealistic one given the problematic status of class analysis in Japan (see Clammer 1995a, 1995b and Chapter 5 below), at the end of his paper Pahl raises a number of alternative possibilities which are significant in a consideration of contemporary Japanese urbanism, not least because they show the gap between Western urban sociological theory and Japanese reality.

If, as Pahl suggests, class is, in practical terms, no longer a useful concept, what can be put in its place? Firstly, Pahl suggests, there is consumption, but he does not see this as providing the basis for any future political action: 'Yet if consumption is the central symbol it is not the main focus for new forms of collective consciousness. Shoppers are rarely bound together in solidarities of shared experiences and aspirations' (Pahl 1989: 718). Instead Pahl sees the basis for the emergence of a common consciousness as based on common dependence on access to credit, especially for home ownership and general consumption. Debt rather than consumption as such becomes the core of his theory: 'Cities are increasingly becoming machines for generating consumer credit dependence' (Pahl 1989: 718). Two immediate comments on this are that, firstly, shoppers in Japan are not so diverse as Pahl might suppose: small income differentials, the tyranny of fashion, the huge influence of advertising and the media, all conspire to produce a remarkably homogeneous market, stratified by age and gender to be sure, but with highly predictable characteristics. Secondly, Japan is still very much a cash society. Credit cards are rarely used, cheque accounts are effectively non-existent and most things are paid for in cash. In some cases even salaries are paid in cash. Electronic banking, now well developed in Japan, is employed mainly to move cash around more efficiently, for example to pay rents or utilities bills, but is not for generating credit. Most 'plastic money' issued in Japan (usually by banks) is not in the form of credit cards, but of charge cards, i.e. debts incurred are automatically deducted from one's bank account. While it is true that consumption does not necessarily create horizontal links between individual shoppers, it may do so in the form of creating networks of friends or members of consumer co-operatives. Furthermore, it is a mistake to confine the idea of consumption to shopping alone. Consumption creates a common culture to a very great extent, and Japanese consumers are certainly aware of links between themselves and other consumers by way of shared information, through purchases of similar items and services and most importantly in a diffuse but real sense of sharing in a common culture. What does one talk about with a just encountered stranger? Almost certainly about consumption:

prices, objects, trends, comparisons. This provides a common language which now displaces any references to traditional culture in everyday Japanese discourse. In a society where debt is low and savings are high, not only is an identity as a debtor unlikely to emerge, but in Japan this would be very socially unacceptable. Even if one is a debtor, and so are one's friends, a conspiracy of silence will keep such an unpalatable fact out of the public domain.

Furthermore, according to Pahl, 'the decentralization of production and the spatial neutrality of many office and service functions makes it very unlikely that a collective consciousness based on workplace relations is likely to be generated in the private sector' (Pahl 1989: 718). Here the operative question is really one of scale. It is true that in Japan the absence of national unions and the so-called vertical organization of society (in which members of an institution or company communicate with those above or below them in the hierarchy, but not very much horizontally to members of parallel institutions – e.g. bureaucrats in one ministry do not talk to bureaucrats in another ministry) makes workplace identification difficult on a national scale. But it is very much the case that workers tend to identify strongly with their individual workplace and with co-workers: indeed workplace identification is one of the strongest forms in Japan and is even instrumental in constructing the sense of self among contemporary Japanese workers (Kondo 1990; Rohlen 1979). Work and workplace identification, although possibly weakening, still provide a vital organizing principle in Japanese society.

Finally Pahl, while indeed suggesting that 'relationships to the means of consumption are of considerable importance in the kind of capitalist society that is moving into the twenty first century' (Pahl 1989: 718) and that the focus of sociological attention should shift from the sphere of employment to the sphere of consumption, also suggests that the focus of social energy is moving to informal social networks and to the institutions of civil society where 'people are engaging in voluntaristic solidaristic and collective activity for a variety of goals' (Pahl 1989: 719). This may be true in Europe, but is at the best only very partially true of Japan. Social movements do indeed exist there (for example, the anti-nuclear movement), but since the students and anti-Japan/USA security treaty activities of the 1960s they have taken on little of the significance of the 'new social movements' in Europe. A central problem with Pahl's approach is that he does not systematically link his critique of class/employment with his hope that 'we may acquire a more robust and vigorous consumption-based theoretical analysis of social power' (Pahl 1989: 719). The working out of this link and of the quasi-groups (even if not Pahl's 'collective consciousness') formed through (or in some cases excluded by) consumption can be seen as the central theoretical issue for both the sociology of consumption and urban sociology. Addressing this question also takes us back to class quite directly, and to repose these questions in the Japanese context (as is done in some detail in chapters 5 and 8 below) is to begin a serious revisioning of the way in which Japanese society might be approached in keeping with the realities of the contemporary era.

If we agree that a consumption-based approach to urban society is necessary, how is it to be accomplished? Initially by considering much more fully than Pahl does the theorizing of the link between consumption and urbanism. Warde (1990) suggests that this has been done in two main ways: through the sociological tradition, which sees consumption as a key factor in social differentiation, and as such connected to the central sociological issues of stratification, work and political divisions, and also as a shared culture on the one hand, and through recent urban theory, which has the option of following Castells's suggestion (Castells 1978) of focusing on collective consumption as the proper subject of urban sociology. Castells, however, with his concern with the way in which labour power was reproduced, was interested primarily in the political implications of the emergence of urban protest movements, something that has rarely been an issue in Japan, although there have been cases of conflict between homeless day-labourers and the police in Osaka and of struggles between the Burakumin Liberation League and the state in many locations. Warde suggests a third viable approach – what he terms a 'sociology of service provision' (Warde 1990: 228) – in which focus moves to the provision by the state and by the private sector of services such as housing, transportation and health care. The analysis of 'consumption cleavages' is important in Britain because of the assumption that voting patterns tend to be split along the same lines. This is not the case in Japan, where in any case the question of provision of services is rarely posed in political terms except by special-interest groups such as the Buraku people (the former 'outcasts' of Tokugawa times) or other minorities (the Korean community being a good case in point).

The position of Warde's main protagonist, Peter Saunders, is precisely that urban sociology should be understood as the analysis of sectoral cleavages, a position that Warde wishes to differentiate from his own conception of the sociology of service provision. Saunders assumes (Saunders 1986), incorrectly in the case of Japan, that leisure has replaced work as the central life issue for people in late modern society and that, because of this, social policy should be reformulated to conform with a purely market model in which 'customers', i.e. consumers, can exert social power through their spending power (1986: 345). Warde's critique of this position is based on the argument that this is just commodity fetishism elevated to a sociological principle – the commodification of everything – and suggests instead his own model of service provision as a rival to a consumption-based model of sectoral cleavage. In the case of both authors some basic premises are left unexplored. These are: that the provision of *services* is the most important aspect of consumption; that consumption is politicized because people expect such services from the state or corporate entities and protest when they are not forthcoming in sufficient quality or quantity; that the welfare state is the context in which such socio-political processes take place; and that consumption for display and status is subordinated to consumption as receipt of services. None of these premises is valid in the Japanese context, and so it is now necessary to turn to constructing a model of urban consumption for Japan that better fits the reality than the versions offered by Western urban sociology.

The 1920s saw both the emergence of large-scale urbanization and the advent of mass industrial production in Japan. By the 1930s city populations had already doubled and transportation networks had improved to the point where large urban concentrations could be sustained. The spatial organization of the larger cities was structured mainly along the routes developed by the railways, a pattern that continues down to the present day. With the rise of the departmental stores (themselves part of railway companies in many cases), consumption itself had become a leisure-time pursuit by the 1930s. The downturn of the war years and the occupation period, seen today with a mixture of horror and nostalgia, actually enabled certain industrial skills to be honed and the urban infrastructure to be reconstructed in those cities badly damaged by bombing. The upsurge in economic activity that got underway in the 1960s again coincides with major population growth in the larger cities, growth originating from rural–urban migration and from movement from smaller towns to the big cities. The problem of rural depopulation which now besets much of the Japanese countryside stems from this period.

This mass migration transformed urban culture. In an analysis of the changing political and social complexion of three Tokyo neighbourhoods (part of the old *shitamachi*, or traditional downtown, of eastern Tokyo, the *yamanote*, or 'high town', district of western Tokyo and a suburban area) under the impact of in-migration, White (1982) demonstrates both the formation and the consolidation of sub-culturally distinctive areas of the city and the ways in which migrants were assimilated into differing urban lifestyles. The present social structure is the result of this mixing of the old residents with the new migrants. The situation described by Robertson for Kodaira has been repeated with interesting variations all over Tokyo and other big cities, and is still occurring in major provincial cities that are growing as companies relocate away from the expense and crowding of Tokyo – in Sendai, for example, currently one of the fastest expanding provincial cities in Japan. This mix has been further complicated by the arrival in recent years of large numbers of foreign workers, whose presence is further complicating and diversifying contemporary social structure (see Chapter 8 below).

This recent formation of the social structure of Japanese cities is important because it means that many of the features of Japanese society that are now taken for granted are actually of very recent origin. The *ichigozoku*, or teenagers, who now feature so prominently in the media and discussions of consumption, are a recent invention as a social category, defined indeed in large part by their relationship to consumption. Many of the economic characteristics of this age group – the tendency of older teens to have part-time jobs, their extensive reading for both pleasure and information gathering, the habit of younger teens to buy lots of small items (snacks, comics, stationery and so on), and their strong tendency to participate in Japan as the *johoshakai*, the information society – are the product of social transformations of very recent vintage and illustrate very clearly the relationship between economic and cultural change. Socialization into shopping rather than into farm or shop work, the existence of a large and segmented magazine market, the adoption of Western consumption occasions such as Valentine's Day or even of birthdays as something to be celebrated, intense interest in fashion (teens are even reported to write about what other people are wearing in their diaries), the concept of the importance of being *machikomi*, or streetwise, in the sense of knowing what is what and what is fashionable; these are all products of an urban culture with its roots primarily in Tokyo, the least conservative of Japanese cities. Tokyo is still the symbolic as well as the political centre of Japan, and trends tend to start first there and then spread to the provinces (often as they are abating in their place of origin.)

The concept of trends or *bomu* (booms), trivial as it might first appear, is actually an important one in the understanding of Japanese consumer culture. Trends are followed partly because it is difficult not to follow them – shops simply cease to carry stock reflecting the previous trend – but equally because to be trend-conscious is to adapt to one of the most powerful mechanisms of social integration in a culture which does not value so much those who stand out. This applies not only to the acquisition of objects: there was a mini-boom in marriages following the marriage of the crown prince to Owada Masako, a diplomat's daughter, whose clothes, hairstyles and make-up were exhaustively catalogued by the media and carefully imitated by large numbers of young women. A decade previously there had ben a similar outbreak of Princess Diana hairstyles in Japan following her marriage to the British crown prince. Such trends and the necessity to bow to convention have substantial economic impact. At *oseibo* some middle-class families spend as much as 10 per cent of their entire income on gifts. A conventional wedding costs upwards of eight million yen (US$80,000), including gifts for the guests, the reception, the wedding kimono and the honeymoon. Even graduation from college is an expensive event, with the necessity of renting a kimono (usually worn by female graduands), make-up and hairstyling, formal photographs and a graduation trip, these days frequently abroad.

Consumption activities thus have a strong group reference. Even regional differences are reproduced on a collective scale. Tokyo fashions, for instance, are generally subdued in colour, with blacks and browns predominating, while Osaka fashions are brighter and often favour shiny materials. National trends sometimes override such regional variations, such as a recent fad for cottons and 'ecological' fashions. There is also a life-cycle to consumption patterns. The conspicuous consumption of teenagers and young unmarried women, in the latter case with the bulk of income going on fashions and luxury items, changes after marriage, especially if saving for a house is an important priority. But even when the focus of expenditure shifts from self to family, trends are still apparent, and the experienced observer can soon learn to spot young married women, especially those who have small children, by their similarity of dress. And if they do have children, the offspring too will probably be dressed fashionably, in whatever style is the craze of the day.

Such young women are important in the total consumption picture because of their control of fashion for their families, because of their concern with interior decoration and the purchase of items for the home, because of their expertise in bargain hunting and knowledge of discount stores, sales, bazaars, promotions and other money-saving shopping possibilities and also because they form the bulk of the membership of consumer organizations, and in particular co-operatives. Such co-operatives are an important part of the shopping scene in any Japanese city, and mid-morning in particular in any suburban area will see housewives clustered around the trucks and vans of the cooperatives that serve their areas. Some of these trucks will belong to co-operatives: organizations to which it is necessary to belong in order to purchase their goods. Others will be from organic farming communes or marketing organizations from which anyone can purchase. An example of the former is the Seikatsu Club, a co-operative and consumer movement of over 200,000 members. Such movements have the dual function of supplying their members with quality produce and consumer information. An example of the latter is the Yamagishi movement, a network of communes that provide a collective lifestyle for their members and which market their produce throughout suburban Japan. All of their produce – vegetables, fruit, milk, meat, yogurt, eggs, jams, bread, and so forth – is organically grown. Purchasing from such organizations is often more expensive than from regular grocers or supermarkets, but large numbers of customers nevertheless buy because of the quality. Such co-operatives actually constitute a real alternative system in Japan and, with their direct marketing to consumers and networks of information, are a genuine social movement, although they are not usually recognized as such.

An important dimension of consumption today is also that of the 'silver industries' – industries that increasingly cater specifically to the aging population of Japan. Fashions, activities, vacations, magazines and consumer items are being tailored for and specifically targeted at this group, which is now very significant in marketing terms. Overall consumption should be seen as structured along the axes of age, gender, residence and seasonality. Residence, and its relation to place of work, places the major constraints on the physical cycles of daily movement. The small size of many Japanese houses and apartments means that much of life tends to be lived outside in the streets and public places, such as restaurants and coffee houses, where most entertaining and socializing takes place. The density of population in major cities creates cities without centres, but with many clusters of small shopping districts serving nearby residents, districts that themselves rise and fall in fashionableness and which are characterized by fluidity and constant regeneration as new business move in and old ones move out or disappear, and as local restaurants or clubs get discovered or forgotten by the consumer nomads. Seasonality too is an important principle in structuring Japanese consumption, and foods, fashions and dominant colours change with the seasons. The analysis of consumption then has to take into account orientations to space, the residues of traditional culture, conceptions of nature and relationship to time. Culture, biology and society intersect most forcibly in consumption, and nowhere is this more true than in Japan.

This fact needs to be combined with a recognition of the *de facto* internationalization of Japanese consumption behaviour. If not the content, then certainly the forms of most of what is consumed has originated elsewhere. How this is conceptualized, however, is of critical importance, and the most extensive recent treatment of consumption in Japan distorts this in serious ways (Tobin 1992). This volume needs some comment. It is a collection of essays devoted to the proposition that contemporary Japanese consumption can best be understood as 'domesticating' the West, following the very conventional argument that Japan has borrowed elements of Western culture and has changed them into something distinctively Japanese. This is hardly news. The editor, however, attempts to construct a conceptual model of this process around what he insists on calling 'domestication', claiming that this is a morally neutral term that simply reflects Japanese ingenuity in borrowing, when actually it is a piece of less than subtle cultural colonialism – a modern version of the Westernization of Asia. Although he is presumably sensitive to this defect, Tobin loudly attempts to deny it (1992: 7-8). In this model the Japanese borrow (from the West and only from the West) and do not of course create.

To be understood at all, contemporary Japanese consumption, including that of the so-called consumption of the West, must be placed in a global context, one in which in fact many elements are no longer 'Western', but part of a cosmopolitan culture which transcends national or regional boundaries. Much of what appears 'Western' in the modern world actually originates in Japan. The fashion being worn by a young Singaporean, the comic being read by a Thai, the TV programme watched by a Malaysian or the piece of medical technology which saves the life of an Australian are today all likely to be Japanese. Baudrillard's idea that Japan is no longer a 'place' but is 'weightless', is everywhere because everywhere it is consumed (Baudrillard 1988b: 76), is very appropriate here. A model which sees 'Japan' as 'domesticating' the 'West' is conceptually very confused and poses the issue in binary terms that simply no longer exist. Similarly Tobin invokes Bourdieu without apparently having understood him, or at least without being willing to carry out in the Japanese context his careful analysis of the relationships between class and taste. In fact Tobin and his contributors do not discuss class at all, and further perpetuate the image of Japan as socially homogeneous and as uniformly affluent, nor do they adequately deconstruct the concept of individualism on which much of their common argument is based. The result is a book which is devoted largely, in postmodern language, to arguing that the Japanese remain Japanese even when consuming the West, something that they do through promoting nostalgia and self-exoticizing activities (departmental stores are seen as a major agency here) and by refusing to be dominated by Western ideologies, but rather differentiating their identity from the West in order to reinforce superiority and cultural uniqueness, an argument which uses consumption behaviour to construct what is close to being a racist position. Thus we find the following statement: 'I argue that the commodified cultural artifacts of Disneyland are recontextualized in a specifically Japanese construction of cultural consumption and take two forms: making the familiar exotic and keeping the exotic exotic' (Brannan 1992: 219). Far from being in any way a critique of *nihonjinron*, the ubiquitous theories of Japanese uniqueness, this book deeply reinforces them in the guise of an analysis of consumption, which at the end remains fundamentally undertheorized.

One fresher and necessary approach to consumption that has not yet been effectively explored is by way of relating it to popular culture, something that the Tobin volume fails to do although it bills itself as being about 'everyday life'. Popular culture and consumption activities are deeply implicated in each other and reflect each other in a continuous dance of mutual influence. This can be seen at every level of the society – in the popularity of *pachinko*, in the *okeikogoto*, or 'lesson culture', in which large numbers of people invest considerable amounts of time and money in learning and practicing ikebana, and other *yugei*, or 'recreational arts', something every bit as popular in Japan as visiting Tokyo Disneyland, and appealing to older women in particular, who have somewhat different ways of constructing their identities than teenagers (e.g. Moeran 1995). Gender and career both affect the life-course very substantially in relation to consumption as with other things. The after-work drinking and recreation of the typical *sarariiman* (male white-collar worker) is substantially different from that of his female counterpart, the 'OL', or 'office lady'. What links them is the common commitment to consumption and the fact that, whether involved in arts or sports, making or listening to music, watching films, videos or TV, reading comic books, science fiction or popular fiction, all are involved in what is essentially an *urban* culture – urban in origin and often requiring for its practice an urban setting: bookstores, cinemas, baseball stadia and, above all, lots of other people (Powers and Kato 1989). The culture of work intersects at many levels with the creation of popular culture – both through the objective constraints, status and salary of one's occupation, and through ideological constraints, factors such as one's perceived location in a social hierarchy – something close to the class perceptions uncovered by Bourdieu in France and which influence musical tastes, reading, preferred sports and eating habits (Bourdieu 1984). Given the central role that work still plays in Japanese culture, work and lifestyle intersect in powerfully deterministic ways, in which subjective taste is strongly influenced by membership in a particular social group with its own mores (Plath 1983). The factor of class is of substantial significance here, and although the consumer-oriented white-collar lifestyle that began to emerge in the late 1950s and early 1960s (Vogel 1963) is seen by many, including many Japanese, as the norm, the lifestyle of blue-collar workers and industrial workers, although it may aspire in many ways to middle-class values and consumption patterns, has always been very different (Cole 1971). Women who do not work in paid employment possess a different relationship to consumption, but an equally important one. 'Being a consumer is a form of self-reflection offered to Japanese women by those media targeted directly at them' (Skov and Moeran 1995: 5), a situation which ties women to consumer trends, but in ways that they find agreeable, and as such creates a two-way relationship between women and the market. For many married women consumption can be a lonely experience, but it is usually an aspect of everyday life that is shared with friends – people who are often friends because they share consumption activities.

Women often also play a more subtle role in consumption. As more women enter the labour force, the dynamics of the household change; patterns of household consumption and social power alter, as women increase their control of family budgets by having a disposable income of their own in addition to managing normal expenditures from the husband's salary. The increasing number of single women with careers is further enhancing women's consumption power. Women are even changing the nature of medical practice in Japan as body consciousness changes and a concern with diet and health as well as beauty becomes a part of female self-identity (see Chapter 6 below). Women have become major consumers of medical products and services, not least as they become the subjects of new medical syndromes that appear to be the products of urban lifestyles and increasing affluence, and as *bunneibyo*, or diseases of civilization, become recognized medical problems by Japanese physicians of both sexes (Lock 1990).

Distribution of expenditure can be seen clearly in figures supplied by the Management and Coordination Agency (1992). Assuming an income of ¥473,738 per month, the breakdown in 1992 was as follows:

Food and drink:	¥83,445
Housing:	¥20,191 (assuming own home or company housing)
Utilities:	¥18,094
Furniture and household Equipment:	¥13,560
Clothing/shoes:	¥24,033
Medical:	¥9,125
Transportation and communications:	¥35,304
Education:	¥18,625
Leisure and reading materials:	¥34,279
Others:	¥96,164

The relatively high expenditure on leisure (including reading material, which is very widely consumed in Japan) and on clothes is revealing, as is the amount spent on transport, showing the commuting lifestyle of many city dwellers, including schoolchildren, who sometimes travel long distances daily if they are in private schools far removed from their homes.

THE SOCIOLOGY OF URBAN CONSUMPTION

Consumption then animates urban life and is itself made possible by the concentration of media sources and consumption sites in cities. The spatial layout of cities is a product of architecture, of social patterns (e.g. daily cycles of physical movement) and of cultural practices, including entertainment, eating and drinking and family activities. What broader sociological issues are implicated here? The first is surely that of the relationship between consumption and postmodernism. One of the principle debates in Japanese studies at the moment is that of whether or not, or in what sense, Japan is a postmodern society (Miyoshi and Harootunian 1989; Arnason and Sugimoto 1996). Interestingly, one of the typical definitions of postmodernity – 'the effacement of the boundary between art and everyday life; the collapse of the hierarchical distinction between high and mass/popular culture; a stylistic promiscuity favouring eclecticism and the mixing of codes; parody, pastiche, irony, playfulness and the celebration of the surface 'depthlessness' of culture; the decline of the originality/genius of the artistic producer; and the assumption that art can only be repetition' (Featherstone 1991b: 7) – fits not Japanese *society*, but rather many, if not most, of its commercial manifestations and mass-media productions. There is in fact a profound continuity between the nature of postmodernity in the arts and the nature of Japanese consumer culture. It would be a mistake to argue, however, that these features extend to the society as a whole, to traditional crafts or to many of the creations of 'high' culture, despite the superficial similarities between traditional aesthetics and a great deal of contemporary Japanese art, film or drama.

A more effective way to approach this question is the recognition that the culture of mass consumption in Japan – the actual practices and experiences of consumption as a way of life – inevitably converges with definitions of postmodernity that emerge from the arts. This is in large part because they are both expressions of the same broader social change which encompasses aesthetic developments as well as developments in taste in the wider society. Consumption in this context comes easily to be conceived of not as utility, but as desire, waste, excess, all this occurring 'within a society where. . . a good deal of production is targeted at consumption, leisure and services and where there is the increasing salience of the production of symbolic goods, images and information' (Featherstone 1991b: 21). Theme parks (now springing up all over Japan), departmental stores and, seaside, mountain and hot-spring resorts all represent controlled disorder, nostalgia and escapism, all fed by the expanding culture industries (including tourism; see Chapter 7 below), the producers of images, who are now at the core of Japanese consumption. The emergence of the culture industries itself signals a major social change from primary production to services, images and information and the creation of a whole new class of cultural intermediaries and knowledge specialists who service this growing sector of TV, book and magazine publishing, advertising and leisure industries, actors, models and designers, interior decorators and hairstylists, teachers of the new skills needed to survive in this new world, including foreign languages, commercial artists, arts managers, tour operators and many functionaries in the catering and hospitality industries. In a sign-saturated society (Barthes 1970) culture itself becomes the core element in a consumer culture, rather than things which, while they may provide a material basis, are often the servants of the signs: one consumes a particular product primarily for its symbolic value.

Seen in this light, contemporary Japanese cities make more sense. Their centrelessness, neon-saturated streets, temporary looking buildings, simulational zones (shopping centres, love hotels, amusement and virtual reality centres, cinemas and phantasmagorical architecture) are both sites of consumption and sites/sights to be consumed, often swamped with the eroticism which is a pervasive element in contemporary Japanese popular culture, but which is strangely rarely commented on or noticed by sociologists or cultural analysts. Crowds, far from being an annoyance in the pleasure and shopping quarters of any large Japanese city, are an essential ingredient, providing the requisite background of noise, energy and sense of something happening. If traditional Japanese culture is one culture of restraint and understatement, contemporary consumer culture is one of excess and visibility, making this aspect of Japan truly a 'society of the spectacle' (Debord 1983). Insofar as such sites of consumption are fluid, temporary and do not constitute a common culture of shared symbols and myths, heroes and villains, yet take place in a nation still very much concerned with its identity as a specific and indeed unique *ethnie*, the question must arise of what kind of social organization exists here: does the consumer society in Japan constitute a definable social structure, or do we need to reconceptualize it in fresh terms?

While few would probably dispute that individuality exists in Japan, individualism in a Western sense is certainly less common. The so-called groupism of the Japanese in large part refers to this fact. The desire to belong to a group, to merge one's identity with that collectivity and to organize one's life around its norms is very strong and can be seen reproduced constantly in endless situations – in membership of voluntary groups, in residential neighbourhoods, in the adopting of the dress code thought appropriate to one's profession and in the careful management of language – men speaking distinctively 'male' Japanese and women 'female' Japanese when they are in a single-sex group. Some commentators have even seen this lack of individualism as retarding Japan's advance to genuine modernity, as with Maruyama Masao's famous argument that the lack of inner autonomy on the part of Japanese was not only the root cause of the rise of Japanese fascism, but is essentially what keeps Japan premodern in social structure (Maruyama 1985). Consumption behaviour involves, at one level, individual choice, but at another level both choice constrained by what is available in the market and the tyranny of fashion and by the willing acquiescence to that tyranny. Much consumption is actually collectivism masquerading as individualism.

Such a view accords very closely with that of the French sociologist Michel Maffesoli whose basic insight has been summarized by Featherstone as follows:

> 'It has been argued by Maffesoli that in the postmodern city we have a move beyond individualism with a sense of communal feeling being generated, a new 'aesthetic paradigm' in which masses of people come together in temporary emotional communities. These are to be regarded as fluid 'postmodern tribes' in which intense moments of ecstasy and affectual immediacy are experienced'. (Featherstone 1991b:101).

In his major work in which he develops these ideas (Maffesoli 1996), Maffesoli develops in detail the notion of 'tribes' as being the concept which best encapsulates the nature of these real but fluid social groupings. The same notion of tribes – *zoku* in Japanese – has been extensively employed in Japan to describe similar groups, a point discussed earlier in this book. The idea of an 'aesthetic paradigm' is also interesting in that it too has obvious parallels with Japan, where aesthetic ideas are quite self-consciously used in consumerist discourse. Maffesoli's work then has many resonances in relation to Japan, so it is worth briefly discussing his ideas and considering the light that they may shed on the question of the social organization of consumerism.

The 'groups' into which Japanese society organizes itself can be seen in the Maffesolian paradigm as 'neo-tribes', as people otherwise unrelated who share common tastes and lifestyles and who are, in Japan, also members of age and gender cohorts. This neo-tribalism is a result of the massification of Japanese society and the influence of the media in segmenting the population into relatively discrete groups. In such a situation individualism, while apparently encouraged by the available plethora of consumption possibilities, is actually channelled and constrained by the ways in which these channels are organized and manipulated by advertising and by the market. The 'communities' (tribes) that are formed in such a situation are not spatially bounded or composed of individuals who have on-going social relationships: they are temporary, to a great extent 'imagined', and are essentially emotional communities: 'In any case, whatever we call it (emotion, sentiment, mythology, ideology), the collective sensibility, by superseding the atomization of the individual, creates the conditions necessary for the sort of aura that characterizes a certain period' (Maffesoli 1996: 13). There are a number of important implications here: that there is something which might be called a 'spirit of the times', although this is not usually part of conventional sociological analysis; that the analysis of the emotions, something again missing from mainstream sociology, needs to be given a central place; that consumption, as the actual activity which animates many of these tribes, is a device against anomie, not a cause of it; that consideration of the media must be a central part of any adequate understanding of contemporary industrial/consumer societies and that the total social structure of such societies should be conceived of as a vast web of networks and associations, many of them temporary and all of them having a transient population. In a sense the appropriate model is more 'ecological' than it is 'structural', one in which the methodological exploration of society requires some new tools, including the transient content of social institutions, a new image of community, the centrality of the emotional and the erotic, and the serious assimilation into the practice of sociology and anthropology of Bourdieu's ideas of habitus, doxa and agency (Bourdieu 1977). In addition it calls for the more central incorporation of the sociology of the body – the social actor as an embodied as well as a thinking subject, a reconsideration of approaches to the analysis of class (especially in non-Western societies) and a recognition of the gendered nature of the perception of social reality which greatly influences the ways in which emotional communities are formed. While Maffesoli himself does not develop most of these ideas, they are certainly implied by much of what he is saying.

Everyday life in consumer societies, and Japan is obviously no exception to this, is organized around materiality and a concern with appearances (the much discussed 'wrapping' phenomenon in Japan?), appearances which create commonalities with others while also potentially concealing the inner self which can maintain its own autonomous imaginative life (what Maffesoli (1996: 90) calls 'secrecy'), allowing the *tatamae* of sociality to be lived out while preserving the inner *honne* of the shadows away from the exhilarating but also exhausting neon-lit public arena. Gossip, friendship and even networks of kinship partake of this materiality, a materiality which is 'spiritualized' by the investment of emotion and its use as the vehicle for the pursuit of far larger goals – the banishment of alienation, a sense of being-in-the-world and the achievement of both internationalization and Japaneseness. The study of consumption, if it is to attain any depth, has to incorporate these factors every bit as much as it assimilates the fashionable language of semiotics and post structuralism. Consumption is as much political as it is cultural, and indeed the new concept of 'cultural politics' is one that must keep both these dimensions in balance, something that will be developed more fully in the next chapter.

Consumption then must be seen as a central part of the culture of Japanese cities: as being both the core and the form of popular/mass culture, as being instrumental in the formation of social groupings organized around consumption, and as being the mechanism which dictates a high proportion of spatial movement and temporal orientation. Economic change in the wider society also tends to show first in cities which are accurate barometers of such fluctuations. Restaurants, which have become major sites of consumption in Japan since eating away from the home became normal, are heavily concentrated in cities, a typical small area of Tokyo having often more than a dozen within the radius of a five-minute walk, and departmental stores usually have one or even two floors at the top of the building given over exclusively to eating places. Urban consumption venues are often combined into a single space, as with the Sunshine City complex in the Ikebukuro district of Tokyo, which contains a hotel, exhibition centre, shopping complex, two floors of restaurants, offices and a very popular aquarium. Nearby is an area of departmental stores, cinemas, numerous smaller shops and love hotels. The entertainment industry, together with the departmental store industry, is one of the major shapers of the spatial layout of Japanese cities and the creator of the visual displays which make those cities so vibrant and, to Western eyes, garish. Culture itself then provides a major economic base for contemporary cities (Zukin 1995: 11-15), with their concentration of museums, cinemas, theatres and populations of cultural intermediaries and in which the 'symbolic economy' is a major part of the total economy. As a result, cultural tourism in Japan is as often to such cities as it is from such cities to the countryside. Experiences are generated, identities framed and connections to society and culture are established through consumption. The cultural industries themselves may be market driven, but it is precisely this nexus of culture (including fashion) and economics that provides the motive power for the Japanese consumer society, a society also framed by its own expectations about taste and behaviour, still deeply influenced by tradition or what it believes to be tradition, and still trying to negotiate a path between the conservatism of the norms at the basis of its social structure and the frenetic hedonism of much of its popular culture.

3

The Context of Desire: The Political Economy of Consumption

Consumption then takes place primarily in an urban setting, the setting in which sites of consumption are concentrated, in which the intensity of advertising and saturation by the media are most pronounced, in which opportunities for gaze and display are best found and in which the crowds, the emotional communities of consumption, are at their biggest. But even urban consumption takes place within a bigger context, a context made up of the economic structures and political trends of the whole society. Changes in the economy which affect the regulation of urban life have immediate repercussions on consumption behaviour, and political policies that influence the rate of savings, the supply of housing, the importation of foreign goods or the nature of work rapidly change the way in which consumption is organized. Macro-economic determinants have implications for the smallest details of everyday life, yet this perspective is often missing from sociological accounts of society in general and accounts of consumption behaviour in particular. In this chapter an attempt will be made to relate them in theoretically revealing ways.

The organizing motif here will be a concept of political economy used in a fairly special sense. Economic and political factors are obviously closely related: in fact in today's world they are really inseparable. Most politics, regrettably, is little more than economic management and manipulation, although it is often not clear which of politics and economics is the master and which the servant. The interplay of economic and political factors sets up the fundamental dynamic of social change in industrialized and industrializing societies. What is often forgotten, however, is that both economics and politics are themselves set in the context of culture. But the place of culture in such macro-social changes is contested both in the wider field of sociology (for example, between Marxists and Weberians, or between structuralists and phenomenologists) and in specific relation to Japan. Much of the controversy surrounding the work of Karl van Wolferen (1989) on the sources of social power in Japan stems from this issue.

Van Wolferen's basic position – that the understanding of social power in Japan has nothing to do with culture, but everthing to do with the domination of the bureaucratic-industrial complex – while very overstated in my view, does provide an antidote to the tendency in a lot of popular Japanology of ascribing everything to culture. The view that everything that is distinctive about Japan comes from some special attributes of Japanese culture is often as unhelpful as it is reductionist. In reality politico-economic factors frame culture in numerous subtle ways. 'Tradition', as is now well known, is usually created by the dictates of political pressures, not because of some inherent dynamic of culture itself. Rituals, myths, ceremonies, dress, even table habits and food preferences are shaped by political developments. Much of what passes as 'traditionally' Japanese is certainly no older than the mid-to late Meiji (Gluck 1985), and many contemporary customs thought to have ancient roots (such as the Shinto-style wedding ceremony) date only from the Taisho and even the Showa period. Partly what is at stake here is the definition of culture itself, and the position being advanced here is that, rather than seeing political economy and culture set over against each other, they are in fact facets of the same whole, interpenetrating at all levels. In reality they contain each other, and no adequate modelling of society can occur without recognition of this fact (Clammer 1985). This conception will be employed in what follows, and it is to be hoped that this might cast some refreshing light on the interplay of economy and culture, and specifically of course on the subject of consumption within this total picture.

THE POLITICAL AND ECONOMIC FRAME

Japan has now reached the top of the league table in terms of per capita income and is, and has been since the 1980s, the major source of capital for much of the rest of the world, in terms of credit, aid and direct investment. This enormous wealth and economic capacity would seem to confer on Japan the status of a superpower. Yet politically Japan seems to be without any clear role in the world community and to be devoid of any coherent foreign policy that transcends purely economic interests; at home it is riven with factionalism, corruption and indecision in basic policy-making, high levels of public apathy (reflected in voting figures) and distrust of politics and politicians, and a basic unwillingness to set out on the course of serious political reform. These factors have created a situation unique among the developed countries: political weakness at home, no or unclear intentions as regards its role in the international community and yet an aggressive presence in the world driven by financial and industrial interests. The result might be summarized as a rich nation with a bored population, an economic superpower that is a political pygmy (to paraphrase the words of Miyazawa Kiichi, a former finance minister).

The two are, however, linked in several significant ways. One of these is the actual control of politics by (non-elected) bureaucrats rather than by politicians. The second is the effective depoliticization of the Japanese population, and the displacement of political ideals by economic goals, including in the now virtually defunct 'left', if such a term can still be used to characterize Japan's highly conservative socialist and communist parties. A third is the pervasive nationalism, cultural as well as political, of Japanese life. Despite more than a decade of *kokusaika* , or propaganda, in favour of 'internationalization' there is little real evidence of Japan's opening to the world except through ways that are unwelcome such as the influx of foreign workers, and through the internationalizing specifically of consumption rather than Japanese life in general (see Chapter 5 below). And the fourth, and one of profound importance, is that Japanese capitalism is simply not the same as other capitalisms – US, German or British, for example – and is actually very different in detail from the capitalism of its East Asian rivals. There are a variety of reasons for this, the main one being the nature of the institutions created to control the economy, such as the Ministry of International Trade and Industry, which link the state bureaucracy and powerful interests in commerce and manufacturing in ways rather different from those of any other industrial nations. This primary factor is supplemented by the sheer size and power of the state bureaucracy, the still strong work ethic and expectations of high levels of quality and service which prevail in Japan, the security of hiding under the umbrella of US military protection, and,despite endless propaganda about its uniqueness and effectiveness (Matsumoto 1991), a labour-relation style and management culture which creates a compliant workforce and greatly reduced union powers.

While debate continues about the reasons for the decline of the political in Japan (the ideological fossilization of the opposition parties, especially those of the left, the success of the Liberal Democratic Party's all encompassing money politics (*kinken seiji*) policy in co-opting or corrupting just about all the major institutions of Japanese civil society, the effects of US policy in creating a political client state in Japan while simultaneously freeing its economy, and so on), the fact remains that, compared with many of the societies of Western Europe, genuine democracy remains relatively underdeveloped in Japan (Masumi 1990).

In this view the pacifism of postwar Japan (despite the actual high level of spending on the large military force known somewhat euphemistically as the Self Defence Forces) and the transformation of the militarist state of the 1930s and 1940s into a *chonin kokka* or merchant state, derive in large part from the dependency imposed on the country primarily by the United States, concerned after the war to suppress socialism and organized labour and to promote Japan as an anti-communist alternative in East Asia. With the high growth policies of the 1960s onwards the path was set for the rapid evolution of Japan into an essentially economic entity, something that both transformed its position in the international system and instituted vast social and cultural changes domestically, not least that consumption began to emerge as a desirable and achievable way of life. Even by the late 1950s, only a decade after Dore's benchmark study, Vogel (1963) could identify a distinct middle class that had emerged in Japanese cities, three decades before sociologists had begun to find new middle classes appearing all over East and Southeast Asia (Robison and Goodman 1996).

The effects of postwar policy on gender, labour relations, patterns of saving and expenditure, class formation and social attitudes were immense (Gordon 1993). Their legacy is still being experienced in the depoliticization and consumption orientation of contemporary Japanese society, which is now attempting to adjust to the emerging forces of 'post-Fordist' capitalism and shifts in the international division of labour occasioned especially by the rise of the newly industrialized economies of East Asia. If Japan is a 'trading nation', a mercantilist state, one would naturally expect to find continuities between external trade and investment policies and internal socio-economic organization. Hyper-consumption in contemporary Japanese cities is not a product of 'postmodernism' so much as the logical outcome of thirty years of policies which have put economics (the economics of the individual as well as the economics of the nation) first and have promoted a pervasive depoliticization, a process which may only now be changing with the faltering of LDP rule, the ideological bankruptcy of the socialists, the realignment of political parties and the slowly increasing public demand for political reform that all began to occur in the mid-1990s. The sacrifices experienced by the working generations of the late 1940s to the late 1970s in the rush to industrialize and to expand the economy are now beginning to bear fruit in international economic domination abroad and the hyper-consumer society at home.

This all has a number of consequences for social analysis. With the collapse of the Cold War paradigm Japan's position in relation to both the United States and the rest of the world has changed, a situation which is forcing the country to face in new ways the problem of defining itself (Miyoshi and Harootunian 1993), a struggle which will be reflected significantly in internal economic arrangements and cultural practices. Furthermore, it creates the possibility of recasting the rather tired categories of Japanological sociology and anthropology into a fresher and rather more dynamic form. All the old discussions of *tatemae/honne* and *omote/ura* take on a rather different complexion if they are rooted in actual practice and in a dynamic perspective. Today these distinctions are embodied (literally in many cases: see Chapter 6 below) largely in consumption practices, not in abstract categories or arrangements of the traditional house (in which, in the cities, virtually no one lives any more). Inside and outside, private and public, are rather defined in terms of property, of control over space and, most significantly, over lifestyle – the right to assert an identity through the establishment of symbolic boundaries. Seen in these terms the conventional categories of Japanology need not be abandoned, but can be radically refurbished.

A clear example of how shifts in the economy are reflected socially is in changes in the employment system and its effects on women's work. In a detailed study of one large company considered to be one of the most progressive in its attitude to promoting career opportunities for women – Seibu Department Stores – Alice Lam (1992) shows that conditions and prospects still lag behind those of companies in the same industry in the West, largely because of structural qualities of the Japanese employment system. These include lifetime employment in the large corporations, promotion by seniority and willingness on the part of management staff to be moved at company's convenience to branches elsewhere in Japan or even abroad. Women who are willing to commit themselves to the same 'rules and practices' (Lam 1992: 221) as their male counterparts in career positions have equal opportunities, but at the price of sacrificing family life and possibly or probably marriage. Actual change then does exist, partly under the initiative of the 1985 Equal Employment Opportunity Law, even though basic structural changes are very slow in coming. Lam makes two strategic errors in her book, for all its virtues. The first is her insistence on explaining present management and employment patterns heavily in terms of continuities with pre-industrial Japanese cultural values without questioning how far these values are still held and to what extent the same words are still used but their semantic content has changed. The result is an uneasy relationship between structural explanation and cultural explanation, and the link between the two is never fully theorized. The second error is that, in simply examining what is, Lam does not explore the wider context, especially the increasing expectations of women (itself a social reality) in relation to receipt and management of economic goods and symbolic power in contemporary Japan. These are contested domains, and the power of women as consumers (fully acknowledged by Lam) has forced departmental stores in general and Seibu in particular to develop the goals of selling 'lifestyles' to customers, especially in ther trendy stores, such as Seibu Loft in Tokyo's Shibuya district, aimed at young and largely female consumers.

Here Lam is making a common category mistake: she is looking for change in the wrong place. While there are glacially slow shifts in fundamental management practices, and more rapid changes in female employment (with larger numbers of women entering the workforce after high school or college graduation and returning later in life when children are grown, albeit in part-time or non-career track work), the real power of women is not as workers, but as consumers. To focus attention on the the employment system, while it is of course a very real issue, is nevertheless not to identify the key point. Women lead social change not through production but through consumption, and major shifts in the market are attributable to this factor, and not to the tastes or creativity of their generally more conservative male partners and colleagues. The analytical focus then needs to shift from work to consumption.

There are sociological as well as economic reasons for this. Work for many Japanese, especially younger ones, is no longer for building the nation. It is for building the self. Work, in other words, is undertaken for motives of consumption. The much vaunted characteristics of Japanese capitalism which are now being given such an airing in the West – flexible accumulation, the 'just-in-time' inventory system and the transcending of the 'Fordist' labour process – and in which information and communication structures (Lash and Urry 1994) have replaced the fixed structures of the older industrial capitalism, are part of a total political economy, some of the features of which were sketched out above. Culture and social organization are profoundly influenced by this informationalized economy. This is reflected in the economic importance as well as the social impact of the media, the expansion of service industries and the creation of whole new sectors devoted to the production and processing of information itself and its applications to areas such as data processing and entertainment – such as the boom in 'virtual reality' centres. Time and space are reorganized around these new forces of production and consumption. Daily schedules become determined by the requirements of transportation, the organization of shopping and frequently by TV or movie schedules, something which in turn transforms popular culture into a form of mass culture based on 'information' or communication of which the content is not fact or even value but 'poetics' – images and insinuations of a kind subversive to tradition and subtly transforming of self and body without themselves being subject to critical evaluation or conscious acceptance or rejection.

> Poetic discourse is constitutive of the rituals through which we operate. It creates the very least mediated universals through which people from now many nations communicate. Globalized popular culture, functioning as poetic discourse, thus becomes everybody's 'elementary forms of religious life'. It imparts form to an unreflected, relatively immediate and internationalized habitus. (Lash and Urry 1994: 29)

Whether or not these transformations can be understood in terms of the concepts of reflexivity and information structures upon which Lash and Urry hang their argument is debatable. The ideal-typical description of the Japanese firm depicted by Aoki (1988, 1989) is accepted uncritically as empirically correct and is not subject to any attempt at deconstruction or investigation of its possible ideological biases (Lash and Urry 1994: 65-71). Nevertheless their account of Japanese-style capitalism shows up many of its distinctive features while failing to depict the workers, who are again the focus of attention (together with management structures) as consumers. The same highly educated workforce that produces also consumes, and applies similar skills and use of information in both contexts. The expanding culture industries in particular, in which the line between production and consumption is blurred, employ workforces whose talents are devoted to the invention of signs. Japanese advertising, often noted for its 'poetic' rather than informational creations, is a good case in point. Things are consumed by the producers and produced by consumers. In a world of signs production and consumption have to be seen as two moments of the same cycle rather than as two spatially, temporally or organizationally separate activities. Indeed the concept of a 'consumer society' is of one in which these distinctions are blurred, production is disguised and the consumption of things and of images becomes an undifferentiated process. Consumption then is the point at which economic activity and cultural practice combine, in which political economy and cultural studies finally talk to each other. A new image of economics is consequently necessary, one which incorporates some rather surprising elements if Japanese consumer society is to be adequately understood. Here I will try briefly to sketch out what these main elements should be.

The question of the 'aestheticization of life' which has exercised so many postmodern commentators (e.g. Featherstone 1991b) is hardly a new issue in Japan. Indeed this fact has provided ammunition for those who wish to argue that Japan has in some sense always been a 'postmodern' society. It is certainly true that in many ways life itself is seen as art, to be enhanced by the practice and application of the specific arts. Levels of taste have accordingly always been high, especially among those with the leisure and wealth to pursue 'taste' as a way of life, but also extend to the quality of everyday objects, practices and services. Not only the cooking but also the presentation of food is considered an art, as anyone who has dined in a Japanese restaurant will be very aware. The design of objects and the quality of finish, even of those bits of an object or structure not visible, is high on average. Japanese economics then involves aesthetics, and it has long done so. This is reflected in the quality of products and services that Japanese consumers expect, even when, as it usually does in Japan, this means high prices.

Aesthetics, however, is certainly not the only factor governing the organization of consumption. An even more significant one, although linked to aesthetics by the concept of design, is technology. The technologizing of desires is a crucial element here. Insofar as desire is socially constructed, it is the product not only of socially derived values, but very much of technological imperatives. Desire is carried by or expressed through some medium, and today most of these media are technological – the film, the book, the video, the Sony Walkman. Disneyland, that grossly over written about artefact of the twentieth century, is pure technology: nothing is 'real'. Structures of meaning are increasingly dictated by advertising and the form and content of the media.

This is not of course to say that there are no underlying cultural values: there are, although the relevant ones might surprise the purists, as they would most certainly include sexuality, power and playfulness and the pleasure principle, not always identified as key features of Japanese culture. However, any reading of modern Japanese novels (for instance the now celebrated ones of Banana Yoshimoto) or *manga*, a little systematic viewing of television or contemporary Japanese films or a browse through many of the magazines available in any bookstore reveal a profound preoccupation with the erotic, with violence and with hedonism (Buruma 1984; 1996: 3-36). Popular culture, far from reflecting the foreign image of Japan as a land of tranquil high culture, reveals a world of sex, death, the bizarre and the fantastic (Napier 1995). Such concerns appear in and constitute a whole area of consumer culture: material containing these themes is what people, or at least a sizable proportion of the population, want to consume. This is important because identity and the reproduction of everyday life are intimately tied to what is consumed in modern societies, where the possession of commodities is largely what defines the self. Playfulness and pleasure, both strongly promoted by contemporary Japanese consumer culture, are culturally defined and include less innocent pastimes and imaginings as well as more *kawaii* (literally, 'cute') ones. Japan combines conservatism and hedonism in a way that few other societies have ever managed to do, a mood somewhat different from that of de Certeau and his argument that everyday life contains the possibility of creative and empowering cultural action (de Certeau 1984). What happens in Japan is that the everyday or its imaginative expression may, as Napier suggests (1995), subvert modernity rather than Japanese society – which of course everyday life actually constantly constitutes and reproduces. Or that it paradoxically supports a conservative sense of public social order by legitimating the free play of a very frequently erotic and violent imagination in areas or compartments set aside for this purpose, something which may have something to do with the absence of violent crime in Japan. The cheek-by-jowl juxtaposition of a district of love hotels and one of Tokyo's premier high-cultural sites (the Bunka Mura) in the capital's Shibuya district is not an anomaly or the accidental result of bad town planning: it represents a fundamental structure of Japanese society at work.

Speaking of structural characteristics, the nature of the system of social stratification is important in relation not only to the distribution of consumer tastes (as in Bourdieu's model), but also to whether they come into being in the way intended by capital at all. Speaking of the West, Lee notes that 'early attempts to institute a mass-consumption norm, as exemplified in Ford's early efforts, tended to founder upon a working-class lifestyle which all too often would display, at best, an ambivalence or at worst, an outright resistance to what were essentially the alien ways of life promoted by the new productive regimes and the advertising imagery surrounding the consumer goods it produced' (Lee 1993: 79). In Japan, however, despite the tensions produced by the early stages of industrialization, there appears to have been little resistance to consumption as a way of life. After the war, as modern-style capitalism began to take root, a rapidly expanding white-collar class eagerly embraced consumption (Vogel 1963).

In Japan then there were few obstacles to the emergence of consumption: an underdeveloped class system, a strong work ethic devoted to rebuilding the nation after the devastation of the war and little resistance to the blandishments of advertising – rather an eagerness to possess the fruits of development. The rapid postwar expansion of the large cities such as Tokyo was the result not of deliberate city planning, but of population influx and growth fuelled initially by industrial and later by consumer capitalism, with its attendant shops and culture industries (Ishizuka 1977). Class differences, such as they are, then came to be distributed geographically, with a differentiated spreading of cultural and economic capital from the *shitamachi*, or old down town of eastern Tokyo, through the *yamanote*, or high city of western Tokyo, and on to the suburbs of western and southeastern Tokyo, there being a general increase in the social indicators of status as one moves west (Kurasawa 1986). But what links all these areas is a common culture of consumption and common access to the same media, the primary former of consumer taste.

The rise of a large middle class and of the 'affluent worker' among the working class has promoted in Japan a movement (now successful) towards embourgeoisement, issuing in the current popular identity of Japan as a classless society. It is not, but what greatly dampens the visibility of class distinctions or the possibility of class conflict is commitment to the same kind of society: Japanese (as opposed to the rest of the world), peaceful and devoted to the arts of consumption. The cultural sphere and the mode of production are then linked and mediating structures. Not only the media itself, but also the family, education, gender relations and aesthetic sensibilities are integrated into this linking function. Out of this arise new values, many of which are 'inscribed' on the body; this then which becomes the vehicle of 'experiental' commodities rather than material ones (Lee 1993: 135–6), in which what is produced is the experience rather than a thing. Whether this represents an 'unease' with the body, as suggested by Featherstone (1991b: 90), however, is questionable in Japan, despite fads in diets, tanning, and healthcare and other 'body maintenance techniques'. That particular problem seems to be essentially a Western or possibly even a British one!

Consumption then needs to be situated in a broad socio-economic framework, and one which comprehends the transition to modernity, which has been the real social revolution in recent world history for those societies that have experienced it. As Lee puts it in very compressed form:

> It is important to stress at this point that the attraction that such cultural products [rock music, TV productions such as *Twin Peaks*, contemporary cinema] have for the new consumer classes cannot be reduced merely to the result of some conscious, quasi-intellectual game-playing on the part of their producers or consumers alike (not least because this would be a great injustice to what are, in many instances, undoubtedly genuine experiments in aesthetic, political and cultural form). Rather, the attraction of such goods to the new consumer classes may stem originally from a profound feeling that they succeed in materializing a particular experience of the contemporary social world in which subjectivity has become parted from the many solid social structures which in earlier times would have given it meaningful shape and coherent substance. Such goods may indeed reflect that structure of feeling born of a certain existential uncertainty and conditioned by contingency. For the new consumer classes, postmodern goods thus represent a vital objectification of a habitus that has been forged from

the material debris of long-forgotten, ancient cultural practices and sev-
ered social roots. (Lee 1993: 175)

While these comments need contextualizing in the specifically Japanese setting, they are highly relevant in pointing out, contrary to a good
deal of postmodernist writing, that consumerism, while vitally linked to
advertising and media, is not only a product of these forces, but must also
be seen in its existential dimension, as part of the search for security and
identity in a rapidly detraditionalizing situation. While Japan has suc-
ceeded in achieving a fairly remarkable balance between, on the one
hand, the integrity of an older social structure and, as we have earlier
noted, a continuity rather than conflict between the generations, and, on
the other, the rapid development of new productive forces, all factors
which have to some extent traditionalized change and maintained a
sense of common history, the stresses of modernization still exist and the
Japanese are not immune to them. The question then becomes one of
how these existential arguments are resolved and whether, as Lee suggests, consumption provides the means to materialize these quandaries
and thus deal with them at the level of social and cultural practice, rather
than merely philosophically.

THE PRAXIS OF CONSUMPTION

It is now well accepted among students of consumption that material
objects or symbolic forms provide a primary means of identity formation
in probably all societies, but certainly in contemporary industrial ones,
where some form of anomie results from lack of embeddedness in a
coherent social and religious structure. In Japan, while this general principle holds true, supported certainly by psychoanalytical accounts of
'object loss' and its psychic effects, the relatively greater degree of
embeddedness, it might be argued, actually allows greater freedom to
consume in two senses. Firstly, that much consumption (gift-giving being
the obvious example) is designed precisely to support that embeddedness;
and, secondly, that embeddedness, by creating a secure social position
and certainty of role, allows greater psychic freedom to explore imaginative and symbolic zones, which is what much consumption actually amounts
to. If culture is understood as practice then daily strategies become of
central importance, as do their relationship to the structuring conventions, or what Bourdieu calls 'structuring structures' that constitute a
habitus (Bourdieu 1977). The interaction of historically created forms
(taken very seriously in Japan) and the strategies of everyday life provide
an essential dynamic in the understanding of culture, which is not a set

of 'patterns' in the sense understood by Ruth Benedict (Benedict 1946), but a set of dispositions formed out of complex historical and social negotiations, without closure and constantly redefined and ascribed new meanings by the intentionality of the actors concerned.

An example of this might be the use of money. Simmel (1978) thought of money as an abstract principle creating impersonal relations between people. Japan today, however, is still very much a cash society. Given the technological sophistication of Japan, there is no reason why this should be the case unless there is an underlying cultural reason. Money need not be so alienating if it is itself incorporated into a social nexus. Thus rents are often paid in cash, in person, necessitating a visit by the tenant to the landlord or agency, an event which becomes an occasion not simply for a financial transaction, but for the drinking of tea or coffee, gossip, discussion of problems that either party might have. Salaries sometimes still are and were certainly until recently paid in cash (now they are usually electronically credited to one's bank account). Resistance to the change to the bank-transfer method has come mainly from wives, to whom the pay packet would normally be turned over and who would undertake domestic budgeting, including issuing husbands and children with pocket money and money for daily necessities. Money, while itself impersonal, can be personalized, and shopping in Japan normally involves face-to-face interaction and payment in cash. Money then can create new social bonds, and ones that are socially valued as well as potentially unequal or exploitative.

What the money example also seems to suggest is that consumption is play, adult play, *asobi*, which carries the argument of psychoanalysts such as Winnicott (1971) that object play is an essential part of children's psychic and motor development. This play does not cease in Japan with the end of childhood, but continues unselfconsciously throughout life, not only in the obvious form of sport, but more pervasively through consumption. For some reason, ever since the Frankfurt School, consumption theorists have tended to be a very serious lot. In reality much consumption is play, and it is precisely this dimension that gives it its subversive edge. The act of buying can be a resistance to work; display can be subversive of convention or established hierarchies. Here lies the essential political paradox of contemporary mass culture. It is certainly true that such a culture is indeed mostly the product of what Adorno calls the 'culture industries'. But this does not mean that it is just passively consumed. Mass culture is double edged, is a mechanism of both conformity and rebellion. And while consumption may be for display, or for resistance, most of the time it has more humble objectives. As Miller put it very succinctly: 'The humility of the common object is especially clear in an area of mass material culture such as furnishing. While it is possible to draw attention to these object frames as forms of display, more commonly they are the appropriate background for living' (Miller 1994a: 101-2).

A number of points, familiar in the literature on consumption, but needing here to be summarized and placed in the context of Japan, can now be mentioned. Initially these may be noted as: the increasing recognition of emotions and affect in explaining people's relationship to consumption; the role that consumption plays in self-expression and the construction of images of the self; and the existence of the life-cycle and the evolving nature of consumption over that cycle – in particular concern with the development of the body as it matures and then ages, and with the recognition of the fact that the project of building the self has become very much a 'body project' in contemporary capitalist societies. To use Lyotard's phrase, the political economy and the 'libidinal economy' are intimately related, and in such an economy the consumption of representations as well as things (which in any case can themselves have representational qualities) becomes primary, especially with the transition from scarcity to abundance which accompanies capitalist development. Desire and its satisfaction become primary motivations for economic activity in such a situation, driven especially by advertising and creating both a society of the 'spectacle' and a society in which experience is actively pursued. Excess and luxury (Falk 1994: 97-9), the pursuit of desire rather than the fulfilment of lack, become attributes of the 'late consumer society', something that is more or less indistinguishable from what is commonly called the 'postmodern' or 'late modern'.

But the reasons for this need not be exclusively hedonistic. Maffesoli suggests that the fragmentation of mass society into a large number of smaller groups makes it possible if not entirely to escape from then at least to diminish the power of dominant institutions. And furthermore in complex societies, where one feels lack of control over the forces that shape one's life, there is the possibility of some autonomy at the micro-level: 'Thus, even if one feels alienated from the distant economic-political order, one can assert sovereignty over one's very existence' (Maffesoli 1996: 44). Depoliticization 'refraining from public expression' goes together for Maffesoli with an "expenditure" in the existential sphere (physical pleasure, hedonism, carpe diem, the body, sun worship)' (1996: 46). The 'popular masses' in this view retain at least a degree of independence from the domination of the mainstream political and economic institutions, a view very similar to that of de Certeau – that, within the tactics of consumption, the consumers invest their own meanings and derive their own enjoyments, which are not necessarily the prescribed or 'official' ones.

The game shows and comedy programmes which occupy so much air time on Japanese television, the comic culture, the huge underground of *butoh*, alternative theatre and music can from this perspective be seen in a fresh light, as pointing to play and festival as a way of managing life in a highly organized society in which power is clearly concentrated at the top of an inflexible hierarchy. So, Maffesoli again:

> Laughter and irony are an explosion of life, even and especially if this life is exploited and dominated. Derision underlies that, even in the most difficult conditions imaginable, one is able, together with or against those responsible, to reappropriate one's existence and, in relative terms, to enjoy it. This is a thoroughly tragic perspective, which is aimed less at changing the world than getting used to and tinkering with it. (Maffesoli 1996: 51)

The reference to tragedy is interesting here, as the dominant theme of a very high percentage of Japanese films, soap operas, *manga* serials and popular novels is tragedy in some form – loss, separation, war, death, unrequited love – a traditional aesthetic tendency that recurs constantly in contemporary popular culture.

Sociality then may take new forms: networks, affective communities, special-interest groups, 'tribes', all of which are alternatives to the 'formal' social structure. The view of van Wolferen that, in Japan, power is concentrated at the top and culture is irrelevant to the analysis of this power, despite its antidotal qualities in relation to the crude culturalism of much Japanology, needs to be rejected in the light of this broader understanding of social power. In reality a form of popular polyculturalism nestles within the apparent hegemony of the traditionalist and elitist definitions of what constitutes Japanese culture and society. An emphasis on the quotidian is not consequently a turning away from an engagement with politics in Japan: it is actually to move towards a model which more accurately reflects the realities of contemporary Japanese life and of the distribution of social power within the society.

The study of consumption then is not a substitute for a critical theory of Japanese society. The analysis of 'play' is every bit as significant as the analysis of 'work', especially as in practice the two are linked, inform each other, intrude into each other's space. Furthermore 'play' (in this context of course consumption) must be situated in relation to changes in labour relations and industrial processes, to internationalization and re-lated structural changes in the economy, to the nature of institutions, the organization of households, and gender relations. For example, as Mouer suggests: 'The consequences of the long hours of work in a Japan are several. First, many Japanese live a highly monetised lifestyle, with high incomes and high living costs. Japanese eat out a lot, and many other household services are purchased rather than being performed by the worker' (Mouer 1995: 55). Commoditization then has broad-ranging effects, not least in relocating the individual in relation to political pressures. The first attempt at *kindai no chokoku* – 'overcoming the modern' – took place in the 1940s as part of the process of ultranationalism. The second attempt took place in the 1980s:

> What is new about the second attempt to overcome modernity launched by the Ohira government in the 1980s is that it explicitly recognizes the destruction that the development of commodity production has had upon tradition, and the way in which it functionally adopts culture to the imperative of control that guides both the state and private business. Hence the aim is not so much to rehabilitate a disappearing national culture, but to instrumentally mobilise its 'simulacrum' – 'the Japanese thing' (*Nihon tekina mono*) rather than 'tradition'. (Harrison 1995: 219)

Civil society in Japan must be seen in this light as well as in the light of the long term effects of being at the receiving end of an imposed constitution (by an occupying force) rather than of an organically evolved one, and to the experience of rapid economic growth. Today the oligopolistic character of Japanese capitalism and its interests in the efficiency of production and the 'rights' of producers is becoming challenged by the power of consumers, who may not be politicized in any traditional sense, but are extremely well informed, highly educated and increasingly internationalized.

These changes can be seen in the way in which they are reflected in intellectual trends within Japan. Some leading scholars of social stratification are switching their interests to the problems of conceptualizing social classes in a situation of affluence in which people seek at least the appearance of difference as a sign of individuality, in which the functionality of consumption is replaced by symbolic factors and in which political culture is transformed from a consensus model to one of the management of individualities and differences (e.g. Imada 1987, 1989; for a discussion of these trends, see Kosaka 1995). Other commentators on contemporary society are turning their interest towards the analysis of lifestyles, especially as they are influenced by scientific and ecological changes (e.g. Funai, Higa and Watanabe 1994).

Certainly it is the case that, whether or not Japan is seen as 'postmodern', the study of the contemporary situation has shifted from that of being a sociology of scarcity to being a sociology of abundance. While it is not yet true that Japan has reached the point of society itself needing to be protected against the aggrandizements of highly individualized consumers, significant political and cultural changes are in train. Politics for many Japanese is increasingly becoming a question of life politics rather than of national ones, of a concern with cultivating the individual body and self rather than with the construction of the nation, and even less the state. Consumption in this situation, far from violating the idea of personal authenticity, comes to constitute it. Given that there is not only one form of capitalism, certain forms or outcomes are not necessarily intrinsic to it: 'Indeed, books on postmodernity with these concerns for global transformation seem even more inclined to talk about "late capitalism" or cultures of inauthenticity as though they represent in their effects the psychic states and generalized experiences of most of contemporary mankind' (Miller 1994b: 11). As Dean MacCannell phrases it elsewhere: 'Postmodern ethnography potentially gives results that are different from postmodern theory, even opposed to it' (MacCannell 1992: 255). In fact there are complex relationships between goods and experiences in differing settings, even though as a general principle it is true that changes in the objective conditions of life create unexpected and unprecedented forms of subjectivity, which in turn reflect back upon and, further, transform 'objective' economic and political conditions.

Consumption then plays multiple roles in relation to the wider social, economic and political processes. Bryan Turner, in explaining the relationship between postmodernism and Orientalism puts it as follows:

> First, we need a dialectic view of the contradictory features of all culture (both high and low), since mass culture contains within itself the potentials of an egalitarian ethic in sharp contrast to the rigid hierarchical divisions embodied in traditional elite culture. Second, we need a more positive view of consumption as a real reward for the deprivations of material production and manual labour, which would avoid the implicit puritanism of the critique of mass culture. (Turner 1994: 119)

– something I am trying to illustrate in this study. Contemporary Japan can be understood as suffering not so much from Galbraith's 'public squalor' as from a public malaise – cynicism over money politics, a growing but unarticulated sense of crisis, rising uncertainty about survival in a complex world and a corresponding unclearness about the image of the self.

The notion of 'risk culture' formulated and popularized by Ulrich Beck (Beck 1994) encapsulates many of these ideas. 'Risk' is clearly related to the image of 'reflexivity' (Lash and Urry 1994: 32-7). Slowly but visibly modern Japanese are floating free of institutional structures and consequently, like their counterparts in the West, are forced reflexively to construct their own biographies. However, compared with many of the advanced societies of the West, Japan is still very stable: individualism as a desired value is downplayed, the labour market is more rigid, divorce rates are low, mobility is restricted and education of a very hierarchical kind is still central. In Beck's thesis the labour market is the motor of individualization, and if this is correct then changes in employment will indeed result in much wider social changes. While individualization in Beck's sense – 'that each person's biography is removed from given determinations and placed in his or her own hands, open and dependent on decisions (Beck 1994: 135) – is much less marked in Japan than it is in parts of Western Europe, North America or Australia, it is increasing, although Beck fails entirely to recognize consumption as an element in this. In Japan the loss of legitimacy of the political centre – the political system is no longer the exclusive focus of politics – the rise of consumption and the slow destandardization of labour are vehicles of change even though what Beck refers to as the 'democratization of techno-economic development' is not yet far advanced. Mary Douglas, in her own discussion of risk, locates the source of change in the market, which sucks us '(unwillingly) out of our cozy, dull, local niches and turns us into unencumbered actors, mobile in a world system, but setting us free they leave us exposed, we feel vulnerable' (Douglas 1994: 15).

While Douglas overemphasizes both the unwillingness and the degree of unencumbered action (at least in relation to Japan, which she does discuss in passing), she locates risk in the larger system of morals and politics:

> Cultural theory does bring us somewhat nearer to understanding risk perceptions of lay persons by providing a systematic view of the widest range of goals that the person is seeking to achieve. Instead of isolating risk as a technical problem we should formulate it so as to include, however crudely, its moral and political implications. Is it possible that the Japanese have a cultural advantage in probabilistic thinking? The reasons would have to do with the teaching of mathematics, with the form of literacy and with the ancient form of society. (Douglas 1994: 51).

Leaving aside the question of ability in probabilistic thinking, two concluding points emerge from this. Firstly, that one of the ways of managing risk is through the consumption of material and symbolic goods which, in secularized Japanese society, take on many of the attributes of religion. 'Risk will produce "religion", by which I mean any generalized view of social reality which emphasizes the meaningfulness of social existence against the threat of chaos and disorder' (Turner 1994: 181). The other is that, if consumption is as much a device against alienation and anomie as it is a cause of them, its particular qualities will be socially rooted and socially expressed, and it is to a range of these expressions that we will now turn.

4

Shopping and the Social Self

Shopping is not merely the acquisition of things: it is the buying of identity. This is true of all cultures where shopping takes place, and the consumption even of 'necessities' in situations where there is some choice reflects decisions about self, taste, images of the body and social distinctions. Japan, a society until recently left out of discussions of the postmodern condition, is well known as a place in which considerations of 'taste' have since earliest historical times entered intimately into both consumption and cultural production. The utensils for the tea ceremony, the colour combinations of *kimono* and *obi* (the accompanying waist sash), the severe economy of traditional domestic architecture, the stress even today on the acquisition of skills in music and calligraphy, and innumerable other instances all point to a culture in which aesthetic values are considered to be not peripheral luxuries, but central to the conduct of social life. But yet they are central in an interesting and perhaps even paradoxical way: firstly, because this aesthetic sensitivity is not necessarily expressed in any conventionally 'artistic' form, but in the mundane activities of everyday life (including, as we shall see, shopping). This feature has led at least one observer to characterize Japanese culture as a whole as one of the everyday, with its lack of an indigenous monumental architectures, its emphasis on the small-scale, the privileged role that it gives to the practical and to feelings rather than to intellectualization (Hasegawa 1982). This is also reflected in many modern Japanese films, especially those now considered in the West to be 'art' films, such as those by the leading directors

Ozu, Itami and Shinoda (McDonald 1983), which seem boring to many non-Japanese viewers because of their slow pace and seeming lack of plot. This, however, is precisely the point: the dwelling in loving detail on the mundane as reflecting the essence of real life, and a concern with images rather than action. Secondly, because of the emphasis on social cohesion in Japan, these 'artistic' activities are not thought of as 'individualistic' in any selfish sense, but on the contrary as creating self-control. Group and individual are not polarized, but integrated in the sense that the social nexus provides the greater context in which the aesthetic activities are carried out. And thirdly, the visitor who arrives for the first time in Japan is often shocked by the apparently anarchic mess that seems to constitute most Japanese cities. But there is a logic here too: interior space, the private, can be managed. Exterior space does not belong to anybody in particular, so can be regarded as purely functional.

It is in relation to these themes that we will discuss Japanese shopping behaviour, especially as it manifests itself in Tokyo. Tokyo of course is not the whole of Japan, no more than London is England. It is a kind of heightened version of what goes on elsewhere in the country: faster paced, bigger, and with an enormous concentration not only of population, but of business, the media, universities, fashion-houses, departmental stores, publishers and booksellers, the government bureaucracies, restaurants, theatres and the other paraphernalia of a major (and very affluent) capital city. It is also in Tokyo that one is constantly made aware of the contrasts of modern Japan: stores and temples, large boulevards and expensive shops and restaurants, behind which still exist the narrow lanes of the old residential quarters with their little neighbourhood shops and itinerant vendors, the most bizarre of Western youth-culture fashion next to ceremonial kimono on the subway. If it is in Tokyo that the consumer culture of modern Japan has reached its apotheosis, it has done so in the context of a society in which both conformity and aestheticism have also reached high levels. It is the dialectic that this creates that makes the Japanese situation so challenging to analysis.

The construction of a sense of self in such a context is an interesting problem, since self is defined not so much in terms of an individual 'essence', as relational. The presentation of the self as both internally integrated and as socially acceptable requires a synthesis, one that when successfully achieved perhaps represents the true genius of Japanese culture. The self can be conceived by analogy with a work of art: as itself the product of a dialectical relationship between interior cultivation and external canons of acceptance. The mask and the reality are thus in a sense the same, or two aspects of the totality. Shopping – the material construction and adornment of this dialectical self – takes on an almost metaphysical significance as a result, since this self-identity must be constantly reaffirmed in ways that are socially visible as well as aesthetically pleasing. Shopping, however, is not just simple acquisition – it has symbolic, spatial, economic, class and gender aspects, and we need to turn to disentangling and clarifying these.

Shopping, although of course men also do it, is regarded largely as a female preserve, both shopping for daily necessities and shopping for major consumer objects such as cars. There are several reasons for this: large numbers of Japanese women are housewives, expected after marriage, or certainly after the first baby, to devote themselves exclusively to the domestic well-being of their children and spouses, and possibly also of parents or elderly in-laws. Not only are women thus 'functionally' associated with shopping, but they are also thought, because of the small sizes of Japanese homes and because their husbands are generally absent, to have both the leisure and the interest. Given also the fact that many Japanese housewives largely control the family budgets, the 'femininity' of shopping comes to be established. And women do often shop for their husbands as well as for their children and themselves. But there are deeper reasons than these operative. Married women are seen as being primarily responsible both for the education of their children and for the physical presentation of their families (in clean, up-to-date and neatly ironed clothes). Accusations of scruffiness – *darashi ga nai* – against one's children or husband involve a serious loss of face for the mother/wife. Japanese houses are frequently crowded and untidy within, but the family will leave the home invariably impeccably dressed (even when in casual clothes). With husbands usually absent for long working days, and children at school (including Saturdays), networks of friendships come into being among women of similar age in a neighbourhood (in addition to kin networks), and shopping together is one of the activities that cement and promote these friendships. Interestingly it is out of these female networks that the albeit embryonic Japanese consumer movement has arisen. Concern about price, quality, safety and durabilty has quite naturally become a major concern of women, who are the primary purchasers of the things that their families consume.

The presentation of self in a very self-conscious culture – which Japan is, and meaning here both concern with the image of the country itself as it is perceived by outsiders and concern, amounting often to anxiety, with the 'correct' appearances of one's individual self – requires the acquisition of the emblems appropriate to both self-image and objective status (as ranked, that is, by the rest of the society, since Japan, while relatively classless, is nevertheless very status conscious). While education, career, travel and cultural accomplishments are also important aspects of this, so is the array of things with which one adorns oneself, one's family and one's home. What one does and what one is are to a great extent the same, and it is thought very desirable to present a rounded or 'total' and consistent image of oneself. A very visible aspect of this are the 'uniforms' that almost everyone in Japan wears (all the more obvious in a society in which 'real' uniforms are rarely seen, except on policemen). Students wear tartan shirts, jeans and clumpy boot-like footwear, and if the weather is cold, bomber-jackets; businessmen and bureaucrats wear suits (blue is the favoured colour) with ties and white shirts. 'Intellectuals', which in Japan mean writers, artists, poets, well-known journalists, classical musicians and university teachers, wear either rather tweedy clothes, possibly with an open-necked shirt, or the same uniform as the businessmen, but with the vital addition of a beret, the sure sign of intellectual status. Youth-culture persons wear youth-culture uniforms, 'office ladies' (clerical workers) wear skirts with white blouses or businesswomen's suits. The key is appropriateness: being not so much tidy as dressed for one's role. In Japan, all the world is indeed a stage.

THE ECOLOGY OF TASTE

This phenomenon creates an interesting mass market of great uniformity, which makes it relatively difficult to buy anything really unusual. Fashion magazines are full of the latest fads, but almost nobody wears them, except for fashion people themselves and a few media people and TV stars. Every Japanese man has a black suit, worn with a white tie to weddings and a black one to funerals. Shopping for originality would seem to be a frustrating experience in Japan unless one grasps the essential point that, while generally acceptable fashion evolves very slowly and is conservative, the secret of shopping is in the quality and the subtle, not the gross, differences. 'Taste' (within one's budget) becomes the vital quality to possess. One of the cognates for good taste (*shumi no ii*) is *johin de*, of which the root *kanji* (Chinese character), means literally 'above' and is also used in writing 'wisdom'. While high fashion is, as in other societies, the preserve of a few, nevertheless high standards of taste usually prevail even in average or 'low' fashion. Perhaps the word that best encapsulates this is *yoshiki* – 'style'. Another characteristic of this kind of relatively homogeneous mass market is, as we have already noted, fads. If a particular fashion variation is 'in' it will rapidly sweep the country, beginning in Tokyo or Osaka and spreading at least to the main urban centres, diffused through the (usually Tokyo controlled) media, which are themselves always alert for novelty.

The rule then is to make a clear statement of gender, occupation and status, to be clean and neat (every Japanese neighbourhood has an amazing number of dry cleaning stores and laundries), but not to be too different from others in your social category, even if that category is only temporary (when golfing wear golfing clothes, when hiking wear hiking clothes). The acquisition of these symbols can be structured in various ways and in various contexts which involve the ecology of shopping and spatial practices.

Several of the same kinds of shopping sites as in any big city in the industrialized world can be found in Tokyo – large departmental stores concentrated especially in such central areas as the Ginza, Shibuya and Shinjuku, smaller but rather up-market boutiques in Aoyama, Azabu, Roppongi and Harajuku, large discount stores selling cut-priced merchandise usually situated in the suburbs, and local stores and small supermarkets scattered everywhere. Then there are the speciality areas – Jinbocho for books, Asakusabashi for toys, for instance; street markets selling cheap clothes, fruit, vegetables and Japanese foods; entertainment districts such as Kabukicho full of bars, clubs, restaurants, theatres and 'adult shops'. Then there are individual shops known for specific wares, including shops selling kimono and their accessories, specialized food shops, stationers, small craftsmen such as name-seal (*hanko*) carvers, who often also design and print the ubiquitous *meishi* or visiting cards. Mixed up with these are a huge number of coffee houses, restaurants and snack places, often physically very small. A distinctive Japanese addition to the shopping scene are automatic vending machines that dispense not only soft drinks and cigarettes, but also beer and liquor, socks, ties, women's stockings, coffee, hot noodles, magazines and practically everything else that can be packaged, including, almost unbelievably, flowers and engagement rings. Such machines are everywhere, and it is reassuring to know that it is possible to buy a rose, a phonecard or a meal in the middle of the night. An important ecological feature of many of these shopping areas is that they are concentrated around the railway stations. The existence of a station, even a quite minor one, is a sure sign of a concentration of shops, coffee houses, eateries, and at least one bookstore. Some of the large stores at railway stations actually own the railway (the station is literally in the basement) – e.g. the Keio or Odakyu stores in Shinjuku or the Seibu store in Ikebukuro) and have branches at suburban stations along the line. In other cases stores have simply grown up around the stations to take advantage of the crowds that flow endlessly in and out. Some of those which at first sight appear to be departmental stores are actually large collections of independent shops and restaurants in the same building (e.g. the My Lord complex at the Shinjuku station). In yet a further variation, huge underground shopping complexes have grown up underneath large stations. The biggest of these appears to be at Tokyo station, adjacent to the Ginza and a large business and government district, where hundreds of shops and restaurants provide all-weather, everyday shopping. This concept has spread to other cities too – Yokohama and Kyoto, for example. Many of these shops also operate for long hours, although the more 'down market' the store, the longer it is likely to stay open, partly because large turnover is necessary to compensate for low profit-margins, and partly because many of these smaller stores are family owned and run. Fast-food restaurants (both Western and Japanese style), 'convenience stores' (i.e. small mini-markets) and neighbourhood bookstores in particular open for long hours.

The form of the last-named appears to be a uniquely Japanese phenomenon. The number of bookstores is enormous, the smallest town or suburb having at least one and usually more. They open long hours, and stock not only popular books but also the ubiquitous Japanese *manga* or comic books. Bookshops are always crowded with browsers, and there appears to be no limit to the time one can stand reading in such a store. The comic books themselves, some of which look like thick or book-length Western comics and are printed on similar cheap newsprint, and others of which are properly bound books, cover a huge range of interests of both sexes and all age groups. There are *manga* for small children, for teens, for adult females and especially for adult males; subjects include science fiction, romance, war, traditional Japanese tales, crime, pornography, economics and politics, humour, animal tales, mixtures of all of these and yet others besides. Given the long commuting distances in Tokyo and other large cities, reading on the train is something of a national obsession – not only the *manga*, but books, magazines and newspapers are all consumed in this way at a prodigious rate, given the large population and universal literacy. Many bookshops also stock magazines, some sell little else but *manga* and magazines, and kiosks at railway and subway stations supply yet a further range of titles. And the range is astonishing, with huge numbers of types of magazines to suit again every age and taste—fashion, travel, sport, news, cars, girls, wildlife, planes, ships, trains, health, children, interior decoration, art, music. More expensive specified magazines – such as on architecture or computing – not available at kiosks, can be bought in bookstores. Almost all are produced to high technical standards of design, printing and paper. Almost all are also discarded immediately on being read. There is only a very small second-hand book/magazine market in Japan, partly because of the Japanese distaste for used items, so most, once read, are either sold for nominal sums to waste-paper collectors or are simply thrown away. And indeed one's impression is that, whether in the bookstore or on the train, browsing is the way most are consumed. Books are read, and some comics too, but magazines and newspapers are scanned and discarded. Most magazines also carry a high volume of advertising, and it often seems to be this that attracts attention rather than the written content.

The bookshop and the big store share a common and desired characteristic – the ability of consumers to browse without any obligation to buy, and a great deal of shopping appears to be what used to be called 'window shopping', which culminates in a small purchase, or the purchase of something that one did not intend to buy, or simply in a coffee house. The act of just going out, to see, to be seen, to see what is new, is an important form of recreation and even exercise. But not all shopping is done in shops. Housewives have only recently but in increasing numbers begun to discover catalogue shopping, i.e. ordering by phone or mail from a glossy booklet provided sometimes by a store, sometimes by businesses that specialize in mail order, and sometimes by other housewives who have a small cottage-industry going collecting orders and distributing a specific range of goods, for example, imported wooden toys, vitamins or handicrafts. Two important varieties of this are door-to-door sales and membership of co-operatives. The first usually involves women who sell, for example, products produced by the handicapped, cosmetics or, rather interestingly, condoms, which are the main means of birth control in Japan. These women, usually middle-aged married women, visit homes and apartment blocks during the day when young housewives are in and their husbands are out. Co-operatives, as we have noted, have become an important part of Japanese retail trade, and it has been recently estimated that as much as 30 per cent of all sales are now via co-operatives. Again these vary: someone joins as a member, and then orders from a catalogue at discount prices, or from the co-op truck which visits members' neighbourhoods at fixed intervals. Others are co-operatives of farmers, frequently those who grow only organic (chemical- and pesticide-free) foods, who sell their products again usually from trucks that tour neighbourhoods at specified days and times. Many of these one does not need to join, but, although anyone can buy, they do in practice tend to develop their own regular clientele for their rather expensive but guaranteed quality produce. A final recent innovation has been the appearance of 'do-it-yourself' stores, where the materials needed for home construction, crafts, home arts such as knitting or oil painting, model making and the like are available. Furniture, bicycle kits, calligraphy equipment and almost anything imaginable that can be put together by oneself can be acquired in these stores, some of which (e.g. the 'Tokyu Hands' chain) are large multi-storeyed buildings resembling departmental stores, which sell high-quality and by no means cheap products.

The symbolism and phenomenology of shopping that exist within these spatial, architectural and economic frameworks is intriguing, and, being in Japan, have their own cultural distinctiveness. To see and be seen, the shopper's 'gaze' directed both at the potential objects of consumption and at the other shoppers, is different in a small town where one is personally known to the vast metropolis. Tokyo contains 12 million people, and the total population of the city and the surrounding Kanto plain is over 30 million. The statistical possibility of meeting anyone you know, except in very well frequented places, is very small. This anonymity has its psychological advantages in a society where, within the residential neighbourhood, one's comings and goings, tastes and activities will be very well known. Shopping, while providing a legitimate and even necessary reason for going to town, is also liberating – one can spend, acquire exciting new things and accordingly fine-tune one's image and be temporarily 'free'. Certainly there are limitations on expenditure based on objective income and consumption decisions based on taste arising from class status, although most people would today expect to possess the 'necessities' such as a TV and washing machine. So although class consciousness is weak, differences in consumption patterns based on economic status are apparent, which suggests that the idea of 'consumption classes' – social groups differentiated by what they consume – is potentially a useful way of looking at social stratification in Japan and may be of greater conceptual utility than Marxist based ones (Steven 1983) as well as an effective way of conceptualizing social divisions within the total political economy (Eccleston 1989). Shopping is not necessarily mundane: it is adventure, safari, carnival, and contains unexpected 'risks' in what you may find and whom you may meet. It is a kind of self-discovery. And by its very nature it possesses theatricality: one dresses up to go out and one shops to acquire the new persona, to modify the old one or to perfect the setting in which one is seen and known. Where one wants to be seen is consequently important. To 'be' among the boutiques of Aoyama or Azabu is phenomenologically different from being among the aisles of a suburban discount store. And since an important task in Japanese culture is to dissolve the distinction between having and being, shopping becomes an important existential project.

CHOICE AND BEING

This project has four key elements – eclecticism, wrapping, choosing and discarding. The modern Japanese house often contains the most amazing collection of artefacts – Japanese dolls, bits of Western furniture, a piano standing on the *tatami* (rush matting), a kitchen containing the latest electrical conveniences and an ancient and primitive stove, pictures and souvenirs representing the spoils of foreign travels or of trips within Japan by family or friends. This wild eclecticism is not just, or even, bad taste: it represents a quality of the Japanese character – the ability not so much to synthesize as to juxtapose the inharmonious, and to live happily with the result because it works. Function is beauty. The excellence of Japanese industrial design is an example of this phenomenon working at another level: it is in the design of the practical and mundane that the merging of the function and aesthetics is most satisfactorily carried out. The first thing that must strike a shopper from a second-or third-world society, or even a neophyte shopper from a first world one, is the sheer profusion of things to be found, a cornucopia and an orgy of overchoice in which practically everything exists in multiple varieties. A visit to the extraordinary 'Electric City' district of Akihabara illustrates this very well. Dozens of stores, many of them multi-storeyed, contain literally millions of items of electrical equipment of all conceivable kinds. Actually choosing one, even a simple item like an electric fan or clock, becomes a feat of decision-making. This range of choice gives a sense of power to the shopper – there is so much to choose or reject – but also a sense of confusion: the thing bought may well not in fact be the best or the latest. The role of the salesperson is important here, and most of them are men, in some cases on loan from the companies that actually make the stuff. They are supposed to know: they have a guru like quality in this existential quandary, and their advice is taken very seriously and rarely rejected. They are not just sales clerks, but priests: mediators between the innocent, ill-informed and choice-fatigued would-be consumer and the plethora of things themselves. Overchoice itself promotes eclecticism, especially in the absence of a central scale of values to structure that choice, and it is for this reason that Japan has been proposed as the pre-eminently postmodern society – as one having no central core of values (say in the Judeo-Christian sense) and as never historically having had one, except for an aestheticism joined to strong pressures of group conformity. According to this argument, Japan has not just become postmodern, it has always been that way ('transmodern'), and contemporary eclecticism is simply an expression of this. But the eclecticism is empirically apparent whatever its origins, and has different expressions: it is not just the random collection of unrelated objects; it differs with class, age, sex and self-image. Seen from one angle, a 'random' collection may be just that; seen from another, it may be an indication of the cosmopolitan character of the individual collector. One may regard oneself as a *kokusaijin* – an international person – for instance, a person of varied cultural persona. Eclecticism would also seem to be a reflection of the Japanese characteristic of simultaneous self-confidence and inferiority complex. For every Japanese who is proud of his/her country's enormous economic success, there is another who is convinced of the inferiority of Japanese culture and character and the superiority of things foreign. Often the two attitudes are found in the same person. The use of things, especially objects that are semiotically ambiguous, to mediate this is an understandable reaction. With careful planning one can be cosmopolitan and indigenous at the same time. Snoopy (of 'Peanuts' fame) is an example of this possibility, and (as a result?) is something of a cult figure in Japan. Little shops everywhere sell trinkets bearing his likeness, and young girls carry his image on bags, keyrings, umbrellas and tee-shirts. He is vaguely American and therefore modern, but he has also been assimilated in the same way that baseball has – indeed both are widely thought to be Japanese ideas borrowed by the North Americans. Above all, however, he is *kawaii* (cute), a concept used with incredible frequency in modern spoken Japanese, especially by young women (Kinsella 1995). Objects then are not neutral, but can be exploited in different and even contradictory ways to illustrate different facets of one's shifting or evolving identity.

The thing bought, however, is not just 'itself'; nor is it just the cluster of symbolic meanings attaching to it. It is indeed all of these too, but it is also transformed by one additional and quintessentially Japanese procedure: its wrapping. This may sound trivial, but in Japanese culture it is not. A serious literature exists in the art (literally the art, for it is so regarded) of wrapping things in paper, straw, cloth, and in packing them in wooden boxes and other kinds of containers (Oka 1967). Shop assistants, assuming they have not already learnt the skill from their mothers, are taught how expertly to wrap and tie the merchandise that they are selling. The cheapest of the ubiquitous *obento* (lunch-boxes) bought at a railway station will be elegantly packaged and its contents laid out inside in an aesthetically pleasing fashion. And a small pair of disposable wooden chopsticks will be included with the purchases, also neatly packaged in a paper wrapping often decorated with elegant calligraphy. A Japanese is as likely to give as much attention to the wrapping – the material, the way it is folded, the ribbons used to secure it – as to the contents of the package. To give a badly or inelegantly wrapped gift, or one not wrapped at all, is both rude and a negative reflection on one's own taste and sensibilities. Stationery stores have large sections for wrapping paper, ribbons, labels, cards and the special kinds of decorative envelopes used for giving gifts of money. The humblest purchase is carefully wrapped, and one is usually asked if it is a present. If it is, it will be wrapped and tied in an even more elaborate way, at no extra cost to the purchaser, the buying and the packaging being intimately linked and both part of the same philosophy of service (Hendry 1993).

This emphasis on packaging is an important facet of the fact that Japan is, on a very large scale, a gift economy of a kind that would be instantly recognized by any anthropologist. Gift-giving and receiving are ingredients of everyday culture. Gifts are given not only for birthdays and weddings, but also for funerals, when visiting someone's home, on the occassion of promotions or other similar events, and especially at mid-year and at new year (*chugen* and *oseibo*) when half-yearly bonuses are paid and when a nation-wide boom in gift-giving occurs – to those who have done you favours, to those from whom you hope to receive favours, to bosses and to one's children's schoolteachers. All the year round departmental stores stock appropriate gifts, but at these occasions they are full of them; advertising appears extolling certain products and parcel delivery companies are inundated with work. Many families keep detailed record books of gifts sent and received, so that mistakes of reciprocity will not be made. The traditional gift-giving seasons are not the only occasions either. The Japanese (almost entirely non-Christian though they are) have discovered Christmas in a big way and even Easter to a degree, as well as Mothers' Day, Fathers' Day, Hallowe'en and Valentine's Day, a point discussed in Chapter 1 above. Life in Japan sometimes seems to be an endless round of gift-giving, reflecting the networks of close social relationships that abound. On moving into a house or apartment one gives to the neighbours on both sides and opposite; on returning from holiday one always brings gifts (*omiage*) for family, friends, secretary, office-mates and neighbours, usually a regional speciality of wherever one has been – cakes, cookies and sweets being common choices. A great deal of shopping activity is not for oneself, but for gifts for others, and shops cater for this huge volume of gift-giving, and every hotel in a resort area has a little shop selling souvenirs and local foods. Even railway stations reflect the gift economy, and in a popular tourist destination such as Kyoto there are gift shops not only around the station but within it and even on the platform, so that gifts for a suddenly remembered acquaintance can be bought at the very point of boarding the *shinkansen* (bullet train) for the ride home. The actual shopping for gifts requires considerable cultural skill – for whom? how expensive? what kind of thing? And yet much of what is received is never consumed – it piles up or is given away again. This perpetual and enormous circulation of commodities – a gigantic kula-ring like cycle of obligations and reciprocities – represents a key dimension of shopping behaviour in Japan, and a fascinating extension of the economics of the gift.

The art of choosing, as we have suggested, is a sophisticated one, whether for oneself or others. In buying a gift, for example, price is important, not only for one's own pocket book, but because to give too expensive a gift is to impose a heavy burden of reciprocity on the recipient, to give too cheap a one is an insult. In choosing for oneself, self-image comes into play. Here there are also some important contextual factors at work. Two groups are among the biggest consumers – youngish unmarried women who are between college and marriage, currently working and living at home, with few overheads; and youngish married or unmarried professionals who, because they cannot possibly ever afford a house in Tokyo, divert what would in other societies be mortgage savings into consumption. Both groups consider themselves sophisticated consumers, for whom consumption is indeed a way of life, and they are aided in this by the huge range of media, not only those carrying general advertising, but specialist consumer magazines and guides as well. The Japanese verb for shopping (*kaimono*) is written with the Chinese character for 'thing', and a leading consumer magazine, on sale at most news kiosks, carries exactly this splendidly practical title – 'Things'. It is, as a representative of its genre, a very interesting magazine – glossy, of nearly two hundred pages per issue, and containing nothing but advertisements and short articles on new products, including TVs and VCRs, cameras, watches, luggage, clothes, chairs, fashion accessories, toys, cars, pens, sunglasses, cigarettes, personal computers, lawnmowers, an endless succession of trivia (jigsaws, kits for making dinosaurs, tissue-holders, tiny first-aid kits, snuff, wild-western style embossed riding saddles, exotic clocks, art nouveau decorations), new product test reports on several items and a lead article – in one particular issue on bourbon, with an illustrated guide to several dozen brands. Product guides of this kind (and there are many others, both rival general ones and ones specializing in cars, sporting goods, bridal wear, etc.) are themselves widely consumed – either for their aid in actually selecting an item or being alerted to the enormous range available, or because they are interesting in themsleves, as attractive and fascinating guides to the inexhaustible range of possibilities – even if you do not actually want or need any of them. Such magazines are also an expression of the fine Japanese art of advertising. Adverts are everywhere – not only in magazines and newspapers and on six of the eight TV channels (two being state run, non-commercial channels), but on walls, telephone poles, billboards, trains and subways, on every available surface, in neon all over commercial buildings and thrust in endless quantities into one's mail-box. As an incentive to consume it is undoubtedly a powerful force, and, like wrapping and the self, it is considered an art form (Moeran 1989).

A thing once chosen, however, will not always be retained. It will, if bought as a gift, be given away. But it is just as likely to be rapidly discarded simply because it is no longer new. A certain day each month is 'heavy rubbish day' when unwanted large objects can be put out on the sidewalk for collection by the municipal rubbish collectors or by private contractors. The most astonishing variety and volume of things are discarded – furniture, TVs, bicycles, golf-clubs, all kinds of electrical appliances and just about everything else that a modern household might possess. Students and poorer people often furnish their dwellings with cast-offs of this kind, which is not a bad idea since the objects are often in almost mint condition. It is not uncommon for middle- and upper-middle-class households to change their furniture, appliances, curtains, even cutlery, every few years. New is good (and there may be a deep seated cultural attitude here possibly originating in Shinto ideas of purity). This high turnover means that constant shopping is necessary, and constant awareness of what is on the market and what is in fashion, which in turn requires a never-ceasing vigilance on the part of the consumer. This mind set produces huge quantities of perfectly serviceable 'junk', and this logic applies even, or especially, to cars. Very few old ones are to be seen on city roads, and those that are are sometimes called *gaijin-kuruma*: – 'foreigners' cars' – as only foreigners, who have little or no 'face', are willing to drive around in them. Even the climate is roped in as a justification here. Japan is markedly seasonal (Japanese sometimes refer to themselves as 'ninety-day people' – fickle and rather changeable, like the seasons, which last only three months each) and certain kinds of clothes are thought appropriate for each season, not only in terms of warmth or coolness but also of colour and style. The non-appropriate clothes are stored and/or discarded, and stores exploit this seasonality by introducing ever finer distinctions. So one finds not only, say, autumn clothes, but 'early autumn clothes'. The logic of consumption expands here in culturally interesting ways. Overnight stores are transformed from late summer to early autumn, and then instantly it is impossible to buy late summer clothes unless one knows the discount stores and boutiques where out-of-season fashion is retailed at knock-down prices. And this transformation is literally overnight. The Christmas season ends on Christmas Eve, when the big stores simultaneously remove Christmas trees, decorations, seasonal music and display themes and replace them by the following morning with decorations and gifts for the much more culturally significant New Year, which again, commercially speaking, ends as the shops close on 31 December.

The situation that we are analysing here, while clearly a recognizable 'culture of consumption' by Western capitalist standards, is also one with its own distinctive characteristics. These include shopping to give away (the gift relationship), the predictability of the shopping cycle (its seasonality, constantly emphasized by the media, and especially on TV every might, where the characteristics of each season are dwelt on at length, and advice is given on where to go to view the best cherry blossoms, plum blossoms or maple leaves, as is appropriate) and in a sense its orderliness. The craziest object bought will still be wrapped in the most traditional manner, and certain colours are still thought appropriate for each age group, season and even occupation. And there are yet other peculiarities. One of these is the travelling abroad for the purpose, essentially, of shopping. Given the very high cost of living and inflated prices of Japanese commodities, it can be as cheap to take a vacation in Korea, South-east Asia, Taiwan or Hong Kong as it is to holiday in Japan, with the added incentive of being able to buy both international 'brand name' goods and Japanese-made products at far below their Tokyo prices (there being big price differentials between the cost of the same Japanese made product at home and abroad). The desire for brand-name goods, especially French, Italian, and British products – watches, luggage, shoes, leather products, perfumes and fashions – is a well-known characteristic of Japanese shoppers, and one thoroughly exploited by shopkeepers in places such as Singapore, Hawaii and Hong Kong. The motive is partly to buy quality goods, something that does, for once, last; and since one's foreign travels are likely to be less frequent after one's brief 'office lady' phase, it makes sense to buy while one can and has the ready cash. And indeed in a sense when one has to. Most Japanese workers still take very short holidays, often less than their official entitlement, and for the great majority of those in working life and their spouses these are concentrated in the few days of 'Golden Week' in May, when several public holidays occur together, in August during *obon*, and at New Year, when many businesses close for up to four days. The major problem with this pattern is that almost everyone is obliged to take their vacations at the same time, leading to massive congestion of roads, airports and long-distance train services. But functionalism is not all: brand names possess a mystique, a cachet that creates the impression of sophistication, of internationalism and of taste. The almost metaphysical levels that this can reach in Japan seem to transcend those found elsewhere, as revealed by the extraordinary success of the best-selling 'novel' *Nantonaku, kurisutaru* (Somehow, crystal) by Tanaka Yasuo, virtually plotless and consisting in large part of lists of brand-name goods and quasi-scholarly notes discussing these commodities; it sold over three-quarters of a million copies and, in doing so, became something of a brand name commodity itself. The big stores in the major cities often have either special promotions of foreign brand name goods or stock them permanently – Harrods of London and Laura Ashley being two currently popular examples in large stores in the Ginza area of Tokyo.

But if the ethnography of shopping in contemporary Japan is undoubtedly of considerable interest, does it help us to move beyond middle-range theory towards a comparative theory of postmodern societies? It would seem that it does, and this reopens the case for regarding, if not Japan as a whole, then at least its urban culture as an example of postmodernism incarnate. To assess this possibility we would have to begin with a subjectively and culturally constructed model for relating self and society – in this case the construction of self as social, that sociality being practised and generated through participation in consumption. This participation both identifies and solidifies the sense of personal self, and confirms it as social through common membership of the shopping fraternity. The image of what one should be like – being fashionable, modern, while also being one's age and status, while continuing all the time to be Japanese (itself of course a social construct) – which is created through an enormous yet remarkably homogeneous media effect, can be fulfilled at a vast range of consumption sites. And here we also begin to see what makes the Japanese case so theoretically interesting. The aesthetics of the self in Japanese culture make that self vulnerable – it is liable to disintegration if it is not located in the social nexus and/or if the subjective means of its identity formation are disrupted. And this sets up what is perhaps the fundamental and persisting tension in Japanese society. The social order, certainly at least since Tokugawa times (the Shogunate of the period 1603–1868 which created and enforced a rigidly hierarchical and controlled social system), has been 'rational', but the basis of this rationality (or 'modernist' project), once one moves beyond mere crude social control, is, and always has been, emotion. The modernist identification of self and task cannot be read in the same way as in the West – as primarily a function of goals and capitalist work relations – but rather on the analogy of the craftsman – a person so dedicated to a task that absorption into it becomes the end result. You do not so much learn a craft as become it. The role of intuition and subjectivity is very strong in Japanese culture – for example, the emphasis, even if often over-rated, on non-verbal communication, *haragei*, 'thinking with one's stomach' (Matsumoto 1988). Mood, atmosphere, feeling, are essential components of this, and this is a major reason why the Japanese are often accused by 'principled' Westerners of being without ethics, or at best being situational ethicists. Feelings, especially considerations of *ninjo*, 'human feelings', are paramount over abstract principles. Shopping then is freedom, but freedom within the constraints so beloved by the Japanese, in which boundaries and limits confer rather than restrict freedom (the economy and restraint of *chanoyu*, the traditional tea ceremony, is a marvellous example of this). Excitement and tranquillity are not, as for most Westerners, opposites, but rather both aspects of an untranslatable 'spirit' in which grace and control are harmonized with pleasure and fun. Many middle-aged people remember the years of postwar privation before the current age of *akarui seikatsu*, the 'bright new life', came about. To be able to shop and choose and to create alternative identities within the bigger framework of a fundamentally conservative society is considered something really quite marvellous.

This expanding range of possibilities, the fruit of affluence, offers new prospects – the increasing public roles of women, the emergence of a distinctive youth culture, a rapidly burgeoning entrepreneurial sector, a flourishing arts and music scene – which, while not necessarily challenging traditional Japanese sensibilities, are certainly extending and redefining them. If this interpretation is correct, Japan would represent a unique experience – the achievement of a form of postmodernity different from that so far described in the West, one without the fragmentary self and in which experiment in architecture, fashion and the arts coexist with pragmatism and the continuous re-creation of tradition (for example, the now almost universal Shinto wedding ceremony, thought by many to be very ancient, was actually invented in 1900 for the marriage of the then crown prince). Certainly the Japanese intellectual community, very well versed as it is with trends of thinking elsewhere in the world, does not tend to theorize the situation so much as an attack on the modern as of the creation of a distinctively Japanese form of modernity. This is perhaps not surprising in a society where media saturation and bullet trains paradoxically coexist with a physical infrastructure that is often positively third world in quality. If the true basis of postmodernity lies not in technology or particular styles of art or design, but in the collapse of meta-narratives (Lyotard 1984), then Japan has, at least in this sense, been postmodern for a long time, since it is widely seen as a society in which such meta-narratives have historically always been weak or absent. But the meta-narrative argument is not all: the corresponding revaluation of self is an equally significant dimension. Although these things are very hard to measure, subjectively at least it appears that alienation is low in contemporary Japan compared with other industrialized countries. The jarring changes of the last half century have not only been assimilated, but have been 'turned round' and presented back to the world as Japan's economic miracle – a success in creating a special brand of Asian capitalism based on a set of cultural and sociological behaviours so different from that experienced in the West that more than one observer has suggested that Japan is in fact the only really 'communist' state in the modern world (Kenrick 1990). Clearly there are critical dimensions to this too, such as whether or not commoditization of a capitalist kind is creating classes in a society that formerly did not have them. Nevertheless, what is interesting about Japan is that certainly the preconditions of postmodernity – the image of self, the central and accepted role of subjectivities, eclecticism, the centrality of feeling and atmosphere, the play element, the love of spectacle and the pose (Edwards 1989) and the existence of a sensual rather than intellectual culture, as well as a materially advanced economy – all flourish. Japanese shopping is situated in this context: disturbingly familiar and yet disturbingly different, in a society semiotically charged, but in unfamiliar ways to the outsider. Here is a society which embodies a sensibility in which aesthetic values and social order continuously interact. Barthes rightly called Japan 'the Empire of Signs' (Barthes 1970), for it is surely a society in which the sign is central (and its ideographic script perhaps ensures this). A recently seen satchel, designed to look like a soap-flakes packet, has emblazoned on it, in English, the following cryptic message, a fitting epilogue to our exploration of Japanese shopping: 'Original Shopper's Bag: American Taste: We give you an answer to everything. You've always wanted to know about LOVE and HAPPINESS. Produced by Super Planning Company. Made in Japan.'

The passage from shopping to even wider considerations must now take us in two directions: firstly into an examination of the internationalization of consumption and its relationship to gender as a key element in social stratification in Japan; and secondly into the question of the body, the site at which gender and consumption meet.

5

Gender, Class and the
Internationalization of Consumption

INTRODUCTION

The theorizing of contemporary Japanese society poses many challenges
to the anthropologist who wishes to understand the realities of everyday
life. Clearly there are many potential angles from which a society as
complex as that of Japan can be and has been approached at the level of
localities – grassroots political organization, the management of *matsuri*,
social movements, the *furusato* phenomenon and religious organization,
to name a few that are currently popular. The theoretical theme of this
chapter is that the analysis of that most everyday and repetitive activity
– consumption – provides a route to understanding local-level Japanese
life in a way that very fruitfully yields a 'way in' to some of the most
intriguing debates and problems in the sociology of Japan – including
questions of class, the continuing viability of local communities and the
real role of women in the Japanese social structure. Ethnographically this
is approached through the analysis of data from a neighbourhood in
western Tokyo which attempted to explore actual economic behaviour
and people's relationship to material objects. In particular, the food and
durables purchasing patterns of housewives, relationships of friendship
and neighbourliness that sprang up around shopping, membership of co-
operatives and networks of local knowledge, and information about the
availability of commodities of various types were focal points in the study.
This is in part because these activities and patterns are of interest in their

own right, but also because, despite their deceptively simple nature they are in fact saturated with symbolic meaning.

This chapter will attempt to theorize these activities in terms of three intersecting models. The first of these is a model of symbolic competition, and an argument will be developed that the concept of class can best be understood in relatively homogeneous Japanese urban neighbourhoods in terms of consumption patterns, and a comparative exploration of the relevance of Bourdieu's work on French social differentiation will be undertaken. The second is a model of the presentation of gender, self and body through the commodity form, where it will also be argued that it is women who primarily control symbolic resources in this area and to a great extent define for their husbands and children the 'correct' means of self/body presentation consistent with social status or anticipated/desired status. The third is a model of neighbourhood co-operation. The potentially damaging effects of too intense symbolic competition are balanced by networks of sharing and common consumption, often centring on clubs or co-operatives.

At all three levels, consumption is often of objects which are not Japanese in origin. Even at the most local level, Japanese families consume the world as much as the world consumes Japan, and this is to be understood both in terms of a material form of internationalization and also as a response to widely held views of globalization and interdependence, and of the management of everyday life under consumer-oriented capitalism. This points to fresh ways of theorizing Japanese society in general.

THE SETTING

There may be no such thing as a 'representative' Tokyo neighbourhood in a strict sense, but the fieldwork site is certainly typical of many other urban localities in Japan. Situated in western Tokyo, Mure 4-*chome* is a district dominated by suburban housing – many detached houses, small 'mansions', wooden apartments, a small danchi zone – together with one busy shopping street, scattered neighbourhood shops, several urban farms, a government elementary school, the campus of a private school (Myojo Gakuen), a small branch campus of Tokyo Joshi Daigaku and a few offices and workshops, including that of a tatami maker. The area is mostly residential and derives much of its character from its proximity to Inokashira Koen, which lies a short distance north and outliers of which penetrate into Mure, so the area is more wooded than many Tokyo neighbourhoods, a feature enhanced by the fact that the Tamagawa Jo-sui bisects the *chome*. Despite the 'villagey' feel of the area, it is on average only a 15- to 20-minute walk or a ten-minute bus ride to Kichijoji, a busy shopping and entertainment area around a major stop on the Chuo line, from which it is only an 18-minute train ride to Shinjuku (one of the main stations on the 'Yamanote' line which encircles central Tokyo).

There is little employment within the neighbourhood, apart from the local shops – a convenience store, mini-market, toy shop, cake shop, video store, two dry-goods stores, two butcher shops, a barber, a coffee shop and several dry-cleaning establishments. The nearest bank is in Kichijoji, the nearest restaurants clustered around Inokashira Koen station at the eastern extremity of Inokashira park, and the nearest area of concentrated shops a five-to-ten-minute bicycle-ride away, across the boundary of Mitaka (the adjacent town), immediately to the west. By day, the area is populated mostly by housewives and young children. The men have gone to central Tokyo, to Mitaka or Kichijoji, where they are employed as bureaucrats or businessmen. Most of the human traffic into the area by day is comprised of students attending the private school or the university branch campus, and a high percentage of these, too, are female. The area then is socially composed mainly of families of the 'sarariman' (salaryman) type – i.e. white-collar commuters and their families. With the exception of the smaller shops and workshops, the area has a distinctly 'middle-class' atmosphere, and house prices are fairly high. Convenient for downtown Tokyo, the physically pleasant character of the neighbourhood and its proximity to one of the city's nicest parks, makes it a desirable place to live. Like many other Tokyo districts it is a mix of old residents (much of the area was farmland until the 1950s and 1960s) and newcomers who have bought property there. It shares the mix of 'native and newcomer' of other parts of formerly rural western Tokyo, but without the sense of social cleavage that Robertson identifies in Kodaira (her fieldwork site just north of the Chuo line, a short distance northeast from Mure) (Robertson 1991). This may be partly because Mure has no distinct sense of being a *furusato* – it has no local *matsuri* (although other people such as the boy scouts use the local forest park for their own *matsuri*), no shrine or temple within its boundaries, and no clear geographical boundaries or spectacular local history of its own. Indeed, administratively, Mure is a sub-district of Mitaka, which is the focus of attempts to generate feelings of belonging to a locality, insofar as this happens at all.

The sense then in which the neighbourhood is a 'community' at all has to be sought in its sociological characteristics – its networks of relationships – rather than in its formal organizations, administrative practices or temple parishes. Some elements of these do exist, of course – for example, as in Kodaira, where the volunteer fire brigade (*Shobo-gumi*) has some part in creating a role for the 'natives' – but here my argument will essentially be that the absence of any kind of *furusato-sukuri* does not create a problem empirically or a vacuum intellectually. Indeed the problematic set up by Robertson, and also by Bestor in his ethnography of another Tokyo neighbourhood (Bestor 1989), centres debate on local-level politics and on the organization of a very visible feature of local activities – the *matsuri*. This is valid insofar as it goes, but it does prevent the emergence of other possibilities – in this case economic and quasi-economic activities which actually constitute networks (and therefore 'communities' in a truer sense than those which administrative or occasional festivals create).

Similarly the 'local' approach clearly has certain benefits for the ethnographer who has as a fieldsite what appears to be a relatively bounded socio-geographical unit. But localism, if not handled realistically, actually excludes what cannot be excluded – the national, which penetrates the local in numerous ways – and (one of the themes of this chapter) the global. The locality is not only defined by its own internal activities; it is also to be understood in terms of its relationship to the international – to the forces that actually shape the consumption which creates the networks out of which local-level communities are constituted on an everyday basis and which animates, in practice, the formal relationships of neighbourliness and residential proximity, especially in areas where people are not in fact linked by kinship, place of origin, or even shared interests.

The hypothesis here is that it is through consumption, and especially through shopping – the primary activity that initiates the cycle of consumption – that networks are formed and friendships cemented. It is through shopping that symbolic competition between households of objectively similar socio-economic status takes place. And as it is primarily the housewives who do the shopping, consumption activities are gendered. Men may consume what is purchased, but they themselves tend to play a subservient role in the actual acquisition of goods except for very high-price items (e.g. houses), those that are considered 'technical' (e.g. more expensive electronic items) or their own clothes, although even in this last case women often buy items for men or play an active role in making the choices, either at the time or by way of finding agreeable styles in magazines or other sources of information. The actual practices of shopping, then, need to be considered.

THE PHENOMENOLOGY OF SHOPPING

We all shop, and probably for most of us shopping has become a commonplace activity, the ethnographic richness of which consequently tends to escape us. Here I will try to describe and analyse some of the salient features of purchasing activity in Mure. For most Mureites some form of shopping is a daily activity despite the universal availability of refrigeration. Fresh vegetables, fruit, bread, milk, meat and fish are acquired on a more-or-less daily basis, mostly as a planned activity for which time is specifically set aside, although often small purchases are made 'because I was just passing' a particular store. Full-time housewives in particular have structured purchasing patterns – at certain stores and at predetermined points in the day, often in the late morning when children are at school or *yochien* and when the day's supply of fresh foods is known to have arrived and been displayed. Men rarely participate in such shopping unless they are students or have occupations with irregular hours, but they do sometimes shop on the way home from their offices in the evening. The bargain hour at the end of the day in departmental store food basements in nearby Kichijoji is also an occasion for a purchasing expedition. Shopping for everyday non-food items takes place less regularly although often still in a limited range of known stores; and shopping for clothes or major durables takes place less frequently still, often at weekends with family or on weekdays with female friends, and often in Kichijoji or further afield, especially in Shibuya (easily accessible by the Inokashira line) or Shinjuku (on the Chuo line): both are only a little over 15 minutes from Kichijoji station.

Men are involved in purchasing mainly large durables or major clothes items for themselves. Clothes for the children and smaller male clothing items (socks, for instance) are usually purchased by the wives. The physical pattern of shopping is based partly simply on ecology – closeness of grocery stores particularly – but also and importantly on networks of information – information acquired either through personal 'purposeless shopping', i.e. going to (usually) Kichijoji and just exploring for the sake of exploring, through advertisements in magazines or fliers put in one's mail box (the amount of unsolicited junk mail, most of it advertising, being as great in Mure as in the rest of urban Japan) or through networks of friends and neighbours. The sharing of information, and sometimes subsequent shopping together, is an important source of neighbourliness in Mure, especially among women living in close proximity. Some purchasing is made by mail order, but most is done personally.

Sometimes these networks go beyond merely sharing information, and involve common membership in a co-operative, usually one specializing in providing organic food products, which are popular in Mure. Networks also ensure knowledge of such important but occasional events as school bazaars, exciting items in the recycle shops (significant institutions despite the Japanese penchant for new things) or new shops. Such purchasing behaviour and the detailing of such networks is of interest in itself, but it is even more interesting if we penetrate a little deeper, which I will now attempt to do.

The interpersonal dimensions of sales interactions have been ethnographically documented (e.g. Prus 1989a, 1989b), but whereas the marketing is seen as a personal accomplishment, purchasing is not. In fact, as my Mure respondents make clear, and as is evident from watching them shop, buying is considered something of an art form. The adepts show mastery of taste, of ability to recognize materials and other physical qualities, of the economics of purchasing (what is good value) and of sheer physical stamina. Setting out on a shopping expedition, especially for clothes or important items in terms of display and self-esteem, is correspondingly an occasion marked by excitement, often planned with friends well in advance and backed up by extensive information from magazine reading and observation of what is in the market and what other people are consuming. What actually happens on a purchasing trip is that marketing practice and the strategies of the consumer intersect in complex ways within the ever evolving matrix of object availability and fashion taste.

To understand Mure shopping behaviour purely in terms of utility would be a mistake. The activity is ludic, hedonic and experiential; it is emotive, multisensory and a fantasy activity every bit as much as it is practical. The 'embedded' nature of consumption must be grasped as much in these terms as in terms of 'culture', or rather a deconstructed understanding of Japanese contemporary culture reveals it to be composed as much of these elements as it is of order, conservatism and high aesthetics. Knowledge of available products, their uses and prices intersects with mental constructs, images of the self as consumer of the product and the simple dimension of *asobi* – play. Consumer goods themselves embody these qualities and also (although not necessarily 'higher level' ones) those such as hopes and ideals (McCracken 1988). Goods are evocative, enable and constrain choice, play a role in both cultural change and continuity; they mobilize behaviour. 'Object codes', understood by Sahlins (1976) as totemic, illustrate yet another facet of the highly complex life of things (Appadurai 1986), all of which are involved in the apparently innocuous act of shopping (or other dimensions of consumption behaviour). Lifestyle, as a result, is increasingly defined by things rather than by beliefs; and indeed, the beliefs express themselves concretely through things.

I would especially argue for the experiential dimension of Mure consumption. Shopping is certainly not life, but it is experience, something that brings one into intimate contact with things, other people, mass culture, Japan and the world; it is, in short, theatrical. It is also active, unlike the more passive possibilities of reading or television viewing, even though both of these act as agencies for acculturation into consumption in the more active sense, and reproduce and reinforce cultural categories deeply implicated in consumption. Image, information and cultural codes are all then involved in product choice and use: things are symbolic at many levels; they are both practical tools and condensed meaning. Not only advertisements resonate (McQuarrie 1989), but, more importantly, so do the objects they promote. Brand-name products, so famously associated with the purchasing devices of Japanese consumers, exemplify this very well, not because they are necessarily more expensive or unique (a lot of people have them), but precisely because they resonate – with ideas of style, desirable foreign places – they have mythic qualities. All consumption choices are within limits – of budget and the worker – but these are subjectively transcended for the Mure shopper by the investment of the object with such powers, for by seeing the object in this way the self is itself extended.

Purchasing then becomes central to the pursuit and experience of leisure. It may also be possible to read it as one of the resistances of everyday life to the demands of the Japanese work culture. But yet, at least in Mure, there appears to be little self-conscious irony: purchasing may be play, but it is, like other expressions of Japanese play, also taken rather seriously. The results of the research findings so far might be summarized as follows.

i) The purchase of objects, while objectively an 'act of consumption', means that, although the purchaser conceptualizes such acts as such, quite different motives may also be involved. The desire may be more important than the acquisition; or the acquisition, whatever its complex strategies, may be merely the means to achieve enjoyment, which itself may be aesthetic or emotional rather than utilitarian, to create personal space rather than to be narrowly functional. In fact, the idea of utility itself in Mure needs careful examination: play, status or cultural capital accumulation may be as important as, or be, 'mere usefulness'. This applies equally to the literal consumption of food, which is rarely eaten only to sustain life, but for reasons of diet or body image, for concepts of health or because certain dishes are currently fashionable. Culture itself is consumed in this way, and Mureites, in common with other Tokyoites, are voracious attenders of museums, exhibitions and art galleries, few of which have any clear 'utility'.

ii) The emotions are probably the most important part of consumer behaviour, but this does not imply, as Campbell suggests, in *The Romantic Ethic and the Spirit of Modern Consumerism* (Campbell 1987: 42), that the emergence of consumer-based mass culture leads to a 'rationalization of emotions'. The centrality of the ludic, especially for the Mure female, who has fewer obvious socially approved opportunities for pure play than do men (who have after work drinking, expense account dining, soaplands and sport, and are less tied to the home), makes consumption the great feminine arena of freedom. This is especially so since the world of things is essentially an imaginative world. And there is a twist to this. The average Mure consumer is, like her sisters elsewhere in Japan, a prophetess of the everyday and its pre-eminent value. But consumption provides the principal means for the imaginative to be incorporated into the practice of everyday life in a largely non-disruptive manner. Objects change space, time, feeling and the sense of embodied self, yet within a framework shared by others. Much of the art of life becomes the art of consumption.

iii) Where there is little real misery, there is little real resistance. Instead, consumption and imagination, rather than being used against the social order, are used primarily to sustain it: space is created for the articulation, not so much of individual meaning, but of shared meaning. But is this simply false consciousness, commodity fetishism hiding behind a cultural façade of harmony? This problem can be approached in several ways, Firstly, the social self-definition of Mureites and their tastes are closely related, but not everyone has the wealth to pursue all these tastes. Such a situation can lead to conflict, or it can lead, as I would argue happens in Mure, to the restructuring of social relationships to emphasize high levels of 'natural equality' ('We are all Japanese') which transcend the 'artificial' inequality of status based on object possession, and to emphasize symbolic competition which allows both the constant contestation of the peripheral codes (e.g. minor fashion possibilities) while ensuring that agreement over the content of essential cultural capital actually allows those with more cultural capital to upstage those with more actual material capital.

Secondly, it is difficult a priori and unadvisable ethnographically to reject what is a mode of life for the Mure inhabitants. In a culture in which freedom is defined largely in terms of controlled restraint (e.g. the tea ceremony) the idea of enslavement to things is not the problem that it might be in more dualistic societies. All things that entail limits constrain, but this is true of all systems of objects, rules or ideas. It is foolish in the view of my informants to oppose constraints as such: the secret is to turn them back on themselves, to find the conditions of liberation where only restrictions could previously be found. So is consumption articulated in Mure. To regard as false consciousness the basis of freedom might be overdoing it a little.

And thirdly, Dean MacCannel has raised the interesting question of the extent to which focus on the everyday, the termination of class and ethnic opposition, and the 'covergence of the libidinal and the actual economy' create the path to what he calls 'soft fascism' of a kind that he already sees flourishing in California (MacCannell 1992: 186-7). His argument is a provocative and telling one, especially as the 'desire to be postmodern' can certainly be found in certain social circles in Tokyo, or among those who argue that Japanese aesthetics with its alleged concern for surfaces, its concern with wrapping and its concern with imperma- nence, have always been 'postmodern'. But his points of reference – Nazi Germany and contemporary California – also suggest important differ- ences from Japan. Germany – 'the ordinary raised to a principle; regu- lative social norms raised to ideals' (MacCannell 1992: 207) comes closest perhaps, and Japan has experienced its own fascism this century. But what is lacking in Japan is: a) the 'death drive' of Nazism; b) the collapse of 'all ethnic, class, regional, gender or other denotation' (p.219); c) the 'discontinuity and schizophrenia at the level of culture' in which 'desire is largely absent' (p.220); and (d) 'superficiality in human relationships' (p.218). These may well be true of California, where postmodernist soft fascism flourishes according to MacCannell, but its inapplicability to Japan throws up a basic and fundamental principle: consumption is not a unitary phenomenon – there is more than one way of being a con- sumer society. Some of these are highly destructive of the human spirit; but others, especially those – like Japan – where the social bonds are already tight, may provide a way out: a zone of liberation, play and the imagination where other expressions of these are circumscribed. And, furthermore, these can be exercised not apart from society (in Japan nature provides that outlet), not as spectacular acts of revolt, but entirely within the practice of everyday life.

We can obviously agree, then, with Douglas and Isherwood (1979) that goods mark social categories and that they also create, through their relationship to those social categories and by the logic of their own connections, an intelligible universe. But we must also go beyond this on the basis of our ethnographic material to suggest three other elements not discussed by Douglas and Isherwood: that goods mark social catego- ries differently in varied cultural contexts; that goods not only render the universe intelligible, but also, if not exactly unintelligible, at least myste- rious; and that they blur as well as mark social boundaries.

The first point is easily explained: the same things consumed in differ- ent (cultural) contexts can, of course, have different meanings in those alternative contexts. The symbolism of colour in relation to clothes, for example, is not universal, so fashion choices will be predicated upon particular cultural codes. To read Barthes (1984) in Japan is an interest- ing experience: the semiotic code so painfully worked out in relation to French fashion behaviour has little utility, except perhaps as a formal model of pure semiotics, in relation to Japanese fashion behaviour. The second is more interesting. The consumption activities from sample households include food; non-food household items (tissue paper, washing powder, etc.); items of non-essential clothing (i.e. not to replace needed, damaged or worn-out clothes) for family members, including things such as children's underwear emblazoned with pictures of the current TV *manga* heroes or heroines; toys; CDs and videos; books and magazines; the occasional luxury item (a new watch or an item of jewellery); make-up; and what can perhaps be described as purely ludic items – whimsical purchases of useless objects that were just bought 'for fun'. Even among the apparent essentials such as food, many purchases clearly were for taste rather than necessarily for nutrition – sweets, ice-cream, fancy cakes, for example. To explain these purchases simply as the acquiring of objects to mark status is inadequate, both observationally and on the accounts of the purchasers themselves. Many such items are perishable and rapidly consumed by the family itself – they are not for display – and others (especially the whimsical ones) are rapidly discarded. Items purchased to be given away as gifts are more likely to be expensive than those consumed at home. In fact, many purchases are for play rather than utility – they are simply fun, tasty, eye-catching. They are consumed for pleasure either with one's family or with friends, and indeed, if they have a 'function' it is as a marker of friendships, since it is only with friends that they are consumed.

The third factor is equally interesting. Foreign-made goods or foods are regularly consumed – Chinese- or Korean-made clothes for cheaper items, European or American (e.g. L. L. Bean) ones for more expensive items; Thai, Indian, Chinese, Vietnamese, Italian, Scandinavian and French food are all available in nearby Kichijoji even without travelling as far as downtown Tokyo, where the range is even bigger; the local supermarkets are full of foreign cereals, chocolates, biscuits, jams, meats, juices and wines. Even locally baked bread is often marketed as 'French'. Clearly some of these things are consumed simply because they are nice; others because they mark status; some because their consumption marks one as a cosmopolitan, as rather international; and yet others precisely because their meaning is obscure. In this last case their unintelligibility gives them an 'aura' (to use Walter Benjamin's term), and it is only foreign goods that have this aura. Their lack of commonplaceness makes them mysterious. This is true across a range of examples, from locally purchased tee-shirts with messages (sometimes obscene) in foreign languages, to European wines which definitely have a mystique. The consumption of foreign goods then fulfils several purposes: as a means of display and symbolic competition (in which rarity value is important as well as price); as a means of establishing one's internationalist credentials;

as a way of reflecting back Japanese culture through contrast and comparison; and as a way of reintroducing the auratic back into everyday life: the foreign becomes a device for the re-enchantment of the world.

Display, then, is many-sided: it is, when done publicly, a means of competition, a potlatch-like activity parallel in many ways to Japanese gift-giving practices. It is also a reflection of one's membership in a particular kind of group. By purchasing and displaying the same kind of objects, belonging is confirmed and the self verified. And at yet another level it reflects the irony that is also potentially or actually present in consumer behaviour. Display can be a form of resistance, of standing against the hegemony of cultural forms by deliberately propagating an alternative code. The Japanese consumer, like consumers in any late capitalist society, is not merely a passive victim, but operates at the nexus of needs, desires, products, taste, information and tradition, and is capable of endlessly restructuring the relationships between these into a kaleidoscope of possibilities. Display of the public self in Japan takes place to only a limited degree through objects (fashion, cars) given the general conservatism in these regards; but the private self can be constructed and verified through relationships to things that are affective and aesthetic as well as practical. Here, the 'audience' is the self itself. What is important is not the viewing of the objects by others, but the sense of personal empowerment that comes from the possession and contemplation of the things. An aspect of this which is somewhat beyond the scope of this chapter is the construction of the body, in relation to which almost all consumption takes place.

THE INTERNATIONALIZING OF CONSUMPTION AND THE REINFORCEMENT OF JAPANESE IDENTITY

The internationalizing of consumption – through purchasing, the media and travel – has paradoxical consequences precisely because it becomes a matter of cultural politics. On the one hand, Japanese life becomes more cosmopolitan in foods, fashion, music, movies and the objects in general circulation. However,this consumption may not necessarily be because of a subjective desire to internationalize, but, on the contrary, may be provoked by nationalist sentiments. Cosmopolitan consumption does not, in this perspective, mean that the world is colonizing Japan, but rather that Japan is consuming the world. From a position of economic strength, and sophisticated taste and knowledge of the products of the rest of the globe, Japanese can plunder the network of international trade in order to support an affluent but still unmistakably Japanese lifestyle.

The average Mure consumer does not consume more American products because of trade pressure from Washington or at the urging of the Japanese government (the resistance to foreign rice in 1994–5 being a case in point), but because they are attractive and because they somehow link the consumer to a mythology of the American way of life. But even this is a stratified phenomenon. At least two shops within a ten- to 15-minute walk of Mure specialize only in American fashion products – meaning jeans and other denim wear, checked shirts, waistcoats, belts, boots and other cowboyish paraphernalia. But this is bought almost exclusively by teenagers. Students and young working adults buy very few American products, although older adults might, though rarely, buy an American car (generally they are considered too big for Japanese roads, to consume too much fuel and not to have the glamour of European ones). Decisions based on taste which is related to personal lifestyle far outweigh decisions based on political considerations or on the specific desire somehow to internationalize oneself. The latter possibility is, indeed, an almost totally unheard of concept except among the occasional *kikokushijo* (returnee from abroad) or the rare aficionado of a particular foreign culture. But even in these cases the behaviour tends to be confined to areas such as fashion or food, as witnessed by the large number of 'ethnic' restaurants and shops in nearby Kichijoji, rather than to fundamental changes in the self.

The deeper reasons for this must be sought in the fact that, even in its most benign forms, nationalist ideologies create themselves at least in part through constructs of culture, and this is nowhere truer than in Japan, where the notion of 'cultural nationalism' (which includes the whole Nihonjinron phenomenon) well describes this style of identity formation (Yoshino 1992). Here, cultural action is used as a primary mechanism for creating what Williams calls 'thinking nationalism' (Williams 1994), which includes the constant reinvention of culture, often in the guise of 'tradition', the *furusato* movement being a good case in point. The normal, moral and real world is thus Japan, and this normalcy is constantly reinforced through mass culture which is replete with images of 'Japaneseness', aimed especially at women, the primary purchasers and the main agents of socialization (Skov and Moeran, 1995). 'Being Japanese' is not an essentialist notion: it is something that requires constant construction and reconstruction, and this is done by a variety of means – through the media; by intellectuals and producers of reflections on Japaneseness; by politicians, especially those on the right; and through consumption and its expression in a lifestyle – in the purchasing of objects, their use in creating a lifestyle and in their incorporation into a semiotic code, the point of stability in which is, for many Mure consumers, self-consciously being Japanese.

This is important, however, not as evidence of some alleged Japanese atavism, but in terms of identity creation in the face of the so-called globalization of culture. Consumption behaviour is, in fact, in the Japanese context a mechanism for the re-creation of ethnicity and for the expression of that ethnicity. Those who see acts of consumption as the search for an authenticity that can only end in an experience of emptiness may be profoundly wrong, both because consumption can satisfy certain existential needs and because consumption can be a vehicle for the achievement of higher level identities than merely individual lifestyles. Consumption, in other words, is complex not only in its practice, but also in the range of purposes – needs, desires, satisfactions and even spirituality – that it attempts to fulfil. Consumption gives space for the play of imaginative possibilities; it does not only trap the consumer in a world of material objects, especially if it is recognized that material objects are themselves symbolic.

If, at the local level, consumption has long been anti-hegemonistic, as Ivy suggests in her analysis of the works of Kon Wajiro and Gonda Yasunosuke – 'that consuming could be a form of challenging the productivist and essentialist ideology of Meiji, Taisho and Showa Japan' (Ivy 1993), at the more global level it allows resistance to certain aspects of Japanese life while simultaneously affirming a primary identity at a more foundational level: meanings are contested, but within a context – the context itself is not. This can be seen clearly in the controversies in 1994 about the importation of foreign rice. The recognition of imbalances in trade has done little to make foreign – especially Thai – rice acceptable. Even arguments about the bad taste of foreign rice and its unsuitability for preparing Japanese dishes do not really touch the root of the problem. For, whereas difference – the other – can be ludic, a source of playfulness, it can also be a threat. If the roots of Japanese culture really are in a rice culture, as Ohnuki-Tierney has argued (Ohnuki-Tierney 1993), then eating the foreign is literally to consume – to ingest – it. Whereas 'ethnic' foods provide, along with their setting in a restaurant decorated to make it appear to be abroad, a packaged experience, a temporary suspension of total involvement in Japanese life, yet in a setting that provides enough clues and signs, allows the ludic to emerge, the eating of foreign rice in a Japanese context is emotive in the opposite direction. In the interplay of the global and the local, rice, above all else, sets limits, becomes the irreducible symbol: the packaged foreign can be consumed, but when what is foreign threatens to become Japanese, particularity defeats the forces of universalism, the local triumphs.

But it is not sufficient to explain this merely as yet another example of 'nationalism' or of ethnocentricity. For what it actually reveals is the problematic nature of universalism. The notion of 'taste' is not irrelevant here. Foreign rice, especially the long-grained varieties, does taste different; it has to be cooked differently and it cannot be used to make, for example, the base of sushi dishes. Literal taste is involved here, but so is symbolic taste. The field of consumption is crowded, and choices have to be made. But how? Many of the objects of consumption no longer have real roots – these days everyone wears trousers. But this universalism creates its own problems – it is 'tasteless', not subjectively satisfying because of its sameness, which generates a need to create contrast and difference through the assertion of particularity, often expressed in Japan as 'tradition' (including the recently invented kinds). And insofar as the project of creating the self is undertaken in relation to objects, the achievement of a relatively integrated self with some sense of cultural identity suggests that a total universalism is not workable. Localization in a particular mode of social being (a culture) is for most people, and certainly for my informants, the only sensible course.

But, as we have been arguing, this particularity is not, and in late twentieth- century Tokyo cannot be, a total immersion: the global intrudes even into the local. But in consumption terms, certain markers are still maintained, at least in Mure, as indicators of everyday Japaneseness. Of these, food is considered important, and no one goes to ethnic restaurants all the time. Reproducing the culture through ingestion is one key; dress less so, since Japanese dress is rarely worn, but the local argument is, and indeed it is supported by visual evidence, that there is a distinctive Japanese 'style' to the wearing of 'universal' (certainly no longer strictly 'Western') dress. The everyday use of language, obviously through speaking, but also through reading, is also important – the consumption of novels, comics and magazines painlessly maintains participation in the broad stream of Japanese mass culture, itself seen as embodying rather than subverting quintessential Japanese values.

All these activities can be seen as part of the construction of the self, especially if one follows the view of Maruyama Masao, who looked on the Japanese self as experiential and 'carnal' (Maruyama 1969), although he did not understand this 'carnality' in terms of consumption, but as a limiting factor preventing the complete realization of modernity in Japan. But it is also part of the construction of gender. The possibility of 'shopping the world' allows men to define their masculinity partly in terms of cosmopolitanness, and women to be feminine in a 'Japanese' way, through the distinctive stylistic codes imposed on foreign fashions. Global consumption provides the major possibility for avoiding entrapment in traditional sex-roles while creating the freedom to define new understandings of gender. Globalization then can be a mechanism of liberation, by allowing fresh definitions of the relationship between *uchi* and *soto*, the inside and the outside. To have both kinds of taste – the Japanese and the foreign – is essential to my Mure informants to the contemporary definition of Japaneseness. This reflects interestingly on debates about mass culture in Japan. Synthetic as the 'choices' of the Mure consumer may be to the purist critic of capitalism, in practice mass culture is unashamedly embraced. Within it, to be sure, distinctions in taste mark a form of class – consumption classes – but in reality most Japanese participate heavily in mass culture. The possibility of global consumption, however, creates the corresponding possibility of transcending, or appearing to transcend, this mass culture and to express a form of creativity-through-consumption, while simultaneously enhancing cultural capital through expression of knowledge of foreign objects. In any society meaning is constructed at least partly through things and their symbolic ordering and evaluation ('taste').

An interesting footnote to this can be seen in the 'international' language of advertising – in the use of foreign languages in advertisements, the prevalence of 'katakana adverts' and in the 'Japlish' used in the labelling of objects as well as in advertising text (Sherry and Camargo 1987). Here, the language is not necessarily meant to be literally understood – rather, it conveys a sense of the desirably foreign (English, French and very occasionally German are used, never Portuguese, Swahili or Malay); it flatters the 'reader' and itself adds something to the 'style' of the object or the advertisement. The 'glamour' of the foreign object labelled in an exotic language also perhaps offsets the fact that the Japanese consumer knows that given the relatively closed Japanese market, s/he in fact has access to only a limited range of genuinely foreign products, and that such products as are available are inevitably priced far above the level that one would pay for the same object in New York, London or Singapore.

Japanese society itself can no longer contain consumption within the old ground rules: new cultural subjects have arisen that were not there previously, shopping, tourism and mass media being among the most significant. The expansion of Japanese capitalism has inevitably brought about both a globalization and a hybridization of consumer culture. Mure consumers utilize French, Italian, Portuguese, Australian and Californian wine, wear clothes made in China and Korea, spray themselves with perfumes made sometimes in France, but often in New York with French brand names, eat Thai, Californian, Australian and Chinese rice, dine in Indian, Thai, Vietnamese, Chinese, French and Italian restaurants in the immediate neighbourhood, read Japanese translations containing numerous foreign words, enjoy Scotch whisky, play games originating in the West (Scrabble and Monopoly as well as baseball) and yet use all these things in their own distinctive cultural ways. The local and the global interpenetrate at almost all levels of everyday life in Mure. Indeed MacCannell goes a step further, to argue that the current dialectic between global versus local, or sedentary versus no-madic or any other dialectic that involves a contradiction between differ-ent levels of socio-cultural organization, is about to be superseded. The emerging dialectic is between two ways of being out-of-place. One pole is a new synthetic arrangement of life that releases human creativity. The other is a new form of authority, containment of creativity, and control. (MacCannell 1992: 5)

Out of this dialectic emerge new subjectivities, new ways of being in the body, new possibilities for social arrangements. One of these is the putative classlessness of Japanese society. This can actually be read in several ways: as pure false consciousness, as ideology, as a genuine em-pirical reflection of the low income differentials in Japan, as a cultural strategy designed to reduce the consciousness of difference in order to allow the free play of a higher level unity (Japaneseness), or, as MacCannell also suggests, as an expression of postmodernism, raising again the inter-esting debate of Japan as postmodern. His view is that, 'to the extent that class differences force themselves on awareness, postmodern propaganda relentlessly promotes the idea of moral uniformity across the classes, and that class is only one among several consequential differences including gender and ethnicity, and by no means the most important of these differences' (MacCannell 1992: 106). While MacCannell intends this as a hostile comment, seen from a Japanese perspective it is remarkably appropriate and positive. Considered from this point of view, it may be that Japan really is a postmodern society!

The expansion of commodities and the increase in their flow also make it harder to read the status of the possessor of the commodities in any consumer society. This is intensified by the internationalization of consumption, which not only makes the range of commodities greater, but also conjures their ranking. In some cases the symbolic value of a foreign object cannot be assessed, and so its part in expanding the cul-tural capital of its owner is ambiguous. But, at the same time, globalized consumption allows Mureites a form of controlled interaction with the world that is not threatening or embarrassing: the dangers of the world and the uncontrollability of the other can be domesticated. Consuming the world is then, in some sense, also to dominate it. This is not the same as global integration and homogenization, however. Internationalized consumption allows the Mureite to enjoy eclectically, to create greater plurality of lifestyle, while clearly distinguishing Japaneseness from the foreign.

CLASS, CONSUMPTION AND GENDER

The analysis of consumption and of the objects consumed should not then be set over against mass culture, but rather regarded as the essence of mass culture both in the post-enlightenment societies of the West (Miller 1994a) and in Japan, which, despite its different experience of modernity, has followed the same route of industrialization and the incorporation of technology into every level of social life. Material objects – their acquisition, display, manipulation and consumption – constitute a large proportion of expressive culture in contemporary Japan. And the social psychology of this is interesting, since, whereas Western anthropological commentators on consumption such as Sahlins (1972, 1976) see consumption as a means of constructing social reality as philosophically essentially unsatisfactory, as it creates a system of infinite but unsatisfiable wants, the possibility that this experience of 'incompleteness' may be read differently in Japan does not occur to them. And I would argue that it can be read differently and represents an important and distinctive feature of Japanese consumer consciousness. There is no expectation that the 'thing' or its consumption will ultimately satisfy: on the contrary, consumption is seen as a process, a continuous activity of self-construction, of relationship maintenance and of symbolic competition. All things pass, including the objects of consumption, and if they did not pass, this would defeat their essential meaning – as transitory powers in a permanent but ultimately non-teleological strategizing.

The question of class must also be further discussed at this point. That Japan is a society in many ways obsessed with hierarchy is beyond dispute. How this hierarchy relates to or translates into class – if it does at all – is a very vexed question. Standard, quasi-Marxist analysis does not seem to solve the problem very well at all, as it simply imposes on Japanese society sociological categories derived from very different social contexts (cf. Steven 1983). Instead, a theoretical model of consumption classes or the empirical analysis of social mobility (Ishida 1992) provide much more fruitful possibilities in terms of the reality of Japanese consumption behaviour.

What needs to be moved beyond is the simple acceptance of the idea of Japan as a 'middle-class society'. The constant repetition of surveys which present this 'finding' should be approached with considerable skepticism. Such surveys ask their questions in such a way as to generate only a very restricted range of answers, occlude intra-class differences and generate or reflect an ideological consensualism which identifies a major quality of being Japanese as 'being middle class', and all this in a society in which class consciousness is evidently very low and in which the word itself (*kaikyu*) is rarely used or heard, except among sociologists. Furthermore, the traditional surveys (especially that of the prime minister's office) do not attempt to relate the abstract notion of class to occupations, gender or social changes, especially changes in the nature of industry.

The suggestion that I have been pursuing in this chapter, however, is that standard concepts of class need fundamental redefinition, and need to be reformulated in a way that is much closer to Bourdieu's position in *Distinction*. That is to say that differentiation through acts of consumption has become the primary means of locating and distinguishing oneself in contemporary Japan. The tendency for consumption decisions (obviously related to income, and income differentials are very low in Japan) to concentrate around a 'middle-class' identity needs further deconstruction. It does not mean primarily a spontaneous identification with the imposed category of class, but the recognition of a reality based on the large but nevertheless surprisingly structured range of consumption choices which is in turn linked to similar incomes, and the desire for homogeneity which is a powerful element in Japanese psychology. What becomes increasingly important, given this situation, is differentiation within an actually very homogeneous social category, which empirically in Mure takes the form of symbolic competition over details (my Golden Week holiday was in a place more exotic than yours) while simultaneously playing down the disruptive and overtly competitive consequences of such rivalry. This is handled not by denying differences, but by regarding them as largely symbolic, which gives every actor the opportunity either to accept or to redefine the code, which is thus inherently unstable. But this instability does not produce symbolic chaos; on the contrary, it tends to promote convergence on a very unity of identity, the parameters of which are set both by convention and by the objective consumption possibilities – what is in the market. The convention itself is something of a 'social fact', understood in Mure both as Japaneseness and as the possession or attempt to acquire universally desired cultural capital, such as education. Consumption and the moral order are not opposed in Mure: they must necessarily fit and sustain each other. A dialectic of homogenization and difference is set up which works itself out in the constant activities of everyday life. As in Kelly's approach, the analysis of this involves the study of the interaction of 'ideological process, institutional patterning and everyday routines of individuals' (Kelly 1993: 192), all set within the context of a form of cultural nationalism, of which, as we suggested earlier, internationalization is paradoxically a part rather than a contradiction.

This is not to argue for the direct applicability of Bourdieu, however. Bourdieu's model, powerful as it is for exploring the idea of lifestyle in relation to taste, does so (it is, of course, based on empirical work in France) on the basis of assumptions about class-conditioned cultural competence. The theoretical question in Japan is not the issue so much of the relevance of distinctions based on taste and the consumption of culture, but the location of these within a context in which class is a taken-for-granted social sub-stratum. Using the concept of habitus Bourdieu has demonstrated the relative autonomy of the cultural *vis-à-vis* the economic: patterns of social classification exist between classes and also (and this is very relevant to the Japanese case) within social groups of the same economic position. The possession of cultural capital – cultural knowledge and competence – allows differentiations to appear among people of the same economic class position. Cultural capital, unlike some forms of economic capital, is acquired over time. Bourdieu sees the chief investment of time as being in education, but from the point of view of consumption behaviour there is also great investment of time in the gathering of information and in the practical aesthetics of monitoring changing taste.

With greater investment in cultural capital, consumption becomes more sophisticated, and since all capital tends to breed more capital, the accruing of yet more symbolic capital occurs as the result of the ability to consume in this sophisticated way. In this manner Bourdieu is able to extend the understanding of the logic of social relations to account for their operation in those social domains where economic position would appear to be less directly relevant in the determination of social position generally. According to Bourdieu, the origin of power lies in the production of social differences, which may be either real or symbolic, economic or cultural (Lee 1993: 33). Given the decline of real economic differences in the determination of class, questions of cultural differences become central, and distinctive modes of cultural consumption are the means through which social differentiation is generated and reproduced. Cultural goods become 'little other than symbolic utilities, valuable not for their inherent properties, but as objective vehicles for the demonstration of the interpretive skills of particular consumers' (Lee 1993: 38).

Class, in this sense, becomes a question not of category, but of strategy: practices, including musical preferences, tastes in food, interior decoration and clothing. Class then is real, but is not be be confused with a purely economic classification on the one hand or with just 'lifestyle' on the other. Indeed, in a little read paper, Bourdieu distinguishes this work from the categorizing tendencies of most class analysis by introducing the concept of class as social space constituted not of essences but of real relationships (Bourdieu 1985: 195). A (Japanese) class is not an 'effectively mobilized group', to use Bourdieu's phrase in the same article, nor is it necessarily a group characterized by consciousness. Rather, it is a field of practices, shared by people, but also used by them to compete, not with other classes, but with other members of the same class. Class is not 'objective' in the sense of being simply the outcome of economic relations, nor is it 'subjective' in the sense of being merely a question of arbitrary dispositions. Real struggle takes place, much of it, however, symbolic, and this struggle, in Japan, is largely through consumption. Yet, such groups, 'sets of agents who occupy similar positions and . . . [are] subjected to similar conditionings', are not really a class; '. . . an actual class, in the sense of a group, a group mobilized for struggle', but 'at most might be called a probable class' (Bourdieu 1985: 185). In Japan then classes exist as social fields, but it can certainly be argued that they do not exist as groups mobilized for struggle: in this respect they remain as potential classes. Choices or dispositions in relation to fashion, food, sport, music, and so on are the practices that constitute a consumption class, but a class so constituted through (and for) consumption has no political agenda. Cultural politics replace 'political politics' in the context of abundance and over-choice. While this is not to argue with Baudrillard for the triumph of the simulcra, it may help considerably in explaining contemporary Japanese political sociology.

Virtue born out of necessity is an old Japanese practice. Constructing 'middle classness' around objective equality of incomes (largely true of Mure) allows an ideology of homogeneity to prevail while permitting and encouraging consumption, consumption being, after all, a hallmark of bourgeois identity. Whatever points of specific difference we might have with Bourdieu, the numerous differences in detail between the French depicted in *Distinction* and the Japanese of Mure, we can certainly agree that in the Japanese context class as practice rather than as category or lifestyle is a valid way to approach the issue.

This view is reinforced by empirical sociological research which strongly suggests that the status homogeneity hypothesis of scholars such as Murakami (1984), that there is a single undifferentiated middle class in Japan, should be rejected in favour of a status inconsistency model of the kind proposed by Tominaga and his collaborators (Tominaga 1979). In summarizing the Tominaga school approach, Ishida states:

> They concluded that the stratification system in Japan could not be repre-
> sented by upper, middle and lower categories along a uni-dimensional
> status scale. The majority of respondents scored high on at least one of the
> status characteristics while low on the others. The status inconsistency
> hypothesis predicts that the various status characteristics of classes are
> inconsistent, so that classes cannot be characterized by consistently high or
> low status attributes. (Ishida 1992: 209)

The dimensions measured in the Tominaga study were occupational prestige, education, income, assets, living style and power. Interestingly, too, in this study, and in its subsequent updatings, the status inconsistency position appears to be especially true of the middle class.

None of these studies, however, incorporates any analysis of consumption. The question of 'power' in the Tominaga study or in Ishida's work fails entirely to include any real analysis of its social qualities. In fact, the Japanese middle class possesses power as consumers, but actually exercises little real power over the forces that really determine social life in Japan, power actually concentrated in the upper reaches of state bureaucracy and the corporate hierarchy. The middle class, which is actually characterized by lack of control over social forces, sees consumption as essential to its 'alternative' (i.e. non-empowered) lifestyle: consumption becomes, in Ewen's useful phrase, a 'cultural warp'. 'The stylish ephemera of the new "middle class" existence was more of a symbolic fringe benefit, a cultural warp, which permitted its recipients to identify with the interests of the upper classes, while occupying a relationship to power that was more akin to that of the working classes' (Ewen 1988: 64). As a class, the Japanese 'middle class' continues its existence, or qualifies as a class, not through its political mobilization but through its symbolic competition with other social groups, its sense of itself as the carrier of basic if 'modern' Japanese values and its emphasis on consumption and the family as its means of self-identification and self-reproduction. The Japanese 'middle class' is actually a social stratum of objectively similar economic characteristics with divided political loyalties, and a 'class consciousness' constructed principally around consumption which allows both symbolic competition and the sense of sharing common interests and a common future pursued through similar means, especially the acquisition of cultural captial.

Consumption, for the new Tokyoites – at least this is true in Mure – is in some respects a substitute for a sense of place. Networks of consumption relations replace the *chonaikai* (neighbourhood association), and these networks, comprised chiefly of women, while largely confined to the neighbourhood, also provide the social basis for the consumer movement and its by-product, membership of consumer co-operatives (Maki 1976). This is not a class movement as such, but it does have the 'mobilized for struggle' characteristic identified by Bourdieu. Like many social movements in Japan, the consumer movement tends to be issue focused and does not contribute all that much to overall social change. But two things are nevertheless significant: the emphasis on consumption places this movement strategically at the centre of one of the most important social processes in Japanese society; and the movement is composed largely of women, who are actually probably the most significant agents of social change in the country.

This is partly because the consumers, contrary to de Certeau's view that they are 'the dominated element in society' (de Certeau 1984: xi-xii), possess knowledge, information, economic power and skill, and are mistresses of the art of using the things imposed on them by the forces of production in ways not necessarily intended by the manufacturers. Practice is now organized precisely around the management of these things, and largely by women. And here, too, we must part company with Lefebvre, who, while correctly arguing that 'everyday life weighs heaviest on women. It is highly probable that they also get something out of it by reversing the situation, but the weight is nonetheless on their shoulders', goes on to state that, as both buyers of commodities and symbols for commodities (in advertisements, for example), 'because of their ambiguous position in everyday life, they are incapable of understanding it' (Lefebvre 1971: 73). My argument here has been exactly the opposite. Consumption and the ambiguities of consumption among Mure women provide precisely a source of knowledge, a means of exercising power and a way of managing sexuality that promotes a deep understanding of everyday life (to say nothing of the associated socialization of children and husbands, management of the home and self-improvement activities). Women in this view hold the keys to understanding everyday life, especially its consumption element: they shop, display, animate the gift culture and are the principal arbiters of taste: their experience is profoundly implicated in any account of late modernity, its social practices, economy, management of the body and the emotions.

The ludic dimensions of consumption are especially important here. The willingness to play with things rather than to see them in terms of crude utility frees people from fetishism and loss of autonomy. Bataille's idea of the importance of 'non-productive expenditure' and of generosity, the gift and 'excess' (non-ultilitarian consumption) as sources of social power, is close to this concept of consumption, which is very much alive in Mure (Bataille 1985: 117). *Omiage*, a necessary accompaniment of travel and, as such, a further expression of globalization of consumption, is an illustration of this. The concept of the *tsukai sutete bunka*, the 'use and throw culture', needs to be relocated in this context: not just as waste, but as excess which promotes precise and specific social goals. Not only use value, but play value, display value and even, as Sahlins would have it, totemic value adhere in the objects of consumption.

Such patterns are underpinned by well-known social practices – the fact that Japan is still largely a cash economy and that women still tend to exercise control over the household budget, which they consume even if they do not produce. Social identities are thus formed largely around consumption for women and around production for men. This has important implications for politics: the struggle for a better life among

Mureites takes place through consumption rather than through attempts to control production. As the locus of struggle is different, so are the means: women's networks, the consumer movement and co-operatives rather than, say, trade unions, become the politically signifi-cant agencies. This non-Baudrillardian separation of people from formal institutional politics may go a long way in explaining the largely unex-plored sociological basis of voter apathy, apparent political opinionlessness and general disillusionment characteristic of contemporary Japanese political culture.

The sub-text of this chapter has not been so much that the study of consumption is important in its own right (something now widely recog-nized in sociology, cultural studies, anthropology and marketing), but that it provides a necessary route not only into the understanding of everyday life in contemporary urban Japan but also into the more ad-equate overall theorizing of Japanese society as a whole. There are sev-eral reasons for making this suggestion. This chapter has tried to demonstrate that, in consumption issues of gender, class, internationali-zation, selfhood, Japanese identity, play and the social organization of the economics of everyday life, all intersect. Consumption is the point at which cultural practice and economic activity meet; it provides the inter-face between political economy and sociology, and is the manifestation of concrete aesthetics. Patterns of life are reproduced through consumer goods, which also provide a legitimate social arena for play, resistance and cultural affirmation. Consumption, which requires the 'production of consumers', is an important dimension of the socialization process in contemporary Japan, and it is closely related to the ideology of the 'classless society', in which everyone is bourgeois, everyone is an affluent worker – mainly (and this is largely true in Mure) employed in the 'new' managerial and the technological professions. The study of consumption also provides a fresh way, when combined with studies of the media and of advertising, into understanding the specific characteristics of Japanese capitalism, which in the existing literature tends to be approached through work organization and practices. In fact, of course, the requirements of production in Japanese industry necessitate a parallel regularization and stabilization of consumption and commodity relations, and, as Marx long ago foresaw, the continuous expansion of consumption, the creation of new needs and the discovery and creation of new 'use values'. Here I have suggested that 'use values' in Japan needs to be expanded to include 'play values' (the ludic dimension of consumption) and to take into ac-count the fact that many commodities are experiential in nature or are used as vehicles for experiential strategies. These strategies reflect, to use Barthes' terminology, the pursuit of *jouissance* – physical sensation, quasi-erotic interaction with the thing, intensity of experience – rather than of *plaisir* – pleasure that comes from the recognition of cultural identity, from the reflection in cultural practices of our own beliefs and values (Barthes 1975).

Consumption can also be located squarely in the middle of many orthodox sociological themes – the production of control and order, the explanation of social change, for example, and even the classical theory of anomie, especially in an area of Tokyo where local traditions, feelings of roots or temple or shrine organization are all weak. As one commentator puts it: 'the attraction of such goods to the new consumer classes may stem originally from a profound feeling that they succeed in materializing a particular experience of the contemporary social world in which subjectivity has become parted from the many solid social structures which in earlier times would have given it meaningful shape and coherent substance' (Lee 1993: 175). The empirical study of Japanese consumption behaviour is also situated interestingly in relation to some equally central anthropological preoccupations, including that of ritual. Consumption behaviour, and in particular its public expressions such as shopping, have in Japan a ceremonial character similar to that of the ritual or formulaic qualities of much of Japanese cultural life. Shopping is a ritual form: it can be performed well or with errors of performance. But beyond this is a more fundamental point: Japanese aesthetic behaviour is characterized by ritual constraint, but this constraint is not read as unfreedom but as the condition of artistic expression and creativity. Small variations within the form become individual achievements. As with art, so with consumption. And the ritual itself is transformed by the penetration of the global: 'One also finds evidence that the entire interaction ritual process (the one Goffman studied) is being rebuilt globally. Rather than just affirming inter-group solidarity, ritual is being creatively transformed to bridge the unknown between groups' (MacCannell 1992: 308). This is true in Mure, not at the level of, say, religious ritual, but precisely in the patterning of consumption.

It is even possible to approach the question of social control in these terms. Featherstone notes the 'increasing capacity of the new middle class to display a calculating hedonism, to engage in more varied (and often dangerous) aesthetic and emotional exporations which in themselves do not amount to a rejection of controls, but to a more carefully circumscribed and interpersonally responsible "controlled de-control" of the emotions which necessarily entails some calculation and mutually expected respect for other persons' (Featherstone 1991b: 59). This in turn points to a whole field beyond the scope of this chapter, but which is very much implicated in the analysis of consumption – the whole question of the anthropology of the emotions. The formulaic nature of Japanese life expressed in language, cultural practices, public emotional responses and consumption is clearly an area ripe for investigation. Maffesoli's suggestion that in the postmodern city individualism is transcended by a new form of communalism of emotional communities of a network-like form, for example, might provide an interesting insight into the nature of quasi-groups as empirical but shifting entities in contemporary Japanese society (Maffesoli 1988).

Consumers, then, form a kind of 'imagined community', one in which symbolic identification with others occurs as a way of ameliorating some of the effects of what Calhoun terms 'indirect relationships', which now challenge the realm of everyday personal existence. But here, again, we must note cultural differences. Calhoun argues that 'we contrast the quotidian no longer with the extraordinary days of feasts and festivals so much as with the systematically remote, with that which "counts" on a large scale' (Calhoun 1991: 96). While it is true that everyday life in the modern world requires constant mediation between the experience and the remote, the local and the global, it is also true that many aspects of Japanese life can be seen as anti-alienation devices, as attempts to make the local meaningful not only despite, but through, the global, to relate experience and system, to dissolve the autonomy of actor and structure which Giddens sees as the fundamental sociological problem. Consumption is perhaps the principal means by which these dichotomies are resolved in Mure, consumption which is itself organized by a set of distinctive social practices. These questions are not only of theoretical interest, but are especially significant in reformulating approaches to Japanese urban life, since central to the study of urbanization is the problem of the nature of the community, of managing everyday life in a mass society, of creating a sense of identity. The study of consumption in the Japanese city allows these issues to be approached in a natural way, while posing in a fresh manner older urban sociological questions, such as the role of cities not in production as such, but in the reproduction of labour power, while avoiding overmuch concern with infrequent events such as *matsuri*.

6

Consuming Bodies: Media and the Construction and Representation of the Body

INTRODUCTION

Open almost any of the widely circulated magazines that appear in abundance in every bookshop, convenience store or railway station kiosk in Japan and images of the body appear. In some cases these images are simply photographs of people in the news, but in many they are in the form of advertisements (which in several of the over 2000 magazine titles currently published in Japan constitute 50 per cent or more of the total content; Moeran 1991) or of posed figures placed there precisely to receive the gaze of the reader or viewer. A high percentage of these images (usually photographs, but in the case of the tabloid newspaper and *manga* or comics, published independently or as part of magazines, also drawings) are of the female body. In the case of women's magazines these images are largely to promote consumption – of fashion, appliances, food, travel or cosmetics especially; in men's magazines the image is itself consumed – by the male gaze.

Japan has often been represented as a society saturated with images – (most famously or infamously by Roland Barthes (1970). Whether or not this is strictly true, the sheer size and power of the Japanese media, and of advertising within the media, make it central to understanding cultural processes in contemporary Japan. But media, especially in a society as large and technologically sophisticated as Japan, form a huge subject. This chapter will take only one aspect of the whole, but one which, it can be argued, illuminates many aspects of the functioning of that whole – the way in which the human body, and in this context specifically the female body, is constructed, represented and, as image, consumed.

This subject would at first sight seem to be a straightforward example of visual ethnography. But in fact behind it or within it are a plethora of questions which go to the heart of cultural theory and to the reasons for the emergence of interest in the body as a major theme in contemporary Western social thought (Turner 1984, 1992; Shilling 1993). This attention to the body has sprung from several sources – from the recognition that the social actor is indeed embodied: is a physical entity with origins in a particular time and place, is gendered and ethnic, occupies literal space, moves, speaks, gestures and is generally active. Social relationships cannot in this view be conceived just as the interaction of abstract categories (classes, castes, occupations, groups, and so forth), but necessarily as processural interaction between embodied subjects, occurring in real time and space, each one of which has a biography, fears, drives, objectives, beliefs. The contemporary sociology of the body then places an experiential view at the heart of its theory of social action.

But in doing so it raises some significant and as yet unresolved questions. The first of these is the relationship of embodiment to selfhood. Are they the same, or does the allegedly Western 'essentialist' view of self introduce a profound epistemological distinction between body as physical and self or identity as somehow not, while the Japanese view sees the self as inherently embodied? Certainly most societies evidence concern with the presentation of the body, and the work of Erving Goffman should suggest that, even in the United States, presentation of the self and presentation of the body are closely related (Goffman 1969) in ways not so dissimilar from those found in Japan (Kondo 1990). Concern with the body in society then necessarily raises philosophical and psychological questions – the issue of selfhood. But it also raises questions of aesthetics (what is beautiful?) or the mechanics of social interaction (in Japan the acute preoccupation with presentation experienced through the wrapping of the body, body 'language' – posture and gesture – and the policing of boundaries) and of nature – of the relationship of selfhood to nature and concern with the 'natural' as a model for the social, including the shape and activities of the human body. Western sociology of the body, while it has transformed our understanding of social action and of the operation of specific institutions within society, such as prisons or the medical system, mostly lacks a comparative angle: it is in many ways ethnocentric in its philosophical assumptions and range of examples. The study of the body in Japanese culture provides perhaps the comparative counterpoint: an industrialized society with highly developed media, but with a distinct and autonomous culture formed by philosophical and religious forces very different from those of Europe and North America. One thing, however, certainly unites East and West, and that is the common devotion to consumption as a way of life. An important theoretical development in the sociology of the body in the West has been the recognition that, of the many social spaces in which bodies interact, consumption is the site of several of the most intensive and meaningful (Featherstone 1991a; Shields 1992).

This is important in the context of this chapter for two reasons. The first is that we are here addressing the question of the handling by the Japanese media, and specifically of the print media, of the representation of the body. And generally the body, and especially the female body, is presented either to promote consumption of services or material objects – banks, clothes, cars, household appliances, for example – or to be consumed itself, most commonly as an image, by the gaze of the beholder, and occasionally, as in magazines, promoting 'soaplands' or massage parlours, quite literally and physically subsequent to a reading of the magazine by those who seek out the proffered services. The media then are not concerned with the pure aesthetics of the body, but with the exploitation of what is indeed an aesthetic canon for largely (however elegantly disguised) commercial ends. Commodity aesthetics reigns, in other words. The second consequence is that, however much the concern of theorists in the sociology of the body is for a full and rounded understanding of the embodied subject – the active and experiencing self – the concern of the print media and of advertising in particular is the presentation of the image. Analysis of the presentation of the body in the media is entirely justified, provided that, as I will attempt here, that analysis both uncovers the suppression of selfhood in the thinking and experiencing subjects, who are constructed or represented as pure images passively before the gazer (who can appreciate/violate at will) and links these objectified images (especially of women) to the mechanisms of representation in the print media as a form (how do they actually so this visually?) and to the concealed patterns of actual or potential domination contained within the representations – patterns of social inequality, race, age, as well as sexuality. Strategically it is necessary then both to see the rich ethnographic data as worthy of treatment in itself, and also to link this material to wider critical issues in the analysis of the Japanese media, of the culture of consumption in contemporary Japan and of feminist debates within the country.

But first some observations about methodology – the delineation of the field and the problem of the 'representation' or even 'construction' of the body. All forms of media present images of the body – even radio, with its use of voice as an indicator of femininity/masculinity, youth/age, social status, ethnicity, and other features of human physical being to be inferred from aural information alone. But clearly film, television and the print media have the advantage of being able to present direct images in the form of pictures. This chapter will concern itself only with a segment of this total media world – the print media, and, within the print media, specifically the magazine. The field is thus much smaller than the total media, but still large given the enormous number of magazines published and their extensive total readership (Moeran 1991: 1). The conclusions reached here, while many may well be generalizable to the other facets of the media, can be asserted with confidence only in relation to the magazines sampled.

But the potential number of magazines available for discussion is itself very great. Here I will concentrate on a small number of titles drawn from three categories: magazines targeted at women, news and current affairs magazines of mass circulation which are read by both sexes, and magazines targeted at men. 'The body' concerned will be that of the adult woman as depicted primarily through photography, and the magazines selected are all of large circulation and are easily available, mostly through bookstores, convenience stores and station kiosks. *Manga*, pornographic magazines and magazines intended for children or teenage girls are excluded, although each category provides materials for a fascinating case study in its own right. Additionally the titles selected here, while by no means the only ones, are intended to supplement the analyses by Moeran of the upper-class housewives' magazine *Katei Gaho* and by White of adolescent targeted media elsewhere in print (Skov and Moeran 1995).

In relation to this admittedly limited sample I will attempt to construct a model, or at least the elements of a model, of the way in which the Japanese female body is defined, identified and presented as part of a larger social code in which ideas about fashion, diet, beauty, shape, size, posture, gaze and 'appropriate' activities are constructed and disseminated through the media and are manipulated, redefined and justified by reference to history and to ideas of what is 'natural'. The analysis of empirical patterns should then provide the basis for a critical perspective allowing the study of the actual or potential manipulation of women through body image and of 'femininity', for the uncovering of dimensions of distinction and stratification in a supposedly classless society and for the development of a critical semiological vocabulary for the identification of typical patterns of representation of bodies in the Japanese media.

But before turning to the ethnography, at least something needs to be said about the theoretical positioning which has dominated much of the debate about the sociology of the body in Western theory to date and the location of this essay within the debate. Much of this has taken the form of a division into two main camps: that of the 'foundationalists', who basically argue for the primacy of the physical body as something prior to and only subsequently affected by the shaping of social and cultural forces; and that of the 'constructivists', who assert that the body is essentially meaningless until it is shaped socially. Radical social constructivists may even go so far as to argue that the biological body as something independent of its social/cultural interpretation does not exist. (For a good review of the debate, see Shilling 1993.)

The position taken in this chapter will be that, while there is of course such a thing as a biological body (the position of the foundationalists), this biological body is at all times presented through clothing, decoration, posture and location in spatial relation to other bodies, and is constantly interpreted. It is this interpretation, which expresses itself in many ways – for example through penal, medical or sexual practices, as Foucault has shown – that constitutes the 'social construction' of the body. This constructing is an on-going project, not an accomplished state, and is constantly affected by factors such as aging (biologically unavoidable but managed in different ways individually and culturally) and by the constant redefinitions of the canons of appearance and presentation. It is here that the media play a major role in almost all contemporary societies, and most certainly in Japan. It is precisely to this shaping-by-media and its relationship to the 'objective' factors (e.g. age or body configuration) that I will direct my attention. A key point, however, that has emerged in these debates is that of the fundamental embodiment of social actors. This is more obvious in the case of say medical practice, but is true in reality of all forms of social interaction and presentations of self and is a constant, if subterranean, theme in all social practices. This is as true in Japan as anywhere else, and so a theme of this chapter will not simply be the uncovering of empirical patterns of the ways in which the (female) body is presented in the media, but of the ways in which these representations of embodiment are actually reflections of patterns of social intercourse and in turn shape the ways that future patterns of relationship are structured.

READING JAPANESE MAGAZINES

Any general bookshop, most supermarkets, every convenience store, many small general stores and all railway station kiosks (of which there is almost always more than one, even at the smallest suburban station) contain racks of magazines, often quite literally stacks of them, together with a large range of comic titles. These are browsed, bought, and shared with friends, neighbours and schoolmates and subsequently appear in huge piles at the roadside on the periodic days when waste paper is collected for recycling by the municipality. They range from the esoteric and minority interest, through popular subject-specific (travel, fashion, cars or sport) or audience-targeted ones (for young working women – the OLs or middle-aged housewives, for example), to mass-circulation news and gossip magazines, the readership of which can run into hundreds of thousands.

Most are visually attractive, with high-quality advertising, graphics, layout and paper. The fact that most magazines are bought directly from newpaper stands rather than by subscription, as is often the case in the West, is attributed at least in part to this visual and indeed even tactile appeal (Moeran 1991: 1).

Magazines are also commodities themselves, and commodities with a short shelf-life which mostly demand only a very short attention span – they are generally looked at and browsed rather than *read* in the sense that a novel might be. With constantly shifting canons of taste, this relative ephemerality is heightened. The sporty look is currently popular, but with the approach of the new university year the co-ed look is quite likely to displace it. In the presentation of the body in the magazines reviewed we see an interesting mixture of issues – of aesthetics, of sexuality, of the use and construction of tradition, of conformity to the uniform of the 'tribe' to which one belongs, to the positioning of the body in space as well as in its own gestures and postures, its connection with seasonality. We may even have discovered the interesting possibility that Japanese feminism expresses itself though femininity rather than through its denial. And that it is unashamedly connected with consumption – of the images of the body, of the body itself and of the wrappings and decorations that enhance it, but which enhance it in ways that correspond both to its biological possibilities and to culturally approved models.

A characteristic of much of the Japanese periodical press is its mixture of genres, with text, advertisements, visuals and comics all in the same publication. The body is presented multiply through these forms – the ritualized pose of pin-ups, the idealized pose of the fashion model, the stylized portraiture of the comic – and through discourse on diet, health care, body decoration and maintenance in the text. The magazine medium furthermore has the advantage of being able to create an interplay between written content, advertising and photographic or graphic content, which adds both to its aesthetic appeal and to the strategic relationship between advertising and text; this is a matter of great concern to advertisers, who appear to have distinct beliefs about the effectiveness of their advertisements, in relation to their placing within a magazine. This interplay is a theme to which we will return later. Out of the vast field of Japanese magazines so widely read in this most literate (and perhaps also visual) of cultures, only a tiny selection of magazines have been sampled for the purposes of this chapter. In the first group are a few women's magazines: *Cancam*, a middle-market fashion magazine with a great deal of visual material; *Caz*, a magazine for white collar working women and younger housewives and containing materials not only on fashion, but on food, travel, make-up, health and similar matters; *Fujin Gaho*, an up-market, long established and quite expensive fashion and lifestyle magazine for older housewives; and, by way of contrast, *Hanako*, a popular and very widely available magazine for young professional women, well-informed housewives and university students which, while it does not contain nearly so much visual material as the others (which are saturated with it), does through its text provide a guide to what Foucault has aptly termed 'techniques of the body' – diet, make-up, medicine, deportment, etiquette and, very much so, food.

In the second group are two men's magazines: *Urecco*, which actually bills itself as soft pornography and which is available in most convenience stores (where much of the magazine and comic browsing in Japan goes on: silent rows of young men before the men's section of the shelves, an equally silent group of young women clustered in front of the women's, and the shop-assistants not caring in the least that no one much is actually buying), and the mass-circulation *Weekly Pureiboi* ('Weekly Play-boy'), which not only contains advertising, but actively advertises itself, especially on commuter trains. Many other men's magazines are interesting because of the *absence* of depictions of women in their pages: widely available examples such as *Popeye* or *Fine Boys* are full of pictures of very fashionable young men, but virtually no women, not even as accessories to the young men.

The third category also explored, but for the purposes of this chapter only as a background phenomenon, are the three rival mass-circulation weekly news, gossip, personality and comment magazines *Friday*, *Focus* and *Flash*. They are included here principally because of their high photographic content, low levels of advertising and inevitable spread of visuals of nude or semi-nude women.

I will provide a rapid survey of the style and content of the various examples before settling into a deeper analysis of their depiction of the body.

Caz evidently has as its target audience 'office ladies' and fashion-conscious younger women, all of whom travel a lot. Its content includes horoscopes, TV, movie, books, art and theatre information, articles on clothes, AIDS, parks in Tokyo, and a range of reports on new consumer items. A high proportion of the magazine is related to travel – airport information, English conversation tips, travel insurance, money, shopping tips in places such as Hong Kong, Bali, Guam and Hawaii, and domestic travel suggestions, for example, for holidays in Okinawa. It has more visual advertising than *Hanako*, concentrating on face products, tea, new entertainment spots, sports gear, hi-fi equipment and telephones of trendy designs. The female body image presented throughout, whether in articles or in advertisements, is of well dressed, but rather girlish-looking women, many with the ubiquitous crooked teeth, and all young – with the exception of one very well-dressed middle-aged women of calm and serious appearance, who appears to recommend moisture lotions and face-creams with a great air of (in the text 'scientific') authority and jargon. Here the use of non-Japanese models is much less frequent, but in a context which soon becomes recognizable as a pattern: adverts relating to body hair, breast-firming devices and underwear feature foreigners. In these polite middle-brow magazines Japanese almost never appear undressed and never have a 'problem' with body hair, although it is obviously Japanese women who buy the products advertised. A discourse of race as class/income enters very obviously into the visual image of advertising – revealing the foreigner both as exotic (those fascinating fruits and cars with Italian names) and as having distinct problems with being or becoming attractive. The general body shape of Western women is attractive – longer legged, bigger-breasted – but the details – body hair, skin – are not. Revealingly, almost no black or non-Japanese Asian models are to be found in the adverts in the specifically Japanese media, although a kind of ambiguous looking Eurasian type is quite popular. But where they do appear (*Hanako*), pushing useful household appliances, they (as is the case with many Japanese models) do so in enormous empty rooms of European design, bearing little resemblance to the reality of the typical Japanese urban interior (and urban is here used advisedly, for it is also quite evident that the image is always of modern, city-dwelling inhabitants, generally of Tokyo, although Osaka or Kyoto will do at a pinch).

But the body image in the *Cancam* case is even more revealing semiotically. Here we have a magazine devoted to fashion – its articles, its advertisements and the photo-spreads which take up most of the space are all about fashion, make-up or diet, except for a tiny number of ads devoted to cars (a fashion accessory?) and gossipy articles on interesting 'boys' in the media and entertainment worlds. Certain images stand out: elegant but conservative; either very dressed up or looking 'natural' with the help of substantial amounts of make-up and carefully chosen clothing; a very standardized physical shape that looks good in tweeds and woollens; dressing appropriately by the season of the year; classical or European settings; and what in Europe would be considered distinctly upper-middle-class accessories – pearls and handbags. Casual in *Cancam* means a studied but simple elegance. Many of these traits are heightened to an even greater degree in *Fujin Gaho*. Here elegant models of distinctly wealthy appearance and often of middle age disport themselves in kimono or very smart Western-style clothes, in spacious interiors or out-doors. The advertisements, which focus on up-market fashion, also relate to fine china, jewels and art works, while articles deal with fine and traditional arts, elegant hotels or *onsen*, 'society' news, Japanese foods and holidays in good resorts. The inevitable consumer guides are a feature too, but of a similar up-market nature. The models are either Japanese of distinctly 'upper-class looks' or very elegant Europeans. All are fully dressed, and the body is presented as groomed – very carefully made-up, wrapped with expensive simplicity. 'Good taste' and 'sensitivity' are hall-marks of the style presented. The world of embassy parties, receptions and society weddings fill these pages, even though in reality they are read by many 'ordinary' housewives and working women.

Hanako, in common with most Japanese mass circulation magazines, is actually primarily a guide to consumption, and has a general content not that much different from many of its rivals – a mixture of brief articles on travel, movies, restaurants, skiing and other sports, plays, books, and a heavy weighting towards news and views on make-up, beauty tips, exer-cise, weight control, and interestingly, I would argue, household appli-ances and hints on storage and organization in the notoriously small Japanese homes no doubt dwelt in by many of *Hanako*'s readers. Much of this information is overt or disguised advertising (presenting itself as information about new products), and in some cases the boundary be-tween the two is very indistinct. One issue (number 234, February 1993, for instance) contains a lengthy feature of six pages on, separated by one page from a full-page advertisement for, a Tokyo 'beauty centre', com-plete with a questionnaire to help assess whether one needs (or rather what one needs) from the range of services provided. Two things in particular stand out. The first is that relatively little of the material actually depicts bodies (there are pictures of products, but not of people), but that almost all of the text is about body management – make-up, diet, weight and exercise primarily, and secondarily to do with fashion, travel and accessories. In the *Hanako* case the text is written and it is the sub-text that is visual, and it is virtually the sole theme of the text that one's primary concern is care for the body, which should be young, smooth, with no visible hair except on the top of the head, well dressed, but not in a distinctive way, and of average size and shape. Interestingly, in all the adverts which do directly depict women, more than half are not Japanese. Young, fresh-faced Japanese models are used to promote prod-ucts as diverse as handbags, banks and face-washes (including one with the unfortunate name of 'Papawash' – the product in question contain-ing papaya extract!). Foreign models, however, are in the majority (all are of a vaguely Italian appearance) and promote foods, fashions, bags and cars (Japanese, but with Italianate names.) Only one of the Japanese models is what would conventionally be described as glamorous: all the others are again 'average' in appearance, which is perhaps 'appropriate', as they are pushing drinks and banks, while the glamorous one is promoting a Shiseido lipstick.

Men's magazines might be expected to depict the female body in a totally different way, but this is not actually the case, despite the fact that here the emphasis moves from depiction through advertising to 'direct' depiction in the form of photos, specifically of clothed, bathing-suited or nude/semi-nude women, always Japanese and usually young – often very young. But in reality the type of woman featured differs little from the average fashion model, except in posture (typically highlighting breasts or buttocks) and, this is important, facial expression. Here two characteristics stand out – the direct gaze and the pout. Fashion models look, and smile, but they do not gaze: gaze and a heightened sexuality go together. Neither do they pout, drawing attention to their lips. Dishevelled hair, a crouching or sprawling posture and a natural setting, particularly one involving sand or water (the latter having its own sexual symbolism in the Japanese movie) are other common characteristics. But any resemblance to Western-style pornography is hard to find. Most of the models are fresh faced and smiling and very much affect a 'natural' look. The name, age, statistics and other personal data often accompany the photographs. Photo-spreads (in *Urecco* for example) are often accompanied by captions such as 'Fresh shot', or describing the model as 'flower girl', 'flower child', 'sweet angel' or 'sports girl'. Many of the models are in any case half clothed or in bathing-suits. There is a fixation on breasts, although whether this reflects the alleged mother complex or the *amae* factor I leave to those more psychologically inclined. And since Japanese censorship ensures the artful concealment of what is plainly revealed even in the kind of soft pornography that one can buy on any railway station news-stand in Britain (although the amount of pubic hair appearing even in mass-circulation magazines has been gradually increasing, despite the official ban and the fact that it is scratched out in imported magazines), much is left to the imagination.

The mass-circulation news and gossip magazines also do their part not only by containing material on health (*Focus*, for example, has a weekly health page), but also, by using their reputation among the Japanese media for being provocative and a little more daring (and no doubt, given their need to compete against each other), gradually to stretch the limits. All of the three surveyed, in the style of a lot of the popular media, have a few pages of nudes. *Focus*, in its issue for 24 September 1993 broke through one limit by having a black model. In the same month *Flash* breached another barrier not only by quite openly detailing pubic hair (formerly a privilege, if allowed at all, confined to 'art' magazines), but by illustrating it on a model in her mid-thirties. Other excuses for depicting the female body in these publications is either in the form of 'news' or in reporting the latest actresses in the vast adult video industry, and of course straight advertising, but even then the rules that we have so far uncovered, for example, the use of foreign models for underwear and sleepwear, still apply. This category, while evidently bought mostly by men, especially salaried workers, is widely read by both sexes.

A number of points of interest can be drawn collectively from these depictions. The first thing that might strike the observer familiar with Western counterparts is that, in general, the images convey a picture of 'wholesomeness', and even of innocence. In fashion magazines they certainly convey impressions of happiness, femininity and marriageability, or if already married, of calm assurance, of being sensible. In men's magazines the models are usually, as we have noted, young, conveying an image of a budding sexuality, attractive but non-threatening. The tendency for models to be dressed, or rather partially dressed, in schoolgirl uniforms or as nurses, intensifies this impression. Where a 'stronger' sexuality is implied, the models will be older, have longer and more unkempt hair, and will pout and gaze with even more directness, or will be foreign women. Even in these cases, as in all pornography, the range of facial expressions and postures is very limited and stereotyped. In traditional Japanese pornographic prints the individuals or couples are always partly clothed, something that has carried over into its contemporary manifestations. Interestingly, however, where a couple appears in the modern version, the woman will be unclothed, but the man partially or even fully dressed, suggesting that the problem of the male body, of its relationship to the female, is also a subject to be put on the agenda of themes in the cultural analysis of contemporary Japan.

READING THE IMAGES

We have then a repertoire of images, surpringly consistent in its iconography, although clearly located along a continuum: the women's magazines concerned with the body as wholesome, and through its wholesomeness promoting 'good taste' (i.e. class-based, and even ethnically-based consumption); the men's magazines representing the body as the object of desire, to be consumed visually and perhaps in the imagination – but yet the desired object is not that much different from the images portrayed in women's magazines, except that they have generally fewer clothes on; the news magazines presenting the body as spectacle, of interest not as a cultural role model or as a physical model, but as an exemplar of the human condition, interesting because of its existential predicaments. The emphasis then is very much on *depiction*. This takes us back to the question of self. Where is the self in the image? It could of course be argued that the preoccupation with representation of the body suppresses selfhood, a suggestion raised earlier in the chapter. But our data by now should have brought us to a rather more differentiated conclusion. The pure image may exist: here is representation but no self; here is a body but not a woman; but this is achievable only in certain contexts. And here we run into a paradox, which is that it is the *women's* magazines that manage the most through suppression of selfhood, re-placed instead by what are really categories – the perfect housewife, the young mother, the elegant professional woman – and this is especially true as women are depicted in advertising. *Fujin Gaho* reaches the apogee here: beautiful women, elegantly posed in fine clothes, in spacious in-teriors or natural settings, representing not themselves but an (ideal) type. If one were to seek anywhere for the alleged lack of individuality in Japanese culture, it might well be here, where self is submerged into the model (in both senses of the word!). But in men's magazines, where it might naturally be supposed that there is much more complete objectification of the female body as purely the object of the gaze (usually male, although they are read by women too), this is not so. Rather two things happen: firstly the model gazes back, often with disconcerting frankness, here there is eye contact which asserts the personhood of the model, even a gaze that makes it clear that here there is power; and it is the woman's, not the man's. Secondly, rather disarmingly, photo-spreads are accompanied by personal information – the model's name (or at least her stage name), her age, her statistics, what she likes doing, where she comes from. She is personalized in a way in which the fashion model in *Fujin Gaho* or *Cancam* is not. In the fashion magazines the selfhood of the women depicted is not in the images; if it is there at all it is in the text: this is so-and-so; she is travelling in Italy/eating organic foods which enhance your personhood by improving your body. Underlying this is a deeper ontology: if in Western philosophy and religion, especially in traditional Christianity, body and self (soul, personhood) are separated and unequally weighted, in Japan they are not. Not only is the body natural, pleasant to see and worthy of care, but the 'true self', even beyond society, is linked to nature. Body, self and nature are thus fused in a way quite alien to anyone but the most thorough-going Western new-ager (Picone 1989; Yuasa 1987).

JAPANESE BODIES/CULTURAL THEORY

At this juncture several main points should be clarified or summarized. Firstly, while it is obviously impossible to generalize about the Japanese media as a whole, and of course no attempt is made to do this here, within the group of magazines examined there are certain continuities. These are expressed in the visual images via concern with fashion in *Fujin Gaho, Cancam* and to a lesser extent *Caz,* with the body itself as the object of desire in *Urecco* and *Weekly Pureiboi,* and in the photo-spreads of the weekly news trio. They are also expressed in the text of *Fujin Gaho* and *Caz* and especially in *Hanako,* the least visual of all the women's magazines, where the female body is not desired but desires, and where selfhood of the female person is represented as being constructed through consumption. And the body is central here: it is to be clothed, fed, decorated, manicured, exercised and protected. Which is of course a very realistic view: the body as the vehicle for the many -faceted interaction with the environment that constitutes actual human experience. The visual representation of the body and the written discourse about it in our sample, while clearly identifying the body as the subject of consumption, do not really lend much support to a manipulative or conspiracy theory of the role of the Japanese media. While the media clearly have a major role in defining and reproducing definition of desirable appearance, the images that they 'construct' seem to correspond closely with the 'folk models' widely accepted in Japanese society.

An important aspect of this is the construction of gender, through both the assigning and reproduction of certain attributes to each sex via fashion, body decoration, ideas of appropriate sports and diet (especially drinks: beer and whisky, for example, being decidedly 'masculine' beverages), and the clear separation of the sexes. This is done again by symbolic means (hairstyles, clothing colours, for instance) and by the extreme segmentation of the magazine market. While the weekly news magazines are bought mainly by men, they are also sometimes bought by women, but otherwise magazines are targeted both by sex and age. Interestingly, men's magazines such as *Fine Boys* are the almost exact masculine counterpart of female fashion magazines, full of images of the (young) male body, advice on hair, clothes, skin, diet and accessories. And all this, almost unknown in the Western media, is aimed at decidedly heterosexual men. The parallels in the print media for women and for men are remarkable. The two categories however, are not duplicated, but entirely separate. But let us return to our main theme: the female body as represented in the sample.

There is clearly an aesthetics of the body at work here. The favoured body is young, firm, fair, middle class, average and cute. The *kawaii* complex operates here with a vengeance (see Kinsella 1995). True sensuality is an attribute of the older woman, glamorous cuteness of the younger one. The text that often accompanies the photos in *Urecco* is revealing in this respect; sometimes it is a vague kind of poetry; at other times it tells you the model's name, age, tastes, hobbies and blood group (itself an interesting minor phenomenon in the sociology of the Japanese body). In fact the impression that comes across very clearly is essentially a juvenile one (all those schoolgirls and panty shots), sometimes mixed with a little minor sadism (the schoolgirls are tied up). The major-league sadism of the pornographic comic book is altogether another thing. As I have suggested, in the mass press, women are not so much humiliated as in control; these are not demon women but mothers and (usually) sisters. While not exactly doll-like, many are immature. Speaking of this phenomenon, Rosalind Coward comments:

'The sexually immature body of the current ideal fits very closely into these ideologies (of women having a sexuality somehow in spite of themselves). For it presents a body which is sexual – it 'exudes' sexuality in its vigorous and vibrant and firm good health – but it is not the body of a woman who has an adult and powerful control over that sexuality. The image is of a highly sexualized female whose sexuality is still one of response to the active sexuality of a man. The ideology about adolescent sexuality is exactly the same: young girls are often seen as expressing a sexual need even if the girl herself does not know it. It is an image that feeds off the idea of a fresh, spontaneous, but essentially *responsive* sexuality. (Coward 1987: 42-3)

Well said.

There are present here a number of factors of great interest not only in the analysis of the Japanese media but for theories of Japanese society in a broader sense. There is clearly an iconography: images of height, weight, size, age, hair colour and body details which, if not created by the media, are certainly disseminated and reinforced through it. While there are variations, there is also a degree of uniformity greater than that which could be explained by biological factors, such as the possession of basically the same hair colour by virtually all Japanese women. This suggests that something even more fundamental is going on.

I have already indicated that there is a real if largely invisible discourse of race apparent in the depiction of the body in the Japanese media, even as there is a not so subtle process of class distinction of a positively Bourdieuian kind at work, evident when one compares the imagery of, say, *Fujin Gaho* with that of *Cancam*. This discourse of race largely takes the form of establishing, principally through visuals and to a lesser extent through text, a notion of what it is to be a Japanese. In *Fujin Gaho* this takes the form of an unabashed traditionalism – features on the kimono, profiles of traditional inns, craftspeople and hot spring resorts, a concentration on Japanese food in the cuisine articles and the use of models of a classically 'Japanese appearance'. 'Japan' here means the very elegant, the traditional, the aesthetically pleasing, restrained, dignified, natural. A certain type of face and body fit this image very well, and, wrapped in right clothing to give the appearance of sophistication with just a hint of internationalism, the picture is almost complete. But it still needs the reinforcement of the right kind of diet not only to maintain that slim body and clear complexion, but also to maintain a sense of almost spiritual Japaneseness. The management of the body is not just to keep fat or age at bay, it is also to enhance the qualities of race. This is equally apparent in the magazines for men, where not only are the models always Japanese, they are written up as such – as representing the essence of Japanese womanhood – and are also often depicted in 'traditional' settings, the *onsen* being an obvious favourite. The diet columns of women's' magazines and the photo-spreads of men's ones both provide a rather fresh angle on the old issue of *Nihonjinron*.

We actually see in these magazines several tendencies standing in a complex and subtle relationship to each other. The primary differentiation by sex we have already noted. Secondarily we see differentiation by race and the establishment of distinct images of 'Japaneseness' parallel to those dicovered in *Katei Gaho* by Moeran (1995). The position of the foreign (almost always Caucasian) models who do occasionally appear in the pages of the women's magazines now becomes clearer: they promote the consumption either of that which is hidden (underwear), or that which is distinctly exotic (such as French perfumes) and as such by definition not Japanese, but enjoyable by the Japanese woman as an indicator of her internationalization and her sophistication. It is no accident that the foreign goods promoted in *Fujin Gaho* are of the same kind as and often identical to those in *Katei Gaho*: expensive, European and clear markers not only of high income, but also of an elegant self-image not very different from that portrayed in distinctly upper-class British magazines – in *Home and Garden* or *Country Life* as opposed to say *Women's Own*. In other words, the concern with Japaneseness (race) also conceals a preoccupation with social distinctions (class). While the two are not precisely conflated, they certainly converge.

But the question of class itself, or even the appropriateness of the word, are thorny questions in the Japanese context. Everyone has heard the endlessly reiterated refrain that the Japanese are all 'middle class', and it is true that, by industrialized country standards, income differentials in Japan are comparatively low. Yet this claim does not sit too well with the fact that Japan is also a society obsessed with hierarchy – of company status, university standing, and so forth. Several factors seem to be at work here. The first is the stratification or differentiation of the media themselves. *Fujin Gaho* is clearly intended for the relatively wealthy, leisured upper-class housewife. Its restrained elegance (both the magazine itself and the things it promotes), its use of older models, the spacious interiors depicted in interviews with successful women, all these speak volumes. This is not the world of the OL, of the university student still living at home or of the young housewife of a junior salaryman in a 2DK (two six-*tatami* mat sized-rooms plus a combined dining room and kitchen). They mostly do not read it; they read *Cancam*, perhaps, *Hanako*, or one of the plethora of family, interior and lifestyle magazines available.

For some, indeed many, of these women the choice of magazine is an indicator of class in its simplest definition as socio-economic status. For the small shopkeeper, the wife of a lower grade manager, the school-teacher or salaryman, the unmarried woman living off part-time work, their class status is not going to improve. But for others, choice of maga-zine is more a function of age. The daughter of the factory-owner may now read *Hanako*, but she will read *Fujin Gaho* in the not-so-distant future. She is also likely to consume travel magazines because she travels, and to be preoccupied with lifestyle decisions involving not breaks with tradi-tion, but her assimilation into that tradition, as signalled by fashion especially. Fashion then is crucial to the presentation of the classed as well as the racialized body. In time she will probably marry, and her concerns will shift from travel and personal consumption to children's fashion and consumption and to interior decoration. But while she is still an elite cosmopolitan (see Rosenberger 1995) her reading will reflect this, just as when she was a teenage or pre-teen girl she consumed the appro-priate magazines, comics and consumer items associated with the other media tie-ins (plastic jewellery, toys, lunch boxes and other items bearing the images of the fictional characters populating the pages of magazines and filling the children's cartoon slots on television). If race and class intersect in the Japanese media, so do age and class. In some, often ideal-typical, respects, increasing age means rising status (income rises and so does respect), and magazine reading progresses appropriately, as do the models depicted in advertisements (even the weekly news magazines often use older models in their photo-spreads, reflecting their diversity and readership – which, while distinctly middle class/working class, is of varying ages). But for others, many others, it does not, and shifts in reading habits, and indeed a decline in readership of magazines of all kinds, reflects a coming to terms with the fact that not every woman does achieve that rise in status. Japan works like an age-grade society in which progress in status is automatic if you can just live long enough.

JAPAN, CONSUMPTION AND THEORIES OF BODY

We started from the assumption that an exploration of even a limited segment of the Japanese media, while interesting ethnographically in itself, also provides a very fruitful way into a dialogue with the burgeoning literature in the sociology of the body that has emerged in the West. That literature is almost entirely concerned *with* the West: most of it does not explicitly make reference to other societies, so except where it claims a universalism, as is sometimes the case (*The* Body and Society), it cannot be faulted for not talking about Japan. My objective in this section is not to charge it with ethnocentrism, but to see where the theoretical dialogue might point us if we do attempt to relate it to the Japanese material that we have reviewed.

Frank (1990) suggests that the media essentially present the body as medicalized, sexual, disciplined and talking. Our review of a range of Japanese material suggests that these categories need to be extended and/or redefined as to their content. Disciplined, for example, needs to contain, or have added to it, the area of 'sportiness'; sexual requires the addition of the gaze and also attention to posture and to the detailing of particular body parts. The medicalized dimension seems to be repressed, but is substituted for by the preoccupation with diet found especially in the women's magazines, including the primarily informational *Hanako*. So while concern with bodily presentation has always been a part of Japanese culture, its centrality in the self-conscious presentation of self appears to be a relatively new phenomenon promoted by the reflexivity of late modernity – to use Giddens's terminology (Giddens 1991) in which 'the body has become a fundamental feature of taste and distinction in which the management of the human form becomes part of the major aspect of cultural or physical capital' (Turner 1992: 47). What Turner does not analyse however, (he sees body management as being conditioned mainly by medical practices), is that the structuring of taste is to a great extent a function of the media. In the Japanese case these media have themselves been deeply conditioned by Western formats and even whole genres (a fascinating history would be that of the evolution of the Japanese fashion magazine). While complexes of images of the 'ideal body' (long legs, round eyes, high noses) have been constructed through the *manga*, with their huge-eyed, tall, slim characters, the baddies are often even more distinctly Western/foreign than the goodies in the conventions of this particular medium. Those who write to the agony columns constantly cite physical 'problems', such as legs, hair and noses, interestingly assuming that non-standard physique would negatively affect marriageability.

There are then interesting paradoxes in the political economy of the body. The body is both biology and culture; it is, or has become as, commodity, while also being a sign. The consumption of the sign then becomes the key characteristic of commodified society: the boundary between the thing and the sign dissolves. This point, one among others stressed by Baudrillard, logically calls attention to another outcome documented by that same analyst – the appearance of simulation and the breakdown in turn of the boundary between the simulation and reality. While Baudrillard seems to see this largely as a function of television, his ideas, at least in their less bizarre versions, can be applied more widely. The craze for 'virtual reality' in Japan at the moment may be an example, but the potential application of the idea is much wider. Here we enter rather uncharted waters – the influence of literacy and of 'visualcy' on behaviour. The consumption of the sign rather than the thing itself (although Baudrillard would presumably deny that there is a distinction) has behavioural and psychological ramifications. It may be that the 'concrete' nature of Japanese culture (Hasegawa 1982) has protected itself from too much damage here yet, or rather that the visual qualities of the culture (from which some trace the origins of *manga*) permit consumption of the sign to have mostly positive or even cathartic effects. Again, some have traced the lack of overt violence in Japan to its open depiction, often in a highly sexualized way, in comics, movies and 'adult videos'. The work ethic and the aesthetic are consequently not opposed, as in a Weberian understanding of the origins of capitalism. In fact, rather than Japan being actually 'communist', as at least one writer has suggested (Kenrick 1990), it would be better to look at it as the most developed example of symbolic capitalism, not only increasingly post-Fordist in its industrial organization, but also devoted to the symbolic consumption of symbolic goods, including symbolic bodies. The presence of these bodies triggers off yet further levels of symbolic activity. Appearance and reality are thus assimilated to each other in culturally new ways (cf. Maffesoli 1990).

Beyond this again lie yet further theoretical vistas. Among these would be the (until recently) hot issue of whether or not Japan is a 'postmodern' society. It may well be that the language of postmodernism, while partly describing the Japanese reality, also does considerable violence to it. The aestheticism and sensuality exalted by postmodernism do exist in Japan, but in a form very different from that imagined by Western postmodernists, and, as we have seen in our magazines, in a much more subdued and even controlled way.

Some aspects of Turner's work have already been mentioned. Another emerging theorist is Chris Shilling who, on the opening page of his book on *The Body and Social Theory*, suggests that 'the position of the body within contemporary popular culture reflects an unprecedented *individualization* of the body' (Shilling 1993: 1) This he relates particularly to the emergence of the 'new' middle class (who presumably have the time, money and education, plus the desire, for symbolic competition). This claim, which Shilling evidently intends to be a universal one, reads interestingly from a Japanese perspective. In Japan too it is the recently urbanized salaried workers, and especially their spouses, who consume the huge amounts of printed material, some examples of which we have examined. And it is on the whole women who pay most attention to questions of fashion, body image, diet and even health, though, in the last case especially, on behalf of their families as much as for themselves. But at the same time the individualization is still limited in fact by the standards of some urban Western social groups. And even when extravagant displays of dress and/or body do occur, they often not only have a ritual quality, but also partake of the common Japanese custom of, in effect, wearing a uniform. If salaried workers wear the blue suit, so members of rock bands wear wild hair, leather clothes and numerous chains, rings and pendants. A strong sense of what is appropriate pervades the Japanese fashion scene and also the presentation of the body. The overall result is an expanding display of the body in the media, and a slow testing of the limits of how much of the female body can be exposed, but very little individuality in the actual expression. A tendency towards normalization prevails, despite the expanded opportunities for display. And whereas Shilling suggests that the body is increasingly in high modernity (obviously Giddens's phrase) constitutive of the self, it is far from clear how far this too is true of Japan. Shilling, following Elias and others, argues as a consequence that the modern problem of death is intimately connected with this phenomenon. If the body is constituent of self, great anxiety is expended on maintaining its health, trim shape and youthfulness. But since this cannot be either guaranteed or indefinitely prolonged, an existential crisis is bound to occur as the body inevitably declines. But aging, the ultimate dissolution of the body, or even voluntary death are not, or certainly not uniformly, treated this way in Japan. The possible connection of these attitudes to religion are left entirely unexplored by Shilling, suggesting yet another gap in the contemporary vision of Western sociology.

The end result of all this is, to return to Frank's ideal types, the appearance of the *disciplined* body, based on what appears to the outsider, and to some insiders, to be a clear example of regimentation, but of a very different kind from the rationalized monasticism which is his model example. Disciplined bodies in Japan coexist with emotionalism, with sensuality and with forms of efficiency which do not exactly correspond to any form of Weberian rationalization. The *mirroring* body, whose medium of expression is *consumption* (the model example being the departmental store), is easily recognized in Japan, although with its culturally specific qualities, some of which we have noted. The *dominating* body (medium: force; model: war), while it is present in *manga*, is largely absent as a type from the rest of the media, no doubt because of a combination of sensitivity to war-time atrocities and to the ornate rules governing activities such as sport, in which overt competition or joy in winning is at least externally subdued. This is not to argue for the absence of conflict, but to draw attention to the social management of conflict and to ideologies of pacifism and harmony, which cannot simply be dismissed as false consciousness. Frank's talking or *communicative* body (medum: recognition; model: communal rituals, caring relationships) is also easily recognized in the images portrayed in the Japanese media.

Critical questions appear at this point, especially from a feminist viewpoint. To what extent do the social patterns of Japanese society in general and their reflection in the media specifically shape the bodies of women, and, in shaping, distort? Do Japanese women have 'natural' shapes and sizes, disrupted by patriarchal media? These questions inevitably draw Foucault into the discussion, for, leaving aside his overly constructivist approach to the body, his emphasis on the institutions which govern the body, the 'discourses' (including presumably, although Foucault does not specifically say so, *visual* ones) which shape thinking or which *are* thinking, and the working of the 'micro-physics' of power through ever more subtle means, indicate the levels at which control and manipulation can take place. And, as he suggests, in the consumer society increasingly control is not through repression, but through stimulation and the creation of desire.

We also see here an issue that we raised earlier: the constructing of *gendered* bodies through images of appropriate fashion, activities, posture, diet, decoration and appurtenances (e.g. cigarettes, cars, golf clubs). Newly created social categories (e.g. the 'sporty' woman) impose new meanings on the biological foundation, which in turn influence behaviour, dress and self-images. The huge-eyed, non-Japanese-looking characters of girls' comics and the androgynous men who inhabit the same pages, the *bishonen*, may not only be, or remain as, figures of fantasy: a parallel phenomenon is reproduced in the very real activities (hugely popular) of the Takarazuka opera company. In other words, such images are manifested in social practices which shape and form particular images of femininity (and masculinity). Specific attributes become attached to each gender. Social inequalities are thus produced and reproduced through, among other means, the social construction of the body, or the social reproduction of 'appropriate' bodies. So women are encouraged towards passive decoration of their bodies (make-up, jewellery), while men are encouraged actively to build up their bodies. When women attempt to do the same through activies seen as masculine, such as body-building, then dissonance, created by social expectations, occurs.

This, as we have seen, applies not only to individual bodies, but to 'collective' ones, reproducing itself through often distinct images of appropriate body presentation based on age, on class and certainly on race, with, in the case of fashion advertising, very distinctive attributes of 'Japaneseness' being conveyed through the type of model, hair style, posture and type of clothes being modelled. Age as such is not abolished, but is presented in a way that clearly links it to class: aging but very well preserved and decorated women adorn the pages of *Fujin Gaho*, and, from their dress, settings and accessories, it is quite obvious that they are not working-class women. The articles that accompany the advertisements and photo-spreads on foreign travel, fancy *onsen*, up-market restaurants and elegant hotels reinforce this status-linked quality of the magazines. Where, in such publications, working women do appear, they are almost always associated with 'tradition' in some way – they are craftspeople whose presence and activities enhance the Japaneseness being projected, or they are there to serve the rich (employers of said hotels, etc.), but they do not appear in their own right. Despite the argument about classlessness the Japanese media are actually highly stratified, although of course there is an element of an age-grade system present – the young OL will change her reading as she ages and marries and as her husband advances through his career, if he does. But for the average urban *danchi* dweller or rural housewife, reading *Fujin Gaho* (which many do, despite its cost) is a form of vicarious consumption only.

A characteristic of bodily presentation is the *regulated* display of class, age, or sexuality. Western writers on the body in consumer society have tended to argue that values about the desirable attributes of the body change rapidly, which leads to uneasiness and uncertainty about being embodied. The evidence would seem to suggest that this process, while not absent, is very much slowed down in Japan, and we could speculate on the reasons for this. For while the Japanese media present, to use Turner's terminology, docile and disciplined bodies, they also present liberated ones: it is no longer necessary to wear a kimono, but shorts are fine. While some of the attributes of all consumer societies are there, including emphasis on body management through jogging, fashion, cosmetics and diet, and with increased emphasis on the performing self rather than the self which just occupies a status or office (although that is still a very real factor in Japan) it needs to be remembered that, while the media present stylized images, they present them in the context of a very stylized culture. The emphasis on the image, which some commentators (e.g. Featherstone 1991b) see as being new, is not new at all in

Japan, and so the argument, subsequently constructed, that this alleged shift from the abstract to the visual produces corresponding shifts in the emotional lives of the people who make this transition, also needs modification.

THE BODY, MEDIA AND CONSUMPTION

In essence then the social construction of the body can be seen as the commodification of the body: its presentation in such a way as to induce desire, to engineer the shape, size, colour, and posture of the body through fashion, decoration, diet, 'fitness' and even surgical alteration, to fit largely media-induced images of what the body 'should' look like. The construction of images – semiotic creativity – is a normal social and human activity. The construction of images directly linked to marketability, either of the body itself or of products to transform it according to ever-evolving and unstable canons of taste, however, is a product of what in generalized terms is known as the 'consumer society'. The analysis of the cultural and economic forms of such societies has itself become a major industry, and here there is no space to discuss the full range of theoretical issues raised by attempts to characterize in detail the qualities of such societies, their genesis and internal socio-economic and political arrangements. (For a good account, see Lee 1993.) But here, beyond simply asserting the generalized commodification of areas of life which have hitherto been outside of the consumption nexus, several points can be made. Firstly, advertising among all manifestations of the media is heavily implicated in this whole process. In the context of the presentation of the body, a much wider range of material, including comics, 'glamour' magazines, the tabloid press and TV, is involved. Secondly, there are cultural variations in the way in which commodification proceeds, as this chapter has attempted to demonstrate. So while commodification has certain qualities that define it as commodification, there are also important local variations, and the tendency in the literature to discuss the consumer society wholly from a Euro-American perspective needs to be resisted, although obviously in this case the interplay between Japanese and other forms of consumer culture is a central theme (e.g. Tobin 1992).

Thirdly, commodification cannot be seen only in the dimension of the imposition by capital of compulsory patterns of behaviour: it also involves freedom, competition and choice. Since Bourdieu (1984) it is necessary to see consumption, even among people of objectively similar incomes, as the principal mechanism of differentiation which allows both symbolic competition for status and relative freedom to define and pursue choice about lifestyle. The question of lifestyle, which can itself be seen as part of the 'reflexivity' of late modern society, is not a trivial issue; it is precisely the means by which a large number of people, including people in Japan, define their relationship to things, and as such constantly make decisions about consumption in general, and in this context their bodies in particular, as the means of symbolizing and manifesting the chosen lifestyle. A decision to use 'natural' cosmetics over 'artificial' ones may signal a complex group of decisions to do with one's appearance, ecological sensibility and desire to support 'alternative' industries, and will probably be found to be connected with other patterns of consumption choice relating to dress (cotton?), diet (organic/vegetarian?), political affiliations, choice of career, etc. And fourthly, advertising and the other manifestations of the media do not just sell things. They also create, to use Judith Williamson's phrase, 'structures of meaning' (Williamson 1978: 11). Commodities function at several levels – as signs and symbols, as regulating agents, as meaning conferring things, as markers of the categories of a culture. As such they connect with many corresponding levels of behaviour and identity, including conceptions of the self, which are deeply embodied. And all these in turn lead back to capitalism, to the products and services that one 'needs' to fulfil to create this self. The very fact that it is possible to talk about the 'creation' of the self (rather than just of the 'having of' self or 'being' oneself) suggests the central role of some form of constructivism at all levels of culture.

All these are connected to shifts in the nature of contemporary capitalism. As Shilling suggests (1993: 35), there has generally been, in advanced capitalist societies, a shift from production, frugality and denial towards a shortened working week, increased leisure and disposable income, and expanding social incentives to consume. While in Japan we can forget the accompanying suggestion that within consumer society the body ceases to be a vessel of sin and becomes an object of display, since it was never generally regarded as sinful in any sense, that consumer culture has sanctioned the presentation of the body in fresh ways. But again a comparative approach is sorely needed, since Shilling at once goes on to claim that, whereas clothes were once seen as 'objects of interest in their own right, inextricably bound to and expressive of social position, the "presentation of self" is now seen as signifying the real character of individuals' (1993: 35), this is hardly true of Japan. The fact that Japan is, sociologically if not physically or geographically, to be seen as a low-risk rather as a 'risk society' (to use Ulrich Beck's now rather fashionable term; Beck 1994), modifies the emergence of extreme versions of Western-style body-based individualism. A point of Goffman's (Goffman 1963), mentioned but not developed by Shilling, of greater relevance to Japan is the pregnant suggestion that, 'as well as allowing us to classify information given off by bodies, shared vocabularies of bodily idiom provide categories which label and *grade hierarchically* people according to this information. Consequently, these classifications exert a profound influence over the ways in which individuals seek to manage and present their bodies' (Shilling 1993: 82). This is in fact correct, and, as such, provides a check on the tendencies in Bryan Turner's work to equate commodification with social fragmentation. Shilling, in a paraphrase to Turner, states that 'commodification is the mode through which contemporary Western societies seek to ensure a minimal continuity in how people present themselves. That is, the means for managing the self have become increasingly tied up with consumer goods, and the achievement of social and economic success hinges crucially on the presentation of an acceptable self-image' (1993: 92). Again, read from a Japanese perspective this presents the same mixture of part truth and misleading generalizing that characterizes some Western (or certainly British) sociology of the body. This is partly because that tradition, commonly given its own social context, has avoided the questions of class and race. Yet, as we have suggested, the analysis of Japanese magazines does imply that, as in Bourdieu's France, there is also constant symbolic struggle for dominance in Japan. This occurs especially through conflicts over taste, which is important where class differences become centred on consumption devices rather than on objective socio-economic differences (Bourdieu 1984).

TOWARDS A CONCLUSION

Japanese media represent a large, diverse and varied field containing the pursuit of many agendas, conflicting ideologies, technical procedures and distinct styles. Here I have explored only a tiny corner of this enormous field: a selection of magazines which nevertheless provide some fruitful ways into the problems of adequately theorizing contemporary Japanese society. This does suggest certain continuities, but also illustrates the differences, even oppositions, within the field, which arise from a number of sources, but especially from the fact that the images within the magazines are targeting specific audiences: they are the outcome of marketing categories. I have also implied questions which are beyond the scope of a single chapter, including that of the social organization of magazine production – notably the gender, educational background, international experience and ideology of magazine editors and publishers.

But what I hope has been suggested is something of the complexity of the relationship between images and practices, including the reflection in the images of questions of class and of race, the manufacturing strategies of fashion producers, the sales strategies of retailers and the visual strategies of their advertising professionals. These, while parading their designs on models (sometimes Caucasian ones), have in practice to cut their cloth to the actual body proportions of the Japanese women who will wear their creations. There is no one Japanese female body and no one homogeneous representation of it. In fact the magazine world seems to reflect, or itself partly creates, a breaking up of homogeneity. Certain codes are still in place: coding of race, class and sexuality, for example, but not in a hegemonic way; the range of body types deemed attractive continues to expand. This is part of a dynamic process: shifting norms within Japanese culture, the influence of foreign experiments, the market-driven nature of much media innovation and the effect that images have in women's perception of themselves and of men's perception of women. The illustrated magazine – a highly visible artefact of contemporary Japanese culture – proves to be a rich field indeed for the exploration of Japanese society.

7

Sites and Sights: The Consuming Eye and the Arts of the Imagination in Japanese Tourism

To assert that identity and the acquisition and possession of material goods are tied up together, while true at one level, is to court the danger of creating a static model – one in which movement, symbolic or literal, is excluded. Consumption itself, however, involves movement – going shopping, browsing, seeking information. Nowhere is this dual process of consumption and movement better expressed than in tourism, in which physical locomotion is the means to both visual and material consumption – the consumption of sights and sites and the acquisition of souvenirs for oneself and gifts for others. And the Japanese are great travellers, in terms of both domestic and overseas tourism. Every day of the week, and especially during 'Golden Week' in early May and the school summer holidays in July and August, roads, railways and airports are packed with urbanites en route to or from scenic spots and historical or recreational sites, including the ever-expanding number of theme parks springing up around the country. And once at these sites, consumption of visual, sporting or cultural facilities of course takes place, inevitably recorded on photographs or videos, necessary adjuncts to Japanese travel, together with the often very extensive purchase of *meibutsu* (local delicacies) and souvenirs, either for personal consumption or more likely as *omiage* – gifts to be taken back to family friends and colleagues.

In some cases shopping is the major purpose of a trip, especially an overseas one. Tours to the nearby cheaper Asian destinations such as Hong Kong and Singapore, while often formally for sightseeing, are often really for the purpose of shopping. Shopping is likewise an expected activity on trips ostensibly of a quite different purpose, such as honeymoons. Japanese honeymooners in Hawaii are estimated to spend as much as 50 per cent of their brief holidays shopping, mostly for relatives and friends, and many stores in Honolulu that cater specifically to Japanese tourists provide check lists of likely candidates for gifts so that no one will inadvertently be forgotten. But clearly the analysis needs to be pushed somewhat beyond the simple description of tourism and the tourist gaze, the (often conspicuous) consumption of foods and services while travelling and the extensive purchase of gifts for those left behind. These activities need to be situated in a wider context which relates tourism to identity, to history and to the embodied nature of experience.

TOURISM AND EXPERIENCE

Tourism, including Japanese tourism, is not a unitary phenomenon. It encompasses both many objective forms (the package tour, the solitary visit to an art gallery, the safari, and so on) and subjective intentions (visual, romantic, escapist, for example). But while contemporary sociology has recovered the social significance of space from the geographers (Lefebvre 1991), the embodied nature of social actors from the phenomenologists (Turner 1984) and the temporal nature of experience from the historians (Gosden 1994), it has not yet successfully dealt with the mediating forces that bind these into a single field. One of these forces is movement. Movement – the physical projection of oneself from one location to another – has many dimensions, and these dimensions are often mingled. Movement can be redemptive (as in pilgrimage), a quest to find the self or to forget the self, purposeful (as on a business trip), to exercise the uncommitted gaze (the *flaneur*), or to seek for some larger sense of identity, personal or national, to give some major examples. It can be literal movement (taking a tour), imaginary (reading a travel book safely at home), or a combination of both. As almost every traveller knows, the trip itself may not objectively be all that much, but the anticipation and the recounting are among its greatest pleasures, regardless of the actual quality of the journey itself. Indeed disasters on the trip can become heroic adventures in retrospect and the drudgery of airports and the boredom of air travel can become romantic. Travel, especially tourism, is strategic movement, with multiple motives and multiple outcomes.

Movement then does not deny identity, but is a form of seeking or creating it, especially when the travel is to cultural or historical sites. Tourism is one of the most important contemporary ways in which the self can be constantly reinvented. Thus it is not only tradition that is invented ever anew, although this too is an important part of cultural practice (Hobsbawm and Ranger 1983), but this reinvention of the self is a strategy for the constant creation of identity, a very unstable entity in a confusing and continually changing social and economic environment. It is also an important form of sociality. The package tour in particular, a favourite mode of travel for Japanese, creates instant and indeed compulsory conviviality, constantly reinforced by the sightseeing, shopping, eating, dancing and even bathing together that is an essential part of the experience, especially in domestic tourism. Travel too provides a way of socializing with those of the same age group or social type, the young visiting ski resorts, beaches and amusement parks, families theme parks and picnic areas and the elderly sites of tradition – reminders of the 'old' Japan. All shop, however, and this itself creates a bridge between the generations.

Tied up with this are complex perceptions of being Japanese, not at all confined to the older generation. While the elderly do indeed seek out sites that confirm a sense of Japanese identity, the weekend crowds at cultural events and museums suggest that this is not an age-specific phenomenon. On a damp spring afternoon the National Museum of Japanese History located in Sakura, a small town over an hour by rather inconvenient trains from Tokyo, is crowded with young couples and families with children as well as retired people. Standing gazing into the meditation hall of the ancient Zen temple of Kencho-ji in the old capital of Kamakura on a late winter afternoon, a young Japanese woman nearby turned to me and said, 'This kind of place makes me proud to be a Japanese.' This is important because it extends the notion of consumption beyond simply 'purchase and use.' While it is widely recognized now that consumption includes imagination and anticipation, it must also be seen to include memory and a way of using consumption (in this case tourist sites/sights) to invent, reconstruct or recover a sense of identity normally suppressed, but which is suddenly called into being by the presence of certain objects or when the spirit of place operates unusually powerfully. Both consumption in general and tourism in particular are significant forms of sociality and social practice. Sites designed for gazing become sites of consumption in multiple senses (every museum in Japan has a shop); spaces designed for consumption (shopping centres, for example) become the contexts for a wide range of other social behaviour: sitting, gazing, wandering, watching other people. Shopping malls in the West have long had these multiple functions; new sites of consumption in urban Japan blend these functions, an excellent example being the Ebisu Garden Place complex in Tokyo (completed in 1995): a huge courtyard-like space on the site of the old Sapporo brewery and beer garden encircled by a group of buildings of eclectic architecture, including a branch of the Mitsukoshi departmental store, an office block, two vaguely German beer restaurants, a cinema, a block of residential apartments, several restaurants, cafes and fast-food outlets, an adjacent hotel and, as its central visual feature, a reconstructed French chateau approached up a flight of steps bounded by fountains, the whole complex connected by covered travellators to the nearby Ebisu railway and subway stations. The result is a huge and sanitized space, Disneyesque in architecture and in remarkable contrast to the narrow streets and crowded sidewalks of the surrounding neighbourhood. The chateau and beer halls and open vistas give the place a 'European' air, and while many people work there, a few live there and others frequent the restarants and shops, many come simply to look: the benches are filled with elderly couples, children run in the huge courtyard covered by a high glass roof reminiscent of old French or British railway terminals, and teenagers sit in groups on the steps.

Tourism itself then is consumption: it is implicated in other forms of consumption: participates in and is itself an important form of popular culture which creates its own 'authenticity'. Wandering from image to image, consuming the surface of things, is one dimension of the activity of the Japanese *flaneur*, but one which, as was suggested in Chapter 4, must be recognized as an aesthetic activity. Wandering in a departmental store and wandering in a museum may not be such different activities. Both are wandering/wondering and both are responses to the skilful and often playful blending of contemporary elements and traditional stylistics common in displays in both contexts (Yamaguchi 1991). Current interest in Japan in the idea of *furusato*, or 'home town' or native place, symbolized by the first Tokyo Furusato Fair held in 1994, indicates this search for an authenticity located in the small towns, villages and countryside of the outer regions of Japan – a blend in practice of nostalgia on the part of urban dwellers, romanticism, and a hard-headed desire to promote tourism to the remoter parts of the country and to popularize their products, especially their foods (Isomura 1981; Sakada 1984).

It has been noted in other contexts in Japanese society that play can be considered a form of resistance. Whereas Western workers may pilfer, loiter or make use of company facilities such as telephones for private purposes, Japanese ones are more likely to resort to forms of play during or after the (by Western standards) very long working day. Drunkenness, mimicry and singing (in the ubiquitous *karaoke* lounges) become forms of protest (Kamashima 1993). Many commentators on Japanese tourism trace the origins of domestic travel to pilgrimages, occasions when, for ostensibly religious purposes, large numbers of people would leave their homes and fields to travel to the great shrines (the grand shrine at Ise being a particularly popular destination). Such pilgrimages in practice often took on the character of extended holidays, free of responsibility and full of potential adventures, sexual encounters, experience of new places and relatively exotic foods (Kato 1994; Vaporis 1995).

Contemporary tourism of course fulfils many of these same functions, and in greater safety. Anticipative consumption – in this case of travel – can be both a genuine form of consumption (in the imagination) and of play/playful resistance, a way of not actually being present on the job. Tourism is to do with dreams as much as with reality, as signalled in the opening line of the theme song of the nostalgia-promoting Japan Railways 'Bound for the Heartland' advertisements: *awaki yume* – between dream and reality. Nostalgia, when more fully deconstructed, turns out to be a complex concept, as evidenced by the frequency with which the idea – itself *natsukashi* – is discussed in current Japanese commentaries on popular culture. One of the genres at which the Japanese excel is without doubt that of the animated film (full length that is, not just the less than 30 minute TV *manga* or cartoon programmes which make up a large part of the early evening viewing diet). While a number of these shorter cartoons deal in nostalgia (*Chibi Maruko-chan*, the story of the vicissitudes of a little schoolgirl, or the enormously popular *Sazae-san* , concerning the life of a middle class family, are classic examples), full length animated movies almost invariably deal either with a past close enough to be remembered as an age of simplicity and civility (e.g. my personal favourite, *Tonari no Tottoro*, the theme of which is the summer stay in a small village of a young family whose mother is in a country sanitorium recovering from TB and the encounter of the two young children with a huge but kind creature of magical powers and his companions who live beneath an enormous and ancient tree on the edge of their cottage's garden) or with a mythical future in which civilization, having passed through some kind of catastrophe, has recovered those values (e.g. the now very well-known *Kaze no Tani no Nauschica*). Nostalgia, while it can be a retreat from the present, also contains utopian themes, and so, like all utopias, represents an implicit critique of the present.

Tourism clearly is escape, and is described by many Japanese in just those terms – freedom from the city, noise, pollution, responsibility. Interestingly that escape contains the same utopian elements, but phrased in a consumer mode – the tourist buys a form of sociality achieved by way of a passage through space, in which experiences can be ordered and in which the body itself can be re-experienced through introducing new foods, enduring physical hardships or by being exposed it to to the sun, sea and wind – elements rarely experienced in urban life. The setting itself is consequently of great importance in tourism. In travelling abroad the different and the exotic present themselves automatically, but increasingly within Japan attempts are being made to create just this kind of difference, not only in enclave-like resort settings, but in particular through the medium of theme parks, many of which combine the different – the illusion of being abroad – with an educational function. And the Japanese do like to integrate fun and learning. A visit to a theme park combines entertainment with information, a good example being the Tobu theme park (operated by a railway line and departmental store company) just outside northwestern Tokyo, in which small-scale model versions of famous buildings from around the world have been reconstructed, all cheek-by-jowl. Here, as the advertising suggests, it is possible to experience a simulation of the great cities of the world all in one place without the inconvenience of actually leaving Japan, and, furthermore, the visitor can 'shop the world' in the stores which of course form an integral part of the complex. Another very well-known example is the Huis Ten Bosch, a reconstruction of an entire Dutch village, with real Europeans walking the streets and working in the shops and workshops. This one is in Nagasaki, historically associated with the Dutch and with the introduction of Western science and medicine into Japan. Elsewhere one can visit an Austrian village or an English village (complete of course with a manor house and where one can very usefully take English lessons), or tour the pre-modern world at the Little World Museum of Man, near Nagoya, which combines an indoor anthropological museum with outdoor reconstructions of full-scale houses dismantled in their place of origin and rebuilt in the hills above Nagoya.

Tourism then is imaginative consumption *par excellence*. It combines physical movement away from one's usual place of residence to some unusual, unknown destination, a movement fraught with the possibility of fresh experiences and with the acquisition of exotic material items, experiences and objects that in some way redefine the self. Travel can be play, the pursuit of identity or rebellion against an imposed identity, and for many Japanese it combines the liminality of the pilgrimage with the relative safety of planned modern travel. Furthermore, while domestic tourism represents play and, for some, especially older Japanese, a search for roots and a national as opposed to purely individual identity – a form of cultural nationalism in fact – foreign travel is often linked with the currently popular idea of *kokusaika*, or internationalization, which was discussed in a different context in Chapter 5. But in relation to tourism it suggests an educational element in the idea of travel. While on the one hand the Japanese government is actively encouraging foreign tourism to help offset (in favour of Japan) the huge balance of payments problem, many Japanese regard foreign travel as the opportunity not only to acquire cheap foreign goods, but also to become *kokusaijin* – international citizens.

While considerable controversy exists over the exact meaning of 'internationalization' (e.g. Mouer and Sugimoto 1986), it certainly does contain at its heart an ambiguity, notably that of wanting to be 'international' (to travel, to learn foreign languages) while at the same time wishing to remain distinctly Japanese. The result is that a good deal of 'internationalization' actually means consuming the world: buying high-prestige foreign goods, wearing Western fashions, eating 'ethnic' foods, travelling in tour groups around foreign countries. Consumption rather than understanding, in other words, actually describes the process. Here the imaginary is very much at play, but an imaginary to a great extent constructed for the potential traveller through advertising in the brochures put out by tour companies. The major forces working against this commoditization of travel are the increasing number of Japanese actually living abroad for purposes of work and the amount of serious information that is available in the form of guide books and academic or semi-academic introductions to particular parts of the world and which are easily available in almost any bookstore. But for the average tourist the information likely to be encountered is actually about consumption, a fact that a quick browse in the travel section of any major bookstore will quickly illustrate. Here I will show how this is done by way of the content analysis of a sample in a large series of such guides, in this case one to Australia, now one of the most favoured destinations for Japanese tourists and honeymooners. This book is typical of a whole genre covering individual countries, whole continents or specific cities frequented by Japanese tourists (for example, Singapore, London or Paris). This particular guide should consequently be situated in a spectrum of material that ranges from magazines such as *Non-no* for women and *Popeye* for men (Nitta 1992: 209), through a large array of guide books specifically for tourists, to travel writings and scholarly surveys of the place or region.

Japanese consumption, including that of tourists, is rarely unguided, but is informed by a large range of data, guides, magazine articles, maps and other aids to efficient shopping. This is very necessary given the short duration of most Japanese holidays, including honeymoons (four to five days), and Japan's status as a society in which gift exchange is still a major factor, of buying for others as well as for oneself. The purchase of gifts is in addition to *tanomare mono* – things one is asked to buy at the request of friends and colleagues. Much of a short holiday or honeymoon is likely to be taken up with shopping, and Nitta (1992: 205) estimates that in the early 1990s the average Japanese honeymoon couple in Hawaii spent US$2111 on gifts and souvenirs. On average Japanese visitors to Hawaii spend well over double per day the amount spent by European and US mainland visitors (US$323 per day compared with US$127 per day), much of it on shopping and the rest on food and services. A lot of this shopping is for brand-name goods, known about and coveted as a result of their coverage in consumer magazines and guide books or from their presence at outrageous prices in boutiques and stores in Japan. European products (perfumes, leather goods and clothes especially) are highly valued and often bought on these shopping safaris.

Practice for such shopping begins early. All Japanese schools organize *shugaku ryoko*, or school excursions, usually to historic centres such as Kyoto or Nara, but sometimes these days even abroad. Graduating university students customarily make a trip abroad or at home in the vacation period between final examinations and starting work at the beginning of April, the date at which new recruits normally enter a company. *Omiage* shopping occupies a good deal of time on these trips too. With the expansion of the middle class in Japan and of its earning power, coupled with the high value of the yen, the average Japanese has become an affluent traveller. Abroad the modest salaryman can feel rich, and the honeymooners can luxuriate in huge hotel rooms, the bathroom of which may be almost as large as the entire apartment into which they will move on their return home.

In this context then we can examine our sample guide book: *Oozutoraria* ('Australia') (Kamitakahara and Kurotsu 1990). A substantial book of 223 pages designed in a slim format that can be slipped into the pocket or handbag, its cover depicts the inevitable koala. Several pages of advertisements for hotels and airlines lead into the text proper: a map of Australia, a dozen pages of information on getting there, currency, shop and banking hours, electricity, useful phrases (mostly in case of sickness or robbery!), travel within the country, some suggestions of exotic things to do such as taking a farm holiday or trying hot-air ballooning, advice about checking in and out of hotels, asking for the bill in restaurants and tips on special Australian customs such as the barbeque and the BYO ('bring your own bottle') rule in certain eateries. By page 26 the guide gets down to the real business: eating and how to read the menu, wines, uniquely Australian souvenirs that should be purchased – stuffed koala toys, opals, sheepskin goods, boomerangs and Australian wines. The rest of the guide is divided into sections by city, starting with Sydney. Each such section follows the same format: a large-scale map of the area, a detailed map of the downtown district, advice on transportation and several pages of information on sightseeing spots. Then a detailed listing of recommended restaurants, with a paragraph of write-up and a photograph of each, information on sports and nightlife and an extensive section on shopping, complete with maps, addresses, telephone numbers, items sold and prices. The book concludes with information about optional tours, advice on entry and departure procedures, including how to fill in the landing card, layout plans of the major airports, a list of recommended hotels and advice on how to get to Narita airport by various alternative routes from downtown Tokyo. What is very conspicuous about this guide book, like many of its genre in Japan and when compared with its European equivalents, is that it contains no information at all about the history, geography, culture or society of the country. It is in effect purely a guide to consumption, with advice on eating and shopping being the main features. Many similar guides give extensive information on hotels and resorts, complete with photographs of typical rooms and even floor plans so that the exact layout is known in advance. These guides assume not that travel means the pursuit of culture, but that travel equals consumption.

In this light the meaning of *kokusaika no jidai*, the 'era of internationalization', supposed to have come to its flowering in the 1980s, is seen from a fresh perspective. The number of overseas Japanese travellers has indeed expanded enormously, from 158,827 in 1965 when exchange control restrictions were lifted, allowing greater freedom of travel to Japanese not on official business, to 6,828,338 in 1987, to an estimated ten million a year today, well over 80 per cent of whom are engaged in 'sightseeing' (*Asahi nenkan* 1995). The high value of the Yen has made foreign travel increasingly cheap, and the desire for foreign travel is reported, in the annual survey of Japanese lifestyle and consumer attitudes carried out by one of Japan's biggest advertising agencies, to be not only very strong, but to be one which most Japanese now hope actually to realize (Hakuhodo Institute 1988). If the origins of domestic tourism are associated with pilgrimage, in which neighbours supported an individual from one household with *osenbetsu* or travel funds, who in return prayed for these supporters at the shrines and temples visited and returned with *omiage* (souvenirs) and *omamori* (charms and amulets) foreign travel still shows many continuities with this traditional past. It is a mixture of material consumption, reconfirmation of Japanese identity, a conferring of status on those left behind, who benefit from the activity when the traveller returns, and a creation of the image of the traveller as a *kokusaijin* (Graburn 1983).

This enormous expansion of consumption-based tourism is closely linked with the expansion of the middle class. While sociologists in Southeast Asia are just now beginning to recognize the existence of new middle classes in such societies as Malaysia and Singapore, such a group has been growing in Japan inexorably since the 1950s. The growth of affluence since then has created a physically expanding group, with more disposable income and with the desire to establish their class credentials with foreign travel, formerly the preserve of the wealthy or the officials. University students (the university and college sector having also very substantially expanded since the war), the children of this new middle class, contribute another major group of travellers, especially during the long spring and summer vacations. 'OLs' – young unmarried women in temporary careers between college and marriage, living at home and with few overheads as a result, are another very conspicuous group. 'Silver travellers' – retired people, now very much targeted by the media as consumers of goods, of culture and of travel through glossy magazines such as *Presidento* ('President') are another, especially in terms of domestic tourism.

Contact between Japanese and other cultures is then most frequently mediated by consumption. Tourism too has other latent functions – it creates a low-key form of Japanese cultural nationalism, by bringing other civilizations into contrast with Japan, and it deflects consumer pressure to bring down the very high domestic prices of goods at home because many of these things can be bought cheaply abroad. Tourism too creates a sense of upper-class status for quite ordinary Japanese when they travel abroad and experience forms of luxury – swimming pools, French food – rarely affordable at home. Foreign travel is politically useful for reasons other than helping with the balance of payments problem. It allows the controlled representation of the Other, whether through the nostalgia of domestic tourism or the construction of the foreign as exotic. Japanese tour brochures and advertisements abound in a distinctive language of representation: the foreign is *ekizochiku* – exotic – or *shinpi-teki* – mysterious, or even *jikan wo koete* – beyond time. Many Japanese see themselves as those whose historical role is to 'gaze' upon the Other in a way that the Europeans used to be able to do (and, interestingly, drawings of Japanese abroad in travel brochures often depict them as having distinctly European features, further reinforcing the idea of travel as part of a class lifestyle). Travel in such cases does not mean the genuine encounter with the Other, but the careful staying within the pre-given meaning system. Internationalization as a result is achieved only on the imaginary plane, while in reality plundering the world for its material riches.

THE CULTURE OF JAPANESE TOURISM

Travel and 'culture' then are not opposed: travel itself is a form of culture, a cultural practice that enters into the way in which a society perceives itself, whether this be occasioned by the travelling of members of the dominant culture to other places or by travllers to that culture who introduce new social practices, mores, ways of life. In Japan this means not so much the management of foreign tourists, who by and large are encapsulated much as Japanese tourists are encapsulated abroad, but from the Other in the form of foreign workers, the new underclass (Clammer 1995b). Movement has become an essential feature of life in the modern world. But whereas many Western sociologists have discovered the 'Other within' in the form of third-world music and literatures, in Japan the discovery has been of the traditional within. This has taken the form, amplified and to some degree created by domestic tourism, of nostalgia, a search for roots and a quest for identity. In many cases these identities are sought in localities, in units smaller than the nation state, and in the peripheral areas of Japan thought still to preserve tradition in a way now lost in the urban centres. Tohoku and Hokkaido in the far north and Okinawa in the far south become the repositories and exemplifiers of this tradition, the 'real' Japan. Japanese culture could be said to have always had strong centrifugal tendencies: originally the province, or *han*, and later, after Meiji, the country itself provides a strong symbolic centre, a situation in which it is difficult for Japanese really to imagine another place, another world. The Chinese have settled worldwide, they make good migrants. The Japanese never have, to anything like the same degree.

There are important implications here for the overall configuration of Japanese society, since such centrifugal tendencies avoid and offset the fragmentations of postmodernity. A strong centre remains. This firmly challenges the ideas of such cultural commentators as Gayatri Spivak and her argument that, 'in post-coloniality, every metropolitan definition is dislodged' (Spivak 1990: 41). While the recognition of the diversity of Japanese culture(s) and the presence of large ethnic minorities is now widely established, centrifying forces are also strong, a fact which contradicts current Western intellectual fashion, as in the claim that the societies of the late modern world are characterized by 'hybridity' : 'This involves the entering into a state of hybridity in which no single narrative or authority – nation, race, the West – can claim to represent the truth or exhaust meaning' (Chambers 1994: 27). Japanese society contains strong antidotes to anomie, but a consequence of this is that the construction of the Other is fundamental to the parallel construction of the Japanese sense of self and of the possession of a distinct, indeed unique, history.

An observation of Chambers is appropriate here: 'We are usually only willing to recognize differences so long as they remain within the domain of our language, our knowledge, our control' (Chambers 1994: 30). Differences are, in other words, permitted a hearing within limits, as evidenced by the management and assimilation of the foreign into Japan since the seventeenth century. Japanese society experiences a permanent tension between the centered nature of the state and the decentred nature of many cultural productions, including film, comics and traditional theatre forms such as *noh* and *bunraku*, where there is no closure: unresolved plots and unfinished stories are normal. Japanese social aesthetics thus represent closure *against* the world, but not *within* the world. But even closure against the rest of the world is increasingly hard to sustain. Tourism, as I have suggested, is not just movement, but a new cultural form, one which is itself changing wider Japanese culture, together with the influx of foreigners and the impingement of TV news and documentaries and debate about Japan's foreign aid policy and world role. This is promoting an unprecedented mixing of cultural forms and cultural performances, the previously discussed examples of Christmas, Hallowe'en and Valentine's Day being instances of this. As MacCannell puts it: 'It would be tenuous and mainly incorrect to frame the interaction as "tourist/other" because what we really have is a collaborative construction of postmodernism by tourists and ex-primitives who represent not absolute differences but mere differentiations of an evolving new cultural subject' (MacCannell 1992: 35). This is an important insight: new cultural forms are no longer just a conflict of differences, but an evolving synthesis of forms in which innumerable influences act synergystically. Japanese consumer society is a prime example of this mechanism at work, and is one that, as MacCannell suggests, forces a radical revision of old models of social change. In particular, as he goes on to propose (1992: 296), it is necessary to be very critical of the idea of 'tradition', something that all groups have, which is constantly reinvented and which is highly ideological. Tourism is a ground of encounter, and as such its functions and outcomes cannot be predicted or catalogued as much of the more conventional sociology of tourism seems to suggest is possible. Those at the receiving end of tourism, for example, may have complex feelings about the constant invasion of their privacy, and may develop strategies to manage this. As Martinez demonstrates in her study of tourism in a fishing village in Mie Prefecture, the 'natives' find the tourists amusing and naive and in some cases simply treat them as if they did not exist (Martinez 1990).

In common with other forms of consumption, Japanese tourism has been transformed and shaped by technological changes, both in terms of specific improvements in transportation technology (the aeroplane, for example) and on account of the large-scale alteration wrought in the society as a whole as the result of technological developments. The appearance of affordable rail travel throughout the country, the technology to reach inaccessible places (it is now possible to get one-third of the way up Mount Fuji in a bus) and marketing techniques through specialist travel agents and the travel departments of departmental stores have revolutionized travel for the average Japanese. The removal of political restrictions on travel between the feudal fiefdoms (*han*, or domains) at the beginning of the Meiji era, the gradual unification of the national language to facilitate communication and the appearance of the concept of the holiday and of Western-style labour laws that guaranteed time off slowly made the possibility of voluntary movement for pleasure both a possible concept replacing the pilgrimage and a physically realizable reality.

The appearance of mass travel for pleasure is a postwar phenomenon, like so much else on the Japanese consumer scene. Before the war, customs that had existed in industrial England, such as bank holiday and wake's week excursions to holiday resorts such as Blackpool, had not developed. As it did begin to develop in the 1950s it soon began to turn into a huge industry, with large travel businesses appearing, bus companies emerging, railways beginning to exploit the tourism possibilities of their rail networks, the design and production of posters and brochures for tourism becoming an important new sector of the growing advertising industry, the publication of tourist guide books developing into a viable activity and a huge expansion taking place of the infrastructure of shops, inns, hotels and restaurants needed to support the growing number of travellers. At the same time the custodians of cultural sites began to realize that they could attract people by improving the facilities at places of interest, and the marketing of *meibutsu* became commercialized. As a result new forms of experience were created and new forms of sociality and social custom invented (most of us familiar with travel have probably forgotten our first-ever stay in a hotel and the difficulty of knowing exactly what the social conventions of behaviour there were).

Japanese tourism was contingent on the appearance of one of the most crucial concepts of modernity – that of *leisure*. Together with the emergence of the idea of free time to be spent on personal activities has gone urbanization, which has created concentrations of population that not only desire entertainment and escape from the city, but which can also be organized. And it is the organized nature of tourism and its professionalization that are two of the most remarkable features of modern travel and the way in which it is experienced: being taken *en masse* to prearranged places, paid for in advance, and in the care of specialists in whom one has invested a huge amount of trust despite the potential risks involved in travel (Lash and Urry 1994: 253-5). And the Japanese are without doubt among the most trusting of peoples in these circumstances, something that has led to the package tour as a major form of Japanese tourist experience: most Japanese tourism is still organized tourism, although the 'post-tourist' – the individual seeker after authentic experience – also exists.

Tourism, like other forms of consumption, is made possible by and in turn contributes to creating new forms of subjectivity. Photography, now an essential accompaniment of Japanese tourism, makes possible the preservation and organization of experience in unprecedented ways. As the consumption of culture itself becomes part of tourism, the recording of sites on film becomes part of the new etiquette of travel. To return without photographs is to have had an experience that it is difficult to then validate in the eyes of others, and photography itself becomes a substitute for memory. Culture and tourism are inseparable: tourism is cultural practice, often that of visiting cultural sites, an activity governed by rules of expected behaviour. Despite claims about the authenticity of tourist experiences, they are actually highly mediated ones. Linked to the huge availability of travel information and integrated into the gift economy, associated with status and perceived as a necessary adjunct to or expression of middle-class life, tourism has become one of the most conspicuous forms of consumption in Japan. As eating out and other forms of literal and symbolic consumption of that beyond one's own place and experience have expanded, so tourism has come to be seen as essentially a necessity – with shopping the pre-eminent marker of membership in the affluent society.

These emergent patterns reflect changes at many levels of Japanese society: a changing class structure, the ability to consume the world at home or abroad, changing understandings of culture and slow but clear changes in attitudes to work. The word leisure (*rejaa* – itself a loan-word) was rarely heard or seen until recently, and even what is believed by many to be the indigenous Japanese term – *yoka* – was not actually coined until the late Meiji era. The concept, in other words, hardly existed in early modern Japanese history. Yet by 1972 the powerful Ministry of International Trade and Industry (MITI) found it wise to establish the *Yoka kaihatsu senta* – the Centre for the Development of Leisure – which produces annual statistics and studies on leisure trends in Japan. The perception has emerged that if the Japanese work seriously, they also play seriously. Leisure – time spent *amaru hima* – not working, has moved from being a problem to being a priority, a question of lifestyle choices for many Japanese and a matter of very big business for the providers of entertainment, sporting, travel and shopping services. Interesting too is the location of the official government leisure centre within MITI. This reflects the foreign policy implications of leisure, not in the sense of the large number of Japanese travelling abroad, but of foreign pressure to curtail Japanese economic competitiveness by reducing working hours and increasing free time. The Japanese, ever sensitive to foreign criticism that they are workaholics and totally economic animals, have established the development of leisure as a national policy priority.

Leisure in contemporary Japan is consequently a many-faceted phenomenon – a statement of affluence, an expression of lifestyle choices, a means of exploring new subjectivities. It can take many forms – from the traditional arts such as the 'way' of flowers (*kado*), tea or martial arts, to participation in high-technology forms of entertainment, two examples being the current boom in virtual reality centres, which for some young people are replacing the cinema as a place of entertainment, and the enormous expansion in the number of theme parks glorifying technology or using it to produce a simulated environment. While Tokyo Disneyland is the grandfather of all of these, other examples abound, Tamatech in southwestern Tokyo being a case in point. Others simulate foreign environments, and theme parks exist evoking, among others, Spain, Canada, Switzerland, Scotland and Holland, as well as and Meiji Mura attempts to re-create the past. All contain shops and 'historical' or scenic attractions, and many include swimming pools, hotels, beauty parlours and golf courses – golf itself being a major feature of Japanese leisure. Many such parks cater for the Japanese penchant for day trips or one-night visits, brief excursions from the pace and pollution of urban life, and have contributed substantially to creating such demand.

Technology is not the only dimension of leisure, however. Japanese have long prided themselves on a special relationship to nature, and a concern with ecology has begun to pervade Japanese attitudes to leisure, with ecology trips, camping, and learning through contact with nature trips having grown in popularity since the late 1980s. This interest has taken a number of forms which deserve comment. Commercial tour companies have been quick to see advantages in green tourism, and some theme and leisure parks exploit this quite consciously, such as Mongoru Mura (Mongol Village), which stresses contact with nature through exposure to a simulation of the lifestyle of the nomadic dwellers of the steppes. But an altogether different form is related to rural de-population in Japan. The huge growth in cities since the 1960s has been fuelled not by natural population increases but by rural – urban or small town – big city migration. The result has been intense urbanization (the Kanto Plain containing Tokyo, Yokohama, Kawasaki and a number of smaller cities, including Chiba in one huge conurbation, embraces almost one-quarter of the entire Japanese population, and the Osaka–Kyoto–Kobe conurbation holds only a slightly smaller proportion). This movement has culminated in the depopulation of villages throughout Japan as young people and able-bodied adults have migrated, leaving the countryside increasingly to the elderly. A downward spiral of decline has resulted in villages and small rural towns becoming relatively impoverished.

Steps to address this have taken two main forms: the *furusato*, or 'home-town', movement based on increasing interest in localities and remote areas of Japan and on promoting nostalgia and nostalgic tourism to such localities; and the economic revitalization of villages through both the provision of government grants and the encouragement of such places to identify their strengths and special advantages, and to build recovery on these. And this has been successful, with villages in Kyushu, for instance, deciding to market themselves as hot-spring resorts, to engage systematically in 'organic' farming in order to cash in on the booming demand for such products in the urban areas, and to exploit the plentiful availability of good scenery and clean air. All this builds on the *shizen to jibun no ittaika* ('being at one with nature') sentiment widespread among disaffected urbanites tired of crowding and too much built environment. In some cases groups of such villages market themselves together to exploit their collective advantage. So one can now visit the countryside, stay in a traditional Japanese inn, eat wholly natural foods and bathe in the hot springs. For many older Japanese in particular this is the perfect recipe for relaxation and health, and fits the preference for a short stay of perhaps two or three days outside of the framework of the group tours, which, while still a huge industry, are beginning to decline relative to other more individualistic options.

The revitalization (*mura okoshi*) of some countryside areas is an aspect of a bigger cultural process: the reconstruction of the countryside as image. The countryside – *inaka* – while it clearly exists in objective form, is to a great extent an urban construction: a place not inhabited by real farmers leading a lifestyle inconceivable to many urbanites, but an image (Ohnuki-Tierney 1993: 92-3). This has led to varying and often contradictory responses in the countryside, from largely ignoring or encapsulating tourists (Martinez 1990) to actively inventing new 'traditions' to promote relations with the cities and to establish the status of villages as (mythical) *furusato* for rootless urbanites nostalgic for a sense of identity with nature (Knight 1993). Domestic tourism is not just an economic phenomenon or even just an example of hedonism disguising a fundamental emptiness of spirit (Koseki 1989); it is also a dual activity of construction: identity construction on the part of tourists and of the construction of the countryside on the part of urbanites with the complicity of the ruralites.

The nature of tourism must consequently be linked to deeper structures of Japanese society and culture, and in the case of eco-tourism to the rediscovery of nature as a social value and of the revaluation of Shinto and of certain aspects of Buddhism as promoting positive images of nature and practices towards nature, something with which notions of Japanese identity are very much tied up (Clammer 1995a: 59-81). Just as the notion of the 'countryside' has evolved in Europe through a long process of social and cultural construction (Berque 1994), so it has been in Japan, although under different pressures. In Japan this is still a relatively unexplored subject, but among the forces that have shaped contemporary attitudes to the countryside are the connections made between nature and the social self; the evolution of ideas about nature, not so much as the result of fluctuations in artistic and architectural sensibilities, but in relation to developing ideas of national and ethnic identity; the emergence of the folklore movement largely under the influence of the bureaucrat-agriculturist-scholar Yanagita Kunio (Tsurumi 1992); the *furusato* movemen;, rural revitalization schemes; and the growth of nostalgia accompanying over-urbanization and commercial forces, including advertising and the expansion of the railways, which are now very active promoters of travel to the hinterland.

If pilgrimage was often a form of tourism, contemporary tourism from the cities is itself a form of pilgrimage, the religion in question being 'Japan' and the underlying motives being not just consumption as such, but also the construction of a postmodern self, one situated in relation to Japanese history and concerns with ethnicity while simultaneously turning towards an increasingly globalized world in which the actual content of everyday life *is* the consumer society, a distinctive form of late capitalism that intrudes on every area of the psyche and society. Studies of advertising and the construction of identity through product and image consumption now illustrate this worldwide. The consumption and the construction of nature go hand in hand in Japanese domestic tourism. Much of such tourism is not a search for the old, but a search for the 'authentic', understood increasingly as the organic, the not-urban, in which technology is used to transport one to the non-technological. The issue of postmodernity once again raises its Hydra-like head. The search for simulation and hyper-reality through technological tourism coexist with nostalgia and the emphasis on localities and authenticity. Both are mediated by consumption: just as Japanese cultural tourism abroad combines sites and shopping, the controlled experience of the Other and its incorporation in many subtle forms back into Japan through fashion, language, architectural motifs, foods and objects of status, so domestic tourism combines many levels of experiences and subjectivities into the encapsulated time-space compression of the tour − the microcosm in many ways of the time-space compression now taken as one of the key defining characteristics of the late modern or postmodern capitalist world (Harvey 1989).

8

Theorizing Consumption in Urban Japan

It has already been suggested that the adoption of capitalism in Japan was successfully accomplished without either basis in or need subsequently to adopt a 'puritan' ethic of any kind. This is not of course to argue against the intense discipline that went into the formation of an industrial economy in Japan and which still prevails in the Japanese work ethic. It is, however, to suggest at least three things. The first of these is that forms of capitalism can vary, not only in terms of structural characteristics (e.g. the nature of institutions or the organization of enterprises), but also in terms of their effective basis and the subjectivities that inform them and provide the basis for participation on the part of workers. The second is that the classical Weberian approach to the role of religion in the origin of capitalism, while it may be of utility in explaining early British or other European capitalisms, is of very limited value in understanding Asian capitalisms, and much of the ink spilled in arguing about variation in the 'Weberian thesis' in Asia could have been saved if some simple empirical and conceptual distinctions had been made. The debate, in other words, needs rephrasing, and to put it in terms of 'religion' and 'capitalism' is inadequate. While religion *per se* is not unimportant it is actually the broader question of value that is at stake here and its connection to ideas of personal and cultural identity. Historically in Japan (or at least through the Tokugawa era) making money and engaging in commerce were not in any moral sense negative activities, even though in the Tokugawa ranking system merchants were relegated to the lowest category, below samurai and farmers. In practice of course many samurai engaged in both farming and commercial activities, especially in the late Edo period, and the glorious culture of the cities (consumed by all classes) was the product of the merchant class. Religion itself reflected this rather than determined it. One of the most popular forms of shrine worship – the Inari cult, often associated with the symbolism of the fox, and which was historically considered a fertility cult, has now taken on the identity of a cult of business and money. The commercialization of desire can take many forms, and religion, certainly in Japan, is not immune to this. Thirdly, the issue of selfhood is linked to economic processes in subtle and often complex ways. Significantly, Giddens, in his book on the self in late modernity (Giddens 1991), does not specifically discuss any relationships between changing forms of economy and changing images of selfhood, but the major extant empirical study of Japanese selfhood immediately does so. In her study of gender and employment in a small factory in the Shitamachi (downtown) district of Tokyo, Kondo sees the self – the self as project – as created through work. Work – its objective conditions and subjective interpretation – becomes in this model the major vehicle through which identity is achieved. Whether ideologically this idea would sell well in the West is unclear, but it makes a great deal of sense in Japan (Kondo 1990). What Kondo fails to do, however, is to move beyond relations of production to consumption – her subjects as exchangers and users of products as well as producers of them. Nevertheless she does clearly establish the connection between work and a sense of identity in contemporary Japan – an image somewhat different from Western preoccupations with 'reflective selves' and with selves formed through the medium of self-help manuals and the like.

Some broad implications for social theory are obviously contained in these observations. The thrust of much that has been said in this study suggests that personal 'authenticity' is not necessarily violated by consumption. There are a number of reasons for this, including the fact that, for many if not most contemporary Japanese, consumption behaviour is the major available form of self-expression. Through it fashions, lifestyles, group identities, gender and sexualities and a range of subjectivities that are difficult to trace are constructed. Also involved is the fact that late capitalism is not just one thing, as was suggested above, and consequently certain predefined experiences are not necessarily intrinsic to it. As Miller puts it in his anthropological analysis of consumption in Trinidad, 'indeed books on postmodernity with their concern for global transformation seem even more inclined to talk about "late capitalism" or cultures of inauthenticity as though they represent in their effects the psychic states and generalized experiences of most of contemporary mankind' (Miller 1994b: 11). Certainly the study of Japan suggests that, there too, experiences generated by or under the Japanese form of late capitalism, with its distinctive institutional structures, patterns of work behaviour and cultural activities – sufficiently different indeed to suggest to at least one commentator that Japan is not really a capitalist economy at all, but a form of disguised communist one (Kenrick 1990) – are sufficiently special to render universalist claims invalid.

This is partly because the objective forms of capitalism vary, both institutionally and culturally, between say Japanese, German, British and North American varieties, to say nothing of emergent forms among the other newly capitalist states within Asia of Taiwan, Korea, Singapore, Hong Kong and, increasingly, Malaysia, Thailand, Brunei and Indonesia; and of course there are other conspicuous examples from elsewhere, South Africa, Brazil and Mexico being good and again varied examples. It is also that alteration in the objective conditions of life because of economic change (new patterns of work, spatial and social mobility, rising incomes, for example) create new forms of subjectivity, forms which are invariably filtered through the history and particular culture of the societies in which they are occurring. Once we have become accustomed to life in one of the extant forms of late capitalism we tend quickly to forget how unprecedented in human history many of these subjectivities actually are – and the experience of mass consumption is surely one of the most significant of these.

Goods and experiences are intimately involved with one another and it is a characteristic of late capitalism constantly to generate new sites/ occasions for such experiences. While the *oseibo* and *ochugen* (new-year and mid-year) gift-giving seasons have long been both institutionalized as social events and commercialized through their orchestration by that most central of consumer institutions in Japan, the departmental store – others have followed as the logic of consumerism creates even more occasions. Valentine's Day, which in Japan is a day in which women give gifts to men (usually in the form of chocolate), its reciprocal occasion White Day (on 14 March), on which men give return gifts to women, Christmas, which has become a very major commercial event in this least Christian of nations, and a number of slightly less important events imported from North America, including Mothers' Day, Fathers' Day and even Hallowe'en, are all occasions constructed largely by departmental stores, but into which Japanese have, quite literally, 'bought in'.

These events, however, do not by any means simply represent American cultural imperialism, but in fact symbolize the expressive transformation of the commodity, often in the form of the creative combining of commodities into a new pattern of signification. Snoopy, that popular symbol of mid-American culture, has become a central cultural icon in Japan, and the image of the lovable beagle can be found on hundreds of different forms of objects – bags, tee-shirts, key rings, mugs, plates, and so forth. He has become an almost indispensable ingredient in the culture of pre-teen and early teen Japanese girls, despite the fact that until recently few books of the Peanuts cartoons were translated into Japanese and sales of the comic-book version were low (in late 1995 there was a boom in sales). The image had become detached almost entirely from its original 'literary' context and the many humorous and quasi-theological commentaries on modern society that it contained. These were most certainly 'lost in translation'.

Property may express a sense of being, an ontology, quite at variance with the intentions of the originators of the product. This simple fact promotes a range of seismic shifts when its implications are traced. To take a rather different example, Bryan Turner suggests firstly in a recent book that, speaking specifically of Islam, 'the main threat to religious faith is in fact the commodification of everyday life' – rather than cognitive challenges, that is (Turner 1994: 9). For Islam, with its doctrinal clarity, central and authoritative set of scriptures and typical form of cultural expression, this is almost certainly true. But, as we suggested above, Japanese religion has often responded to the threat of commodification by commercializing itself. This can be seen in many of the *Shin-shukyo*, or New Religions, some of which, such as Soka Gakkai, have promoted a system of ethics very convergent with the demands of business existence and a materialistic lifestyle. In a religious culture in which memorial services, or *kuyo*, are held not only for the dead and for *mizuko*, or the foetuses of aborted children, but also, on occasions for used needles (*hari kuyo*), tea whisks, eels (a favourite item in the Japanese diet) and even used brassieres, the commodification of everyday life has a quite different impact on religion (LaFleur 1992: 144-6).

Such considerations take us to the issue of the general configuration of intellectual culture in Japan and its political orientation. Lifestyles, or at least images of possible lifestyles, are formed out of such material. Japanese political culture is characterized by the absence of ideologically motivated political conflict, the lack of involvement on the part of the average citizen in wider political or even community life and the general organization of lifestyles around consumption rather than issues or religious motivations or identities. But, at the same time, Japan is enmeshed in the global network of knowledge, money, media and styles that influences, in varying degrees, every society. The result is that in innumerable subtle ways the relationship of the individual to the 'system' has altered.

The movement from the primary orientation to work as the central value to consumption in the market place is one of the most important indicators of such a shift in contemporary Japan, in which 'seduction' rather than repression becomes the main form of social control and in which a bigger range of more individual lifestyles that deviate from traditional social forms begins to take place. But again the specific characteristics of this transition as it occurs in Japan need to be directly addressed. So when Callinicos speaks of the defining feature of post-modernity as being 'the fragmentary, heterogeneous and plural character of reality' marked by the shift from structuralism to post-structuralist epistemology (Callinicos 1989: 2), three questions arise when this definition is applied to Japan. The first is the question of epistemology. Philosophical discussion in Japan has never been dominated by questions of epistemology, but rather by ontology. Japanese discourse is closer to the ideas of the human's relationship to the world sketched out by Heidegger and Wittgenstein than it is to the logical positivism or analytical theorizing of many Western frameworks. Concern is with being rather than knowing, with practice (doing) rather than knowledge. The primary philosophical relationship to the world and the phenomenal is consequently very different, and this is presumably part of the basis of the idea that Japan not only is, but always in some sense has been, postmodern: something akin to the postmodernist stance in the West is already an intellectually dominant tradition.

The second question relates to the nature or conception of time. In traditional Japanese aesthetics time is understood not as duration, but as transience, and in religion (specifically Buddhism) as cyclical. It is often not appreciated by social scientists how deeply images of the nature of time enter into the phenomenology both of everyday life and of the structuring of social systems. The understanding of time, culturally conceived, is one of the main forms of orientation to social life. In many Western and Middle Eastern traditions time not only represents progress, but contains a moral purpose either (or both) in the macro-sense (as the medium of Revelation) or in the micro-sense (saving time, using it efficiently, refusing the temptations of idleness). But where these considerations do not apply, an individual's relationship to social practice changes. The enjoyment of the ephemeral, the recognition of transience as all pervasive and the unwillingness to ascribe any particular moral content to the use of time, all create exactly the conditions in which consumerism can flourish. A concern with the temporary, a preoccupation with fashion, a passion for novelty, all are expressions of a temporal orientation as much as they are of economic attitudes or forces.

The third question relates to social practice. Elements of relativism and provisionality may be present in 'post-structuralist' Japanese culture, but this has not led to a fragmented social world. The link between culture and social organization is not the one that might be expected – a very important theoretical point suggesting that the relationship between ideology and practice is an oblique and rarely, if ever, a direct one.

The lifestyles that are constructed from the elements on offer in late Japanese capitalism are formed within a framework which, if undergoing its own subtle transformations, nevertheless provides a fairly constant template for social relations. Cultural 'postmodernism' takes place within the boundaries of a sociological 'structuralism'. Much of the theoretical and comparative interest in Japan on the part of sociologists should stem precisely from this fact. So while the boundaries of the socially acceptable in Japan are slowly extended, they are by no means abandoned, and civility still rules. Many of the characteristics of postmodernity identified by Jameson (1991) – depthlessness, the stressing of surfaces and images, ahistoricism, subjectivist epistemology, stress on technology, the employment of pastiche, the play of invention rather than realism, episodicity rather than coherent sequential discourses – are indeed present in Japan as cultural themes. But Jameson, in common with many postmodern theorists, does not adequately distinguish the cultural expressions of postmodernity, often in any case confined to an artistic elite, and their relationship to social organization. The precise theorization of this link is a major challenge, since it remains as a central problem for sociology and has done so since it was first systematically identified by Weber in his analysis of the origins of capitalism.

The postmodernity question also raises the issue of resistance in a post- (or, in the Japanese case, non-)foundationalist situation. How, in other words, might one construct a critical sociology of emancipation in Japan? The Japanese political economy is characterized by its mass-production methods, corporatist industrial relations, statism, bureaucracy and substantial systemic corruption in the political and industrial systems. Furthermore, the old potential organizing symbols – emperor, nation, fascism – have proved to be historically very unsuccessful. Dean MacCannell's provocative idea that the appearance of postmodernity in the midst of such conditions leads to the emergence of what he terms 'soft fascism' (MacCannell 1992: 187, 211), with its own distinctive aesthetics, has considerable applicability here. Norma Field's suggestion in her study of modes of resistance in contemorary Japan (Field 1992) that, especially for young Japanese, consumption is the only available form of opposition to this 'soft fascisim' is an interesting one that potentially expands the idea of consumption-as-expression into the idea of consumption-as-resistance.

At least since Tokugawa times the ordinary Japanese has experienced top-down control, intensified after the Meiji Restoration by the establishment of a centralized bureaucracy and compounded by the pressures of capitalist work with the emergence of industrialization. Even during the Tokugawa period consumption was experienced as emancipation, and the flowering of townspeople's culture, especially in Edo (Tokyo) and the other castle towns, partly reflects their status at the bottom of the Tokugawa social hierarchy. Unable to penetrate the samurai class, townspeople turned their energy to commerce and culture, and many of the forms of Japanese 'traditional' arts and theatre (for example Kabuki) were the result of the flowering of a consumer class cut off from meaningful political participation. If the modern rationalist project was never fully accepted in Japan, something that created other spaces and other meanings than in the West, its positive advantages including fairly clear notions of social 'justice', were not imported either. The continuous succession of scandals which marks public life in Japan (in early 1996, for example, the collapse of *jusen*, or savings and loans companies, across the country, the discovery that a major TV company had leaked sensitive information to the Aum Shinrikyo religious cult resulting in the abduction and murder of an anti-cult lawyer, his wife and young child, and the revelation that the Ministry of Health had been knowingly importing HIV-injected blood that had subsequently been administered to haemophiliacs and that government ministries involved in the first and third of these scandals were engaged in massive and systematic cover-ups) has deeply undermined public confidence in institutions.

The project of democratization, very high on the agenda after the war and during the movement against the security treaty and among the student movement of the 1960s, has been buried in the co-opting techniques and corporatist politics of the 1970s through to the 1990s. Freedom for many has consequently come to be seen as freedom of consumption, despite the recognition that the market is itself constructed, and manipulated by the media and by capitalist enterprises. Such media-carried consumerism, while fostering the illusion of free choice of lifestyles, actually promotes both mass narcissism and historical amnesia. A real grasp of modern Japanese history has been replaced by a fantasy history expressed through the medium of theme parks, many of which are actually a disguised form of nationalism. The lack of access to real power for the average Japanese, the blandness of most broadcasting and the interlocking structure of the media (with TV, newspapers, magazines, book publications, sports and numerous derivatives such as toys representing the figures in cartoon stories), together with the enormous lack of real educational alternatives or experiments, provides a comfortable and, for most people, except the failed consumers or those for some reason outside of the nexus of consumption (foreign workers, daily-rated labourers, the handicapped), an affluent environment, but, as the Japanese so often complain, also a stifling one. The *furusato* movement can be seen partly as the local and the particular striking back – as a form of local democracy somewhat beyond the centralizing and urban-dominated forces of the cities.

At one level this all simply reflects the paradoxical nature of the media

– owned by big business yet capable of creating a public sphere (of consumption) that lies beyond politics. Seen from this perspective, consumerism actually trains people in the techniques of argument and knowledge acquisition denied them by both the political and the educational systems. Civil society in Japan therefore has its sources outside of political processes proper and in some cases in opposition to them. 'Depoliticization' then takes on a special meaning in Japan, where there is strong public sentiment about, for example, political corruption and where there is a huge amount of information in circulation – information that can be employed for a vast variety of purposes. It results, for example, in the widespread character of popular culture, a world that contains its own 'experts', and can be seen, together with consumption, as constituting a form of 'positive politics'. So while there is indeed expressive consumption in Japan (the creation of individual identities through consumption), it is also the case that political issues increasingly tend to be expressed through the market place. Concern with industrial pollution and waste has bred green politics which in turn has bred green consumption (health foods, recycling, non-animal-tested cosmetics, the wearing of natural fibres, etc.). All freedoms are constrained by a wider context in which they are exercised, and freedom as consumption or choice of lifestyle, while new to Japan, is still a 'freedom' that occurs within the framework of a capitalist and media-dominated society in which the workplace remains a potent factor and where hierarchy if not class is still a central organizing principle.

IDENTITY, MODERNITY, CONSUMPTION

The relationship between the global and the local again becomes important here. International forms are assimilated to the local culture, and that 'local culture' is now 'Japanizing' the world. Foreign models too are significant in promoting the construction of new images of and possibilities for selfhood, and new strategies of individualism have appeared, especially in the last two decades. So while Japanese society as a whole may have no ideology of individualism, there are many individualistic practices. Self-cultivation, a practice (or wide range of practices) with its roots in Confucianism, is, for example, an ancient art in Japan, and is not confused or identified with narcissism. Selfishness is condemned, and strong social sanctions exist to minimize its manifestations, but auto-development is a duty. What is interesting about the contemporary situation is that modern subjectivities are constructed in ways rather different from those of the past, and are constructed principally through consumption. Such self-cultivation needs then to be seen as a dynamic process in two dimensions – historically and in terms of the life-course, both set in the context of social values (which are themselves not essentialistic, but evolving). Notions of aesthetic transience and institutional (especially kinship) permanence can go together, a further rejection of the indirect links between culture and social structure, related by an inner logic of several dimensions.

Consequently identity itself can be constructed in more than one way. In his analysis of consumption in Trinidad Miller demonstrates how, in that ethnographic context, identity is tied to the event. Status, in other words, does not accrete and is not permanent, but must be constantly created anew at the next carnival, the next dance party, with the next purchase, in a preoccupation with 'style'. At first sight this would seem to be the obverse of the Japanese situation, and so at the level of the continuity of social roles it is. But at another level the logic of cultural relations links the two situations geographically and social-structurally so remote from each other. Japanese culture is often accused of being obsessed with 'surfaces', with appearances and with 'wrapping', as being a culture of depthlessness. In its concern with 'style' Trinidadian culture has many of the same features, but, as Miller points out, their consequences for an analysis of what he calls modernity are subtle but extremely important.

> The concept of the superficial is entirely inappropriate here. Certainly things are kept on the surface, and it is style rather than content that counts . . . This is because the surface is precisely where 'being' is located. It is the European philosophical tradition, and in particular the ultra-conservatism of philosophers such as Heidegger, for whom being and rootedness are effectively synonymous, that makes it difficult to understand how the very possibilities of modernist speed and ephemera can become the vehicles for both viable and authentic existence. (Miller 1994b: 311)

They clearly can, especially when, as in Japan, they are located within a social structure that stresses continuity. The changing and the relatively unchanging, agency and structure, are related often in ways undreamed of in conventional structuration theory (Giddens 1983).

Modernity then, as we have stressed before, is experienced in different ways and coped with in varying fashions. And the present and its objective conditions (capitalist, dominated by consumption and staged by the media) is where daily life and 'lifestyles' are fashioned, and where tradition is, at least in Japan, not replaced but transformed. New subjectivities made possible through the existence of such opportunities as travel come into being as a result of changes in objective conditions, but in turn modify and reinterpret those same conditions. The attempt to construct identity through objects (consumption, in other words) inevitably comes up against the problem that objects never quite fulfil expectations. This self-limitation of consumerism is balanced in Japan, however, by the recognition of the need for an inner life, the primary orientations of which are towards some idea of the deep self (as in some forms of Buddhist practices) or towards nature. The self as it appears in public encounters (the 'role') is still very important in Japan, even though it increasingly coexists with the idea of a genuine inner self separate from its public presentation (an old theme in Japanese literature). Such a model of the self allows for the embracing of conformity together with space for expression of individuality. The extraordinary prevalence of the erotic in contemporary Japanese popular culture, especially the *manga*, the popular novel, and movies, is a clue to this, the erotic being the space in which social rules and nature coexist and interact, as well as being a zone of freedom (like drunkeness in Japan) in which a deeper self can emerge and be recognized by others as valid.

Self-creation, whether pursued through consumption, the erotic, work or the traditional arts (in practice usually through all or most of these), takes place within boundaries. This of course is not unique to Japan. As Foucault tirelessly pointed out, there are powerful controls within what appears to be freedom, but what he did not often mention was that the disenchantment of the world resulting from the rise of abstraction and abstracted rationalities can be very much held at bay by the concreteness of everyday life, the way of life most celebrated in Japanese indigenous identity. This suggests that the 'premodern' and even the 'postmodern' can nestle within the modern, or rather that the concrete can exist within a universe of abstracting forces without it being necessary to invoke the language of pre/modern/post at all, probably a clarifying move in the linguistic and conceptual confusion of so much contemporary cultural studies.

The commodity then is linked to actual lifestyles – daily lived experience – and is not simply reducible to abstract rationalities. People's awareness of alienation is countered not primarily through political action but through the management of lifestyles. As Miller again suggests in his study of mass consumption in Trinidad, 'it is quite possible for a group of people, who focus their sense of identity upon strategies of fashion and style, to use these same elements of the modern as their main instrument of identity construction. Mass consumption itself may serve equally well as an instrument for confronting as the medium for creating the sense of alienation' (Miller 1994b: 74). If alienation arises mainly through a sense of disempowerment, control of one's everyday world, and of skill in the management of objects and symbols, is a powerful antidote. As Miller shows, and as MacCannell demonstrates in his analysis of contemporary tourism, the theorist of the modern or the postmodern must confront individual and particular instances. General theory can be enlightening, but the besetting sin of most postmodernists is to hide behind it rather than to use it as a way of illuminating the particular. Consumption can be expressive in different ways; values are implicated in it in varying forms. Societies which, like Trinidad, have experienced colonialism, dependency and underdevelopment, and are in addition fundamentally multi-ethnic, have radically different experiences from a society like Japan. The sense of the creation of identity through possessions and the acquisition of possessions as expressions of personality, role, status, age and gender are real (Dittmar 1992), but nevertheless need to be contextualized in a wider cultural and political setting, specific in many cases to individual societies and the peculiarities of their unique historical experience.

COMMODITY, AESTHETICS AND EVERYDAY LIFE

Everyday life is not just daily grind: it is also the arena of play and pleasure. As Maffesoli suggests in his study of the sensibilities in contemporary life, 'Donc voilà l'hypothèse: il y a un hédonisme du quotidien irrépressible et puissant qui soustend et soutient toute vie en societe. Une structure anthropologique en quelque sorte' (Maffesoli 1990: 13). This 'hedonism of the everyday' is expressed in the pleasures of the senses, the play of forms and the intrusion of the 'futile' – the non-utilitarian – into daily life, and occurs in relation, most of the time, to quite ordinary objects. The attraction to spectacle is for Maffesoli an important aspect of this. In such a world aesthetics rather than ethics becomes the primary mode of relating to the social environment, a tendency promoted by the complexity of modern society and the failure of the big solutions to its accumulating problems. This 'reign of appearances' promotes a culture concerned with elegance, with the erotic, with emotions, and creates a mode of being deeply concerned with the body. And it expresses itself in effervescence, in a serious concern with the aesthetics of food (Mitsukuni and Tsune 1989) with *asobi* – 'play' – and the proliferation of images, and in the continual stimulation of both the senses and the emotions (Mitsukuni, Ikko and Tsune 1987). The result is the exaltation of everday consciousness, considerable reverence for *mingei* – folk art – an art without dominant figures – a lack of any monumental architecture and a society without heroes. This privileging of the phenomenal world is perhaps best traditionally expressed in *ukiyo* – the idea of the 'floating world'.

The commodity then is not necessarily something needed, but is the expression of desire and fantasy approachable often only through a (culturally contextualized) semiotics rather than through economics. Here at least we can agree with Baudrillard that consumption has become the basis of the social order and its internal classifications. But when he goes on to argue that consumption is to be analysed by linguistic categories rather than Marxist, Freudian or needs theories (Baudrillard 1988a), he traps himself typically in Western logocentrism. He does not sufficiently pursue the idea of desire, and, while consumer objects up to a point constitute a system of signs, these signs must also be read culturally, and the logic of particular systems explicated ethnographically. Those who consume also labour, for instance, and while there is a problem of creating communication in a world dominated by media, it clearly does occur, especially at the level of everyday life. The pessimism of Baudrillard's ideas, and especially the victory of 'hyper-reality' and the domination of simulacra, where the distinction between objects and representations is no longer valid as the image absorbs the real into itself, does not by any means map fully onto Japanese society, where the concreteness of everyday life and the continuities of social structure compete with the 'virtual' quality of only some aspects of mass culture. The position of de Certeau that people in practice reinscribe their own meanings onto the manifestations of mass culture and thus achieve a means of resistance is more realistic. Baudrillard's finding of only system in the clutter of objects that provide the material framework for daily life is over-optimistic: 'The system of needs has become less integrated than the system of objects; the latter imposes its own coherence and thus acquires the capacity to fashion an entire society' (Baudrillard 1988a: 14). Not entirely, and in any case Baudrillard sees needs rather than desires as the basis of practice – a view that requires challenging.

In fact, of course, many, possibly most, objects do in some sense fulfil needs of some order, and objects themselves do not, as Baudrillard suggests, 'tyranically induce categories of persons' (1988a: 17). Of deeper interest in Baudrillard than these flights of hyperbole is the very real insight that consumption is the basis of the whole cultural system in the affluent industrialized societies: 'We are living in the period of the objects: that is we live by their rhythm, according to their incessant cycles' (1988a: 29). The pregnant suggestion that consumption is 'a frustrated desire for totality' (1988a: 25) certainly provides a potential perspective on this cultural system that avoids the moralizing stricture of the Frankfurt school approach to mass culture.

Aesthetics may involve or promote new relationships to ethics. It also implies a central place for that most neglected of elements in Western sociology – the emotions. Desire by definition involves feeling: it is feeling. It is an orientation of affective intention towards objects, other people or states of mind. Desire can be for other desires – the pursuit of happiness, for example – and its fulfilment is supposed to bring satisfaction and its frustration negative states felt both mentally and somatically. Although usually understood as feeling and as a psychological disposition, it also in practice very much involves the body. The desire to do things with the body and for the body – to feed it, decorate it, touch or be touched, to have erotic encounters – is among the primary desires, although desires of the mind and sensibilities are also important. However, these too usually turn out to be mediated by the body – enjoying music for example. Desire, consumption and embodiment are three aspects of the same whole.

The analysis of consumption places the emotions back at the centre of the sociological enterprise. Just as the last decade has seen the body reintroduced into social analysis, now it is the turn of the emotions, even though their sociological treatment remains difficult. At the very least, the study of consumption demonstrates that the presumption, whether in sociology or in economics, of the purely rational actor is false. Rationality, the sifting of information, the making of informed choices, exists as a central part of the consumption process, especially when needs are involved. But where consumption is dominated by desire, altogether other factors come into play: fantasy, imagination, erotic yearnings, utopian expectations. Indeed consumption is now the primary mechanism through which new structures of social relations, affectively and subjectively, come into being. These new relations are literally 'inscribed on the body' in many cases, and new forms of physical behaviour (e.g. in shopping, fashion, diet, cosmetics, exercise, eating) express new social patterns, attitudes and dispositions. Rhythms of social life are changed and new cycles instituted. What Bourdieu calls the 'structuring structures' of social life – the means by which societies reproduce themselves – come no longer to be dominated by agricultural cycles, but by cycles of consumption. Seasonality is no longer just a product of climate, but of the shopping calendar. Spring becomes a time of new sales rather than new life; rather, perhaps, new life is symbolized by new purchases. Seasonality is governed then by the cycle of fashion, and the old (in this case a genuine concern in Japan with the changing of the seasons and with wearing 'appropriate' clothes for the time of year) intersects with the new in subtle and complex ways. Nature and consumption interpenetrate each other as fashion and food (such as eating *unagi* or eel in the hot season) rather than ritual marks the transitions of the year.

Seasonality is but one example of the intersection of a 'commercial logic' with a 'practical logic', and in the process the system of symbols is transformed by being employed in new and different social contexts – inside or outside the home, for example, where the traditional distinction between *uchi* and *soto* is inscribed in new forms of practice (advertising,

youth behaviour), something that has still not occurred to many anthropologists of Japan, for whom these terms remain classifications. Symbolic
power is not created just by the accumulation of cultural capital, but
increasingly through the ability to manipulate and negotiate these border
areas of symbolic transformation.

A 'traditional' society for Bourdieu (Bourdieu 1977) is one in which
'practical logic' (which implies a multiplicity of sometimes confused and
contradictory, but always commonsensical and strategic, approaches to
meaning) dominates. Actions in such a society are neither specifically
'economic' nor 'religious' nor anything else: they merge with one another. Japan in these terms is a 'traditional' society, not in the sense of
being dominated by custom or by the past, but in terms of possessing and
employing multiple points of reference. The possession of an object or its
aesthetic qualities are fluidly independent of any fixed meaning. It is for
this reason that Japan has been able to imitate the lifestyles of the capitalist West without generating the puritanical ethos associated by Weber
with capitalist behaviour. What becomes necessary is to insert an analysis
of aesthetic culture into the study of 'general' and economic culture. The
dawning recognition of this requires the incorporation of the study of
body practices such as eating habits (Falk 1994) into the sociological and
anthropological analysis of contemporary society. Where Weber saw the
basis of capitalism in a system of ethics, in late capitalism in general and
in Japan in particular it is more realistic to seek it in a system of aesthetics.

THE COMMODITY AND THE GIFT CULTURE

On a number of occasions it has been necessary to discuss the nature of
the gift relationship as it expresses itself in Japanese culture, and here I
must return briefly to this point again. Seen from one perspective Japan
is clearly a society dominated by the commodity form. But at the same
time the gift relationship remains as extremely important and almost an
index of morality. Any idea of a 'pure commodity' economy is profoundly modified by this fact. Just as the continuities of social structure
set limits around the deconstructive potentialities of postmodern cultural
forms, so the gift relationship constrains and orders the seductive capitalism of the commodity form. Indeed it channels them in what might in
functionalist terms be seen as 'socially useful' directions – the creating
and sustaining of relationships, the creation of networks and the bonding
of groups (say secretaries and their bosses) who might otherwise be separated and even antagonistic. But of course these gift relationships today
take place within the commodity form, utilizing commodities in some
sense to transcend the commodity.

A number of important anthropological consequences stem from this. Consumption becomes primary, rather than accumulation, both in the consumer society and in the gift economy, the first through purchasing and using and the second through exchange and prestation. In both there is a strong element of hedonism: in the first the economy of leisure is central and in the second excess, the potlatch principle. In both, in Japan, bargaining is non-existent. Waste and expenditure are the essence of both. The priority of social relationships over the needs of the market is at least symbolically stressed in Japanese society in general and in the gift relationship in particular. Japan demonstrates very clearly the 'uneven development' of modern societies in which commoditization is by no means fully triumphant, at least in that its forms are modified and reorganized by the presence of older and possibly more persistent values.

There is a convergence in this reading of the place of the commodity in Japan with some of Baudrillard's early ideas. A question raised by Baudrillard as early as the 1970s was that of the effects on social structure and culture of the rise of consumption and affluence, a question that precipitated his break with Marxism. For Baudrillard this issue raised the problem of the relation of symbolic exchange to commodity exchange, which for him is more fundamental than the classical Marxist distinction between use value and exchange value. Baudrillard's conclusion of the superiority of the symbolic order (the gift) over the semiotic order (the cash nexus) is a telling observation in relation to Japan (Baudrillard 1972), as was his suggestion that it is through consumption that social integration in class societies is now achieved (Baudrillard 1970), bringing with it resistance through passivity and hyperconformity. For Baudrillard, however, affluence is also repression, but a repression that moves from physical force to 'seduction'. The potential abstraction of modern life – leading rapidly to alienation – is, however, as I have suggested, resisted in Japan both through the continuing concreteness of everyday life and through the gift relationship. The successful maintenance of social relationships in a commoditized economy has become, one might argue, the 'goal' of contemporary Japanese society and insofar as it is successful, its greatest achievement. Baudrillard's own growing pessimism is perhaps partly the product of his lack of any comparative perspective. His suggestion that, 'in the immense polymorphous machine of contemporary capital, the symbolic (gift and counter-gift, reciprocity and reversal, expenditure and sacrifice) no longer counts for anything, nature . . . no longer counts' (Baudrillard 1993: 35) is precisely the opposite to the interpretation being advanced here.

To find out why it is necessary to burrow a little deeper. Freudianism has made little inroads into Japan, which might be said to be a culture in which the unconscious does not exist. Emotions yes, and certainly will, emerging from what is essentially a Buddhist conception of mind. But an 'inner life' in a Western sense is not high in the agenda, and Japanese intellectual culture is not given to psychologizing, surely one of the chief deficiencies of Western social science. 'Depth' is not sought in the unconscious, but rather in social forms. As MacCannell very perceptively notes in relation to postmodern theories in general, 'The claim to 'depthlessness' on a theoretical level appears as an alibi for some older cultural forms: the honouring of fathers and families and the ancient power arrangements between them, and a mythic sense of a deep convergence of biological and cultural reproduction' (MacCannell 1992: 288). A similar point can be made about the alleged aesthetic of depthlessness or of the purity or specificity of art in Japan. In fact, as Moeran notes, 'what often passes for 'aesthetic' is, in fact, an amalgam of what the Japanese themselves refer to as 'aesthetic' (*biteki kankaku*), 'commodity' (*shohin kachikan*), and 'social' (*shakai kankaku*) values' (Moeran 1990: 132). Presenting a surface, even aesthetically, may conceal depths that may turn out to be not necessarily aesthetic at all, but social, or once again the commoditized.

The act of consumption then is not just one thing. It can be an expression of the self or an attempt to create an identity; it can be a gesture of nostalgia or evidence of 'competence' – the ability, socially very valued in Japan, to produce a 'correct performance' in a given setting; it can be a way of dealing with the internal tensions of contemporary Japanese society, a way of accumulating cultural capital and of achieving status in a society that denies the validity of class. For some theorists in the West the consumer society, the ability to construct identities and lifestyles out of consumption choices, has come to be dubbed 'post-industrial'. In fact in Japan modes of production (work) and modes of consumption coexist and interpenetrate, as they presumably do in all capitalist societies. The rationality of consumption presupposed by liberal individualism in the West is modified by the non-existence of that identity in Japan. Japan is perhaps not so much 'post-industrial' as 'post-individualist'. Indeed in some wider sense one does not need the individual at all, not only in the way that Maffesoli argues in his theory of neo-tribalism, but in the sense that commodities need not refer to human needs at all, but begin to reproduce themselves according to a logic not simply of economic expansion, but of the proliferation of novelty on a principle analogous to that of the growth of cancerous cells: there is no need, and they may eventually destroy their host and hence themselves, but nevertheless they grow, impelled by some fierce inner logic.

The mass consumer society is still a very new phenomenon in Asia. Even in its beginnings among the Edo townspeople of the seventeenth century it was concealed, restricted by sumptuary laws and the rural nature of most of the society. If the prototype consumer society was England, in Japan its rapid and unprecedented expansion has flowed along other channels. In both consumption meant the liberation of desire (and imagination) rather than its containment. But this liberation, although it has brought about competitiveness in the economy, has done so while minimizing the envy and avarice thought by early Western capitalist theoreticians to be the necessary basis of the consumer society. Consumption and civility, expressed in ideas of service, quality, the gift relationship, the suppression of overt displays of status difference and public policy such as the punitive inheritance tax, coexist. Contained within this is the fact that consumers do not only act rationally, but are impelled by emotion, imagination, the erotic and the 'darker' sides of the human character (tribalism and display, for example) in a continual dance of creativity within and beyond the market. Consumption prevents one from being excluded from the club; consuming the same things as everybody else reinforces this sense of belonging. It is, furthermore, an evolving phenomenon: the very ephemerality of taste not only drives consumption forward, but prevents any one of its forms ever becoming totalitarian: fashion may create temporary bonds, but it also creates long-term diversity. Symbols not only decend from above, but are constantly reframed anew by those who consume them.

The consumer society is still new in Japan: it is very dynamic, heterogenenous and, like all mass societies, contains elements of contradiction. No closure can be imposed upon its direction or interpretation. Two major questions nevertheless weave themselves throughout its analysis. One is empirical: how is the management of consumption (and of its specific elements like leisure and travel) organized in terms of its relationship to the logics of Japanese culture? The second is theoretical and comparative: with mass consumption becoming a universal fact of life, does Japan demonstrate a way in which the economics of affluence and the culture of civility can be combined?

References

Aoki, M. (1988) *Information, Incentives and Bargaining in the Japanese Economy*. Cambridge: Cambridge University Press.

Aoki, M. (1989) 'The nature of the Japanese firm as a nexus of employment and financial contracts: an overview', *Journal of the Japanese and International Economies*, 3, 345–66.

Appadurai, A. (ed.) (1986) *The Social Life of Things*. New York: Cambridge University Press.

Arnason, J. and Sugimoto, Y. (eds) (1996) *Japanese Encounters with Postmodernity*. London: Kegan Paul.

Asada, A. (1984) *Tosoron*. Tokyo: Chikuna Shobo.

Asahi nenkan (1995) Tokyo: Asahi Shinbunsha.

Ashihara, Y. (1989) *The Hidden Order: Tokyo Through the Twentieth Century*. Tokyo: Kodansha International.

Barthes, R. (1970) *L'empire des signes*. Geneva: Les Sentiers de la Création.

Barthes, R. (1975) *The Pleasure of the Text*. New York: Hill & Wang.

Barthes, R. (1984) *The Fashion System*. New York: Hill & Wang.

Bataille, G. (1985) *Visions of Excess: Selected Writings 1927–39*. Minneapolis: University of Minnesota Press.

Baudrillard, J. (1970) *La société de consommation*. Paris: Gallimard.

Baudrillard, J. (1972) *Pour une critique de l'économie du signe*. Paris: Gallimard.

Baudrillard, J. (1988a) *Selected Writings*, ed. M. Poster. Stanford, CA: Stanford University Press.

Baudrillard, J. (1988b) *America*. London: Verso.

Baudrillard, J. (1993) *Symbolic Exchange and Death*. London: Sage.

Bauman, Z. (1994) *Postmodern Ethics*. Oxford: Blackwell.

Beck, U. (1994) *Risk Society: Towards a New Modernity.* London: Sage.

Befu, H. (1968) 'Gift-giving in a modernizing Japan', *Monumenta Nipponica*, 23, 445–56.

Benedict, R. (1946) *The Chrysanthemum and the Sword: Patterns of Japanese Culture.* Boston: Houghton Mifflin.

Berque, A. et al. (eds) (1994) *Cinq propositions pour une théorie du paysage.* Paris: Editions Champ Vallon.

Bestor, T. C. (1989) *Neighborhood Tokyo.* Stanford, CA: Stanford University Press.

Bocock, R. (1993) *Consumption.* London: Routledge.

Bourdieu, P. (1977) *Outline of a Theory of Practice.* Cambridge: Cambridge University Press.

Bourdieu, P. (1984) *Distinction: A Social Critique of the Judgement of Taste.* Cambridge, MA: Harvard University Press.

Bourdieu, P. (1985) 'The social space and the genesis of groups', *Social Science Information*, 24/2, 195–220.

Brannan, M. Y. (1992) 'Bwana Mickey: constructing cultural consumption at Tokyo Disneyland', in J. J. Tobin (ed.) *Remade in Japan: Everyday Life and Consumer Taste in a Changing Society.* New Haven,CT: Yale University Press, 216–34.

Buruma, I. (1984) *A Japanese Mirror: Heroes and Villains of Japanese Culture.* London: Jonathan Cape.

Buruma, I. (1996) *The Missionary and the Libertine: Love and War in East and West.* London: Faber & Faber.

Calhoun, C. (1991) 'Indirect relationships and imagined communities: large scale social integration and the transformation of everyday life', in P. Bourdieu and J. S. Coleman (eds) *Social Theory for a Changing World.* Boulder, CO: Westview Press, 95–121.

Callinicos, A. (1989) *Against Postmodernism.* Cambridge: Polity Press.

Campbell, C. (1987) *The Romantic Ethic and the Spirit of Modern Consumerism.* Oxford: Blackwell.

Castells, M. (1978) *City, Class and Power.* London: Macmillan.

Chambers, I. (1994) *Migrancy, Culture, Identity.* London: Routledge.

Clammer, J. (ed.) (1978) *The New Economic Anthropology.* London: Macmillan.

Clammer, J. (1985) *Anthropology and Political Economy: Theoretical and Asian Perspectives.* London: Macmillan.

Clammer, J. (1995a) *Difference and Modernity: Social Theory and Contemporary Japanese Society.* London: Kegan Paul.

Clammer, J. (1995b) 'Discourses of ethnicity and the international division of labor: migrant workers, state and society in contemporary Japan', *Japan Christian Review*, 61;19–33.

Cole, R. E. (1971) *Japanese Blue Collar.* Berkeley, CA: University of California Press.

Coward, S. (1987) *Female Desire.* London: Palladin.

Cybriwsky, R. (1991) *Tokyo.* London: Belhaven Press.

Debord, J. (1983) *The Society of the Spectacle.* Detroit: Black and Red.

de Certeau, M. (1984) *The Practice of Everyday Life.* Berkeley, CA: University of California Press.

Dittmar, H. (1992) *The Social Psychology of Material Possessions.* Hemel Hempstead: Harvester Wheatsheaf.

Doi, T. (1973) *Amae no kozo.* Tokyo: Kobundo [Eng. trans. as *The Anatomy of Dependence.* Tokyo: Kodansha International, 1988].

Dore, R. P. (1967) *City Life in Japan: A Study of a Tokyo Ward.* Berkeley, CA: University of California Press.

Douglas, M. (1994) *Risk and Blame: Essays in Cultural Theory.* London: Routledge.

Douglas, M. and Isherwood, B. (1979) *The World of Goods.* New York: Basic Books.

Eccleston, B. (1989) *State and Society in Postwar Japan.* Cambridge: Polity Press.

Edwards, W. (1989) *Modern Japan Through its Weddings: Gender, Person and Society in Ritual Portrayal.* Stanford, CA: Stanford University Press.

Ewen, S. (1988) *All Consuming Images.* New York: Basic Books.

Falk, P. (1994) *The Consuming Body.* London: Sage.

Featherstone, M. (1991a) 'The body in consumer society', in M. Featherstone, M. Hepworth and B. S. Turner (eds) *The Body: Social Process and Cultural Theory.* London: Sage.

Featherstone, M. (1991b) *Consumer Culture and Postmodernism.* London: Sage.

Field, N. (1992) *In the Realm of a Dying Emperor: Japan at Century's End.* New York: Vintage.

Frank, A. W. (1990) 'Bringing bodies back in: a decade review', *Theory, Culture and Society,* 7/1, 131–62.

Fujioka, W. (1984) *Sayonara taishu.* Tokyo: PHP.

Fujita, K. and Hill, R. C. (eds) (1993) *Japanese Cities in the World Economy.* Philadelphia: Temple University Press.

Fukutake, T. (1982) *The Japanese Social Structure.* Tokyo: University of Tokyo Press.

Funai, Y., Higa,T. and Watanabe, S. (1994) *Honmomo no seiki: paradaimu ga kawaru, ningen ga kawaru.* Tokyo: PHP.

Giddens, A. (1983) *Central Problems in Social Theory: Action, Structure and Contradiction in Social Analysis.* London: Macmillan.

Giddens, A. (1991) *Modernity and Self-Identity: Self and Society in the Late Modern Age.* Stanford, CA: Stanford University Press.

Gluck, C. (1985) *Japan's Modern Myths: Ideology in the Late Meiji Period.* Princeton, NJ: Princeton Universty Press.

Goffman, E. (1963) *Behaviour in Public Places.* New York: Free Press.

Goffman, E. (1969) *The Presentation of Self in Everyday Life.* Harmondsworth: Penguin.

Gordon, A. (ed.) (1993) *Postwar Japan as History.* Berkeley,CA: University of California Press.

Gosden, C. (1994) *Social Being and Time.* Oxford: Blackwell.

Gottdiener, M. (1995) *Postmodern Semiotics: Material Culture and the Forms of Postmodern Life.* Oxford: Blackwell.

Graburn, N. (1983) *To Pray, Pay and Play: The Cultural Structure of Japanese Domestic Tourism.* Aix-en-Provence: Centre des Hautes Etudes Touristiques.

Greenfeld, T. K. (1994) *Speed Tribes: Children of the Japanese Bubble.* London: Boxtree.

Hakuhodo Institute of Life and Living (1988) *Seikatsu shinbum.* Tokyo: Hakuhodo.

Harrison, P. (1995) 'The Japanese postmodern political condition,' in J. P. Arnason and Y. Sugimoto (eds) *Japanese Encounters with Postmodernity*. London: Kegan Paul, 213–36.

Harvey, D. (1989) *The Condition of Postmodernity*. Oxford: Blackwell.

Hasegawa, N. (1982) *The Japanese Character: A Cultural Profile*. Tokyo: Kodansha International.

Hendry, J. (1993) *Wrapping Culture: Politeness, Presentation and Power in Japan and Other Societies*. Oxford: Clarendon Press.

Hernadi, A. (1990) 'Consumption and consumerism in Japan', in A. Boscaro, F. Gatti and M. Raveri (eds) *Rethinking Japan*, vol. 2: *Social Sciences, Ideology and Thought*. Folkstone: Japan Library, 186–91.

Hobsbawm E. and Ranger, T. (eds) (1983) *The Invention of Tradition*. Cambridge: Cambridge University Press.

Horioka, C. Y. (1993) 'Consuming and saving', in A. Gordon (ed.) *Postwar Japan as History*. Berkeley, CA: University of California Press.

Imada, T. (1987) *Modan no datsukochiku*. Tokyo: Chuo Koronsha.

Imada, T. (1989) *Shakai–kaiso to seiji*. Tokyo: Daigaku Shuppan–kai.

Imamura, A. (1987) *Urban Japanese Housewives*. Honolulu: University of Hawaii Press.

Ishida, H. (1992) *Social Mobility in Contemporary Japan*. London: Macmillan.

Ishizuka, H. (1977) *Tokyo no shakai-kezai-shi*. Tokyo: Kinokuniya Shoten.

Isomura, E. (1981) *Chiho no jidai: sozo to sentaku no shihyo*. Tokyo: Tokai Daigaku.

Ivy, M. (1993) 'Formations of mass culture', in A. Gordon (ed.) *Postwar Japan as History*. Berkeley, CA: University of California Press.

Jameson, F. (1991) *Postmodernism, or the Cultural Logic of Late Capitalism*. London: Verso.

Kamashima, J. (1993) *Nihonjin no hasso*. Tokyo: Kodansha Gakujitsubunka.

Kamitakahara, M. and Kurotsu, T. (1990) *Oozutoraria*. Tokyo: Kadokawa Shoten.

Kato, A. (1994) 'Package tours, pilgrimages and pleasure trips', in A. Ueda (ed.) *The Electric Geisha: Exploring Japan's Popular Culture*. Tokyo: Kodansha International.

Kelly, W. W. (1993) 'Finding a place in metropolitan Japan: ideologies, institutions and everyday life', in A. Gordon (ed.) *Postwar Japan as History*. Berkeley, CA: University of California Press, 189–216.

Kenrick, D. M. (1990) *Where Communism Works: The Success of Competitive Communism in Japan*. Tokyo: Charles E. Tuttle.

Kinsella, S. (1995) 'Cuties in Japan', in L. Skov and B. Moeran (eds) *Women, Media and Consumption in Japan*. London: Curzon Press, 220–54.

Kondo, D. (1990) *Crafting Selves: Power, Gender and Discourses of Identity in a Japanese Workplace*. Chicago: University of Chicago Press.

Kosaka, K. (1995) 'Changing status perceptions in contemporary Japan: a debate on modernity and postmodernity', in J. P. Arnason and Y. Sugimoto (eds) *Japanese Encounters with Postmodernity*. London: Kegan Paul, 194–212.

Koseki, S. (1989) 'Japan: homo ludens Japonicus', in A. Olszewska (ed.) *Leisure and Lifestyle: A Comparative Analysis of Free Time*. London: Sage (Sage Studies in International Sociology 38), 115–42.

Knight, J. (1993) 'Rural *kokusaika*: foreign motifs and village revival in Japan', *Japan Forum*, 5/2, 203–16.

Kurasawa, S. (ed.) (1986) *Social Atlas of Tokyo*. Tokyo: Tokyo University Press.

LaFleur, W. R. (1992) *Liquid Life: Buddhism and Abortion in Japan*. Princeton, NJ: Princeton University Press.

Lam, A. (1992) *Women and Japanese Management*. London: Routledge.

Lash, S. and Urry, J. (1994) *Economies of Signs and Space*. London: Sage.

Lebra, T. S. (1982) *Japanese Patterns of Behavior*. Honolulu: University of Hawaii Press.

Lee, M. J. (1993) *Consumer Culture Reborn: The Cultural Politics of Consumption*. London: Routledge.

Lefebvre, H. (1971) *Everyday Life in the Modern World*. London: Allen Lane.

Lefebvre, H. (1991) *The Production of Space*. Oxford: Blackwell.

Lock, M. (1990) 'New Japanese mythologies: faltering discipline and the ailing housewife in Japan', in A. Boscaro, F. Gatti and M. Raveri (eds) *Rethinking Japan*, Vol. 2: *Social Sciences, Ideology and Thought*. Folkestone: Japan Library, 197–215.

Lyotard, J.-F. (1984) *The Postmodern Condition*. Minneapolis: University of Minnesota Press.

MacCannell, D. (1992) *Empty Meeting Grounds: The Tourist Papers*. London: Routledge.

McCracken, G. (1988) 'The evocative power of things: consumer goods and the preservation of hopes and ideals', in *Culture and Consumption: New Approaches to the Symbolic Character of Consumer Goods and Activities*. Bloomington: Indiana University Press, 104–17.

McDonald, K. I. (1983) *Cinema East: A Critical Study of Major Japanese Films*. Rutherford, NJ: Fairleigh Dickinson University Press.

McQuarrie, E. (1989) 'Advertising resonance: a semiological approach', in E. Hirschman (ed.) *Interpretive Consumer Research*. Provo, UT: Association for Consumer Research, 97–114.

Maffesoli, M. (1988) 'Affectual postmodernism and the megapolis', *Threshold IV*, 1.

Maffesoli, M. (1990) *Au creux des apparences*. Paris: Plon.

Maffesoli, M. (1996) *The Time of the Tribes: The Decline of Individualism in Mass Society*. London: Sage.

Maki, S. (1976) 'The postwar consumer movement – its emergence from a movement of women'. *Japan Quarterly*, 23, 135–9.

Management and Coordination Agency (1992) *Annual Report on the Family Income and Expenditure Survey*. Tokyo: MCA Statistical Bureau.

Martinez, D. P. (1990) 'Tourism and the *ama*: the search for a real Japan', in E. Ben-Ari, B. Moeran and J. Valentine (eds) *Unwrapping Japan: Society and Culture in Anthropological Perspective*. Manchester: Manchester University Press, 97–116.

Maruyama, M. (1969) *Thought and Behaviour in Modern Japanese Politics*. London: Oxford University Press.

Maruyama, M. (1985) 'Patterns of individuation and the case of Japan: a conceptual scheme', in M. B. Jansen (ed.) *Changing Japanese Attitudes toward Modernization*. Tokyo: Charles E. Tuttle.

Masumi, J. (1990) *Hikaku seiji: seio to nihon*. Tokyo: Tokyo Daigaku Shuppankai.

Matsumoto, K. (1991) *The Rise of the Japanese Corporate System*. London: Kegan Paul.

Matsumoto, M. (1988) *The Unspoken Way: Haragei*. Tokyo: Kodansha International.

Miller, D. (1994a) *Material Culture and Mass Consumption*. Oxford: Blackwell.

Miller, D. (1994b) *Modernity: An Ethnographic Approach*. Oxford: Berg.

Mitsukuni, Y and Tsune, S. (eds) (1989) *Naorai: Communion of the Table*. Hiroshima: Mazda.

Mitsukuni, Y., Ikko, T. and Tsune, S. (eds) (1987) *Asobi: The Sensibilities at Play*. Hiroshima: Mazda.

Miyamoto, K. (1993) 'Japan's world cities: Osaka and Tokyo', in K. Fujita and R. C. Hill (eds) *Japanese Cities in the World Economy*. Philadelphia: Temple University Press, 53–82.

Miyoshi, M. and Harootunian, H. D. (eds) (1989) *Postmodernism and Japan*. Durham, NC: Duke University Press.

Miyoshi, M. and Harootunian, H. D. (eds) (1993) *Japan in the World*. Durham, NC: Duke University Press.

Moeran, B. (1989) *Language and Popular Culture in Japan*. Manchester: Manchester University Press.

Moeran, B. (1990) 'Making an exhibition of oneself: the anthropologist as potter in Japan', in E. Ben-Ari, B. Moeran and J. Valentine (eds) *Unwrapping Japan: Society and Culture in Anthropological Perspective*. Manchester: Manchester University Press, 117–39.

Moeran, B. (1991) *Media and Advertising in Japan*. Copenhagen: Nordic Institute of Asian Studies.

Moeran, B. (1995) 'Reading Japanese in *Katei Gaho*: the art of being an upper class woman', in L. Skov and B. Moeran (eds) *Women, Media and Consumption in Japan*. London: Curzon Press, 111–42.

Mouer, R. (1995) 'Postmodernism or ultramodernism: the Japanese dilemma at work', In J. P. Arnason and Y. Sugimoto (eds) *Japanese Encounters with Postmodernity*. London: Kegan Paul.

Mouer, R. and Sugimoto, Y. (1986) *Images of Japanese Society*. London: Kegan Paul.

Murakami, Y. (1984) *Shin Chukan Taishu no Jidai*. Tokyo: Chuo Koransha.

Nakamura, H. (1993) 'Urban growth in prewar Japan', in K. Fujita and R. C. Hill (eds) *Japanese Cities in the World Economy*. Philadelphia: Temple University Press, 26–49.

Napier, S. J. (1995) *The Fantastic in Modern Japanese Literature: The Subversion of Modernity*. London: Routledge.

Nitta, F. (1992) 'Shopping for souvenirs in Hawaii,' in J. J. Tobin (ed). *Remade in Japan: Everyday Life and Consumer Taste in a Changing Society*. New Haven, CT: Yale University Press, 204–15.

Ohnuki-Tierney, E. (1993) *Rice as Self: Japanese Identities Through Time*. Princeton, NJ: Princeton University Press.

Oka, H. (1967) *How to Wrap Five Eggs*. Tokyo: Bijutsu Shuppan-sha.

Pahl, R. E. (1989) 'Is the emperor naked? Some questions on the adequacy of sociological theory in urban and regional research', *International Journal of Urban and Regional Research* ,13/4, 709–20.

Picone, M. (1989) 'The ghost in the machine: religious healing and representations of the body in Japan', in M. Feher (ed.) *Fragments for a History of the Human Body*, part 2. New York: Zone.

Plath, D. W. (ed) (1983) *Work and Lifecourse in Japan*. Albany, NY: State University of New York Press.

Powers, R. G. and Kato, H. (1989) *Handbook of Japanese Popular Culture*. Westport, CT: Greenwood Press.

Prus, R. (1989a) *Making Sales: Influence as a Personal Accomplishment*. Beverly Hills, CA: Sage.

Prus, R. (1989b) *Pursuing Consumers: An Ethnography of Marketing Activities*. Beverly Hills, CA: Sage.

Robertson, J. (1991) *Native and Newcomer: Making and Remaking a Japanese City*. Berkeley, CA: University of California Press.

Robison, R. and Goodman, D. S. G. (eds) (1996) *The New Rich in Asia: Mobile Phones, McDonalds and Middle Class Revolution*. London: Routledge.

Rohlen, T. P. (1979) *For Harmony and Strength: Japanese White Collar Organization in Anthropological Perspective*. Berkeley, CA: University of California Press.

Rosenberger, M. (1995) 'Antiphonal performances? Japanese women's magazines and women's voices', in L. Skov and B. Moeran (eds) *Women, Media and Consumption in Japan*. London: Curzon Press, 143–69.

Sahlins, M. (1972) *Stone Age Economics*. Chicago: Aldine.

Sahlins, M. (1976) *Culture and Practical Reason*. Chicago: Chicago University Press.

Sakada, T. (1984) *Atarashii chiiki shakai-zukuri*. Tokyo: Gyosei.

Saunders, P. (1986) *Social Theory and the Urban Question*. London: Hutchinson.

Seidensticker, E. (1983) *Low City, High City: Tokyo from Edo to the Earthquake*. Tokyo: Charles E. Tuttle.

Seidensticker, E. (1990) *Tokyo Rising: The City since the Great Earthquake*. New York: Alfred E. Knopf.

Sherry, J. and Camargo, E. (1987) 'May your life be marvellous: English language and the semiotics of Japanese promotion', *Journal of Consumer Research*, 14/2, 174–88.

Sherry, J., McGrath, M. A. and Levy, S. J. (1995) 'Monadic giving: anatomy of gifts given to the self', in J. Sherry (ed.) *Contemporary Marketing and Consumer Behavior: An Anthropological Sourcebook*. Thousand Oaks, CA: Sage.

Shields, R. (ed.) (1992) *Lifestyle Shopping: The Structure of Consumption*. London: Routledge.

Shilling, C. (1993) *The Body and Social Theory*. London: Sage.

Simmel, G. (1978) *The Philosophy of Money*. London: Routledge & Kegan Paul.

Skov, L. and B. Moeran (eds) (1995) *Women, Media and Consumption in Japan*. London: Curzon Press.

Spivak, G. (1990) "Reading *The Satanic Verses* '. *Third Text*, 11.

Steven, R. (1983) *Classes in Contemporary Japan*. Cambridge: Cambridge University Press.

Tobin, J. J. (ed.) (1992) *Remade in Japan: Everyday Life and Consumer Taste in a Changing Society*. New Haven, CT: Yale University Press.

Tominaga, K. (ed.) (1979) *Nihon no Kaiso Kozo*. Tokyo: Shuppankai.

Tsurumi, K. (1992) 'A theory of endogenous development with reference to Japan', in C. Nakana and C. Chiao (eds) *Homebound: Studies in East Asian*

Society. Tokyo: Tokyo Bunko.

Turner, B. S. (1984) *The Body and Society.* Oxford: Blackwell.

Turner, B. S. (1992) *Regulating Bodies: Essays in Medical Sociology.* London: Routledge.

Turner, B. S. (1994) *Orientalism, Postmodernism and Globalism.* London: Routledge.

Umesao, T. (1987) *Nihon santo ron.* Tokyo: Kadokawa.

van Wolferen, K. (1989) *The Enigma of Japanese Power.* London: Macmillan.

Vaporis, C. (1995) 'The early modern origins of Japanese tourism', in T. Umesao et al. (eds) *Japanese Civilization in the Modern World,* ix: *Tourism.* Osaka: Senri Ethnological Studies, 26, 35–38.

Veblen, T. (1953) *The Theory of the Leisure Class: An Economic Study of Institutions.* New York: Mentor Books.

Vogel, E. F. (1963) *Japan's New Middle Class: The Salary Man and His Family in a Tokyo Suburb.* Berkeley, CA: University of California Press.

Warde, A. (1990) 'Production, consumption and social change: reservations regarding Peter Saunders' sociology of consumption', *International Journal of Urban and Regional Research,* 14/2, 228–48.

White, J. (1982) *Migration in Metropolitan Japan.* Berkeley, CA: Institute of East Asian Studies.

White, M. (1994) *The Material Child: Coming of Age in Japan and America.* Berkeley, CA: University of California Press.

Williams, D. (1994) *Japan: Beyond the End of History.* London: Routledge.

Williamson, J. 1978 *Decoding Advertisements.* London: Marion Boyars.

Wimberley, H. W. (1973) 'On living with your past: style and structure among contemporary Japanese merchant families', *Economic Development and Social Change,* 21, 413–28.

Winnicot, D. W. (1971) *Playing and Reality.* London: Tavistock Press.

Yamaguchi, M. (1991) 'The poetics of exhibition in Japanese culture', in I. Karp and S. Levine (eds) *Exhibiting Cultures: The Poetics and Politics of Museum Display.* Washington: Smithsonian Institution Press, 57–67.

Yoshino, K. (1992) *Cultural Nationalism in Contemporary Japan.* London: Routledge.

Yuasa, Y. (1987) *The Body: Towards an Eastern Mind–Body Theory.* Albany, NY: State University of New York Press.

Zukin, S. (1995) *The Cultures of Cities.* Oxford: Blackwell.

Index